Indians in
Eighteenth-Century
Eastern
Massachusetts

Behind *the* Frontier

Daniel R. Mandell

UNIVERSITY OF NEBRASKA PRESS

Lincoln & London

∞

First Bison Books printing: 2000
Most recent printing indicated by
the last digit below:
10 9 8 7 6 5 4 3 2 1
Library of Congress
Cataloging-in-Publication Data
Mandell, Daniel R., 1956–
Behind the frontier:
Indians in eighteenth-century
eastern Massachusetts /
Daniel R. Mandell.
p. cm.
Includes bibliographical references and index.
ISBN 0-8032-3179-2 (cl: alk. paper)
ISBN 0-8032-8249-4 (pa: alk. paper)
1. Indians of North America—Massachusetts—
History—18th century.
2. Indians of North America—
Massachusetts—Social conditions.
3. Indians of North America—
Cultural assimilation—Massachusetts.
I. Title.
E78.M4M32 1996
974.4′00497—dc20   95-20900
CIP

CONTENTS

PREFACE

Textbook Indians disappear when conquered. Real people are not, however, quite so obliging. Today the Pequots operate the most lucrative casino in America (perhaps the world), gleefully winning a measure of restitution from the inheritors of the Puritans who supposedly wiped out that tribe in 1637. And soon the Gay Head tribe, a community that you will frequently encounter in this book but was believed to have "died" in the late nineteenth century, will build its own casino.

Historians generally close their studies of Indians and colonists in southern New England with the colonists' military triumph in 1676. But I find more fascinating the continued struggles of the "losers": how they survived by shaping new cultures and communities that absorbed a multitude of changes while maintaining essential traditions. This study examines the process of adaptation and persistence among the natives of eastern Massachusetts in the century following political and demographic subordination.

After 1676, Indians were but a few scattered islands in the English sea of eastern Massachusetts. This helpless, conquered minority may seem inconsequential. Yet the natives remaining within the Bay Colony posed a significant concern to the governor and General Court, even threatening the relationship between the colony and the Crown in 1760 when a lone Mashpee carried his community's complaint to London. Indians were also dominant in a number of villages. People in towns around Mashpee, for example, remained anxious about their unpredictable neighbors into the nineteenth century. Between 1744 and 1805, Natick Indians held most of the political cards in the town's dispute over its meetinghouse location — even when fewer than a dozen individuals remained. While the numbers and resources of Indians shrank during the eighteenth century, some groups still controlled important resources: Chappaquiddick held some of the best grazing lands on Martha's Vineyard, for example, and Mashpee became one of the few places east of the Connecticut River where deer could still be hunted.

"Indian" has become a controversial word in the late twentieth century, as Native American activists work to increase our understanding of this continent's first settlers. But I find the term quite useful for this study. Others have pointed out that "America" is hardly a native word, and that there is no untainted noun that refers generally to native peoples in North America. For me, "Indian" is a useful reference, for a major theme of this work is how that multiracial ethnic group emerged in eastern Massachusetts, transcending old divisions between clans, villages, and tribes.

Scholars who study the history of nonliterate groups are inevitably constrained by inadequate and biased documentation. Although some Indians in Massachusetts were literate, they left few records of their lives. I am fortunate that there is a rich body of records and accounts from eighteenth-century Massachusetts. A potential pitfall is that the overwhelming majority of documents, including many Indian complaints, were written by Englishmen. Yet the events reported by these records are fairly reliable, even when their language is clearly biased. In fact, colonial authorities were sensitive to the accuracy of letters and petitions. Whites accused of misdeeds often defended themselves by charging that the Indians' complaint was fraudulent or forged. Such countercharges were seriously investigated, and sometimes rejected and at other times upheld. These complaints, countercharges, and investigations can be evaluated to determine the truth. Unfortunately, the records are primarily about things going bad: a family's misfortunes, problems within communities, and conflicts with outsiders. Of course, not all was grim; people had joys as well as sorrows. I try to avoid distorting their lives, but sometimes their story is unavoidably one of epidemics, wars, trespass, poaching, fraud, and other evils.

Acknowledgments

During the many years in which this project evolved, James Axtell, Constance Crosby, Stephen Innes, Ann Plane, and Neal Salisbury provided moral and critical support. John Brooke arranged precious library privileges at Tufts University and frequently reviewed my work. Jack Larkin, director of research at Old Sturbridge Village, helped me develop the picture of African–Native American intermarriage. Ann, Colin Calloway, and Peter Hoffer provided useful readings of various chapters. I owe a special debt for the advice and editing given by Michael Winship, who enthusiastically plunged into a world far different from that inhabited by his stern Puritan theologians.

Several institutions provided vital financial support. The city of Malden and the Commonwealth of Massachusetts awarded me a timely Massachusetts Arts Lottery Grant. Old Sturbridge Village conferred a fellowship to study New England Indians in the early nineteenth century, which shed light on some "invisible" Indian communities and long-term trends during the previous century. The Department of History at the University of Georgia graciously provided the grant to produce the map that graces this book.

Part of this work has been published as " 'To Live More Like My Christian English Neighbors': Natick Indians in the Eighteenth Century," in the *William and Mary Quarterly*, 3d ser., 48 (1991): 552–79. The exceptional editorial work by Michael McGiffert and Ann Gross at the *Quarterly* dramatically enhanced the article and helped me to improve the entire work.

Numerous individuals and institutions have been helpful in my research. William Mulhomme, Reference Supervisor, and others at the Massachusetts State Archives have been especially warm and generous in their assistance, and this book would not exist without the documents in their collections. Librarians at the Massachusetts Historical Society and American Antiquarian Society have also been helpful. Peter Heaney provided access to the New England Native American Institute's genealogical data on Nipmuc families. Constance Crosby shared her transcripts to the SPG records, and Julia Caldron Walker shared her transcripts of Gideon Hawley's papers from the Congregational Library in Boston.

This book would not have been possible without my wife Barbara's many years of love and support (and welcome distractions). Over the past few months the two of us have had a joyful race to see whether I could produce the manuscript before she could produce our first child. As I finish this preface and the conclusion amidst David's nighttime feedings and diaper changes, I can say that this was a race I was happy to lose.

Indian Enclaves and their Neighbors, 1676–1776.

ABBREVIATIONS

AR   *Acts and Resolves, Public and Private, of the Province of Massachusetts Bay*

JME   John Milton Earle Papers, American Antiquarian Society, Worcester, Massachusetts

MA   Massachusetts colonial records, Massachusetts Archives, Boston, Massachusetts

MCP   Middlesex County Probate Court Records, Massachusetts Archives, Boston, Massachusetts

MCD   Middlesex County Deeds, Middlesex County Court House, Cambridge, Massachusetts

MHS   Massachusetts Historical Society, Boston, Massachusetts

MHSC   Massachusetts Historical Society *Collections*

NEC   New England Company (Society for the Propagation of the Gospel)

NEHGS   New England Historical and Geneological Society, Boston, Massachusetts

SPG   Records of the Society for the Propagation of the Gospel, Guildhall Library, London, England

WCP   Worcester County Probate Court Records, Worcester, Massachusetts

Behind *the* Frontier

Introduction

As the American Revolution erupted in Massachusetts, some who rioted in the streets of Boston or watched their husbands and sons join the patriot militia looked back at a century of their own struggles within the now-rebellious colony. Crispus Attucks, a "mulatto" mariner in Boston who became one of the first martyrs of the Revolution; laborer Joseph Aaron from Grafton, the son of a Hassanamisco woman and an African servant; widow Sarah Wamsquam, who traveled throughout the region begging from or working for white families; the Rev. Solomon Briant of Mashpee who preached in Wampanoag to the largest native community in the region; these Indians were part of a regional ethnic community that shared a common identity and a unique culture. During the one hundred years between the start of King Philip's War (20 June 1675) and the Battle of Bunker Hill (17 June 1775), an Indian ethnic group emerged in eastern Massachusetts. New England's law, economy, and wars combined with internal demographic and social pressures to destroy some native enclaves, to combine others, and to reshape Indian culture and affinity.

The encounter of natives and Puritan colonists in early New England is a source of folklore, scholarship, novels, and movies. The story usually ends with the defeat of Metacom (King Philip) in 1676, and tells of the collision of two forces, native and colonizer, that overwhelmed the former. That picture, while rich and deeply tragic, is misleading. Scholars now examining Indian groups that survived King Philip's War are finding adaptability and persistence rather than "demoralized and dispirited remnants" that "sank ever deeper into subjection and debauchery."[1] This study takes a new look at the century between that terrible war and the American Revolution, and develops a picture of the internal dynamics and external pressures that led Indians in eastern Massachusetts to redefine their communities, transform their loyalties, and forge a regional ethnic network. Individual choices, family concerns, divisions within groups, collective decisions, and networks between native enclaves are all part of this picture. Regional events and trends helped reshape Indian groups just as they did colonial communities.

The Indian population of eastern Massachusetts ebbed and many native villages disappeared during the eighteenth century. Indians had fewer children and a higher mortality rate than colonists. Those who remained after the 1675 revolt were battered by changes in the colonial economy, by the terrible effects of epidemics, alcoholism, and indebtedness, and by the loss of men to wars and migratory labor. Swelling white racism isolated Indians with African Americans in a scorned underclass, abetting fraud, poaching, and trespassing by settlers. Indian enclaves frequently petitioned provincial authorities, not only seeking protection from white neighbors—usually to little avail—but also for the resolution of factionalism that threatened community peace and resources. These were neither the "Peaceable Kingdoms" nor the vibrant, quarrelsome-yet-productive eighteenth-century New England towns often depicted by social historians.

The story of Indian communities in colonial Massachusetts is not, however, that of a helpless descent into extinction. While natives declined in numbers and circumstances during the century, and many villages dissolved, survivors adapted by reshaping their communities while maintaining key elements of aboriginal culture. Indians teetered along the line between isolation from and immersion in colonial society and culture, seeking to satisfy their needs in the new environment while maintaining critical boundaries against white settlers. They looked to sustain themselves and their families in accustomed ways and within the borders of their villages, even as they were increasingly forced or enticed into seeking employment on Anglo-American farms or whaling ships.

Some of the more destructive aspects of the period actually facilitated Indian survival in the region. When threatened by white trespassers or poachers, Indians often gained the sympathy of provincial officials. While the political connections rarely solved native problems and in fact strengthened colonial power over Indian communities, outside authorities became potential allies. Those forced from their communities by economic problems or the pressures of white settlers helped form new regional ties that transcended old boundaries between tribes, clans, and villages. Native enclaves also developed new means to sustain themselves in the face of colonial dominance, most notably churches whose congregations maintained native languages and customs and whose preachers began to knit distant congregations and households into a new Indian ethnic community.

The history of the experiences of the Indians during this century can be divided into two eras. During the half century following English victory in King Philip's War, surviving Indian enclaves enjoyed a high, though increasingly threatened, degree of political, social, and economic autonomy. Native villages on Cape Cod and the islands survived the war without major disruptions, and the "praying Indians" who had been interned near Boston resettled some of their towns. While some war captives (including children) and indebted adults lived with English families as servants or apprentices, Indian groups continued many aboriginal subsistence ways even as they maintained ties to the colonial economy by working for white farmers or selling their surplus in regional markets. But native autonomy was gradually undermined as Anglo-American investors and settlers purchased "vacant" Indian territory. In newly annexed New Plymouth, Nantucket, and Martha's Vineyard, the number of Indian villages declined as the Indian population concentrated in a few enclaves of reserved territory.

After the Treaty of Utrecht in 1713, Indian communities throughout eastern Massachusetts experienced a drastic loss of autonomy as English settlements multiplied rapidly with the end of the frontier conflict with France. The Indian population plummeted as epidemics scourged native enclaves, and tuberculosis and alcoholism weakened the survivors. After many native men failed to return from the colonial wars at midcentury, the women increasingly married African-American men, bringing a new and potentially disruptive element into Indian communities. At the same time, the growing population of white settlers exerted pressure on resources both within and without the boundaries of native enclaves, forcing Indians into a greater dependence on the colonial economy. The combination of economic and demographic problems compelled Indians to sell more land, leading many to leave villages increasingly dominated by white settlers. The few enclaves that survived the period in good condition had at least two hundred members, owned land protected by provincial law, and held their resources in common.

Indian leadership and polity groped to meet the period's extraordinary pressures. The colonists' demand for Indian resources generated internal conflicts within many native communities, including those that survived the Revolution, as the few remaining sachems used their traditional authority to sell their communities' land and wood to outsiders. Some groups dealt with the conflict by deposing the offending individual and electing new leaders. The efforts of others to prevent these assaults by appealing to the governor and General Court usually resulted in the appointment of white guardians to protect Indian enclaves; unfortunately, most guardians were either ineffective or corrupt, and the involvement of colonial authorities further undermined Indian autonomy. Indian ministers took up the mantle of leadership in many communities as the aboriginal leadership degenerated and the arrogant outsiders misunderstood and mismanaged their responsibilities.

While differences between Indians and Anglo-Americans were legion, regional trends and problems affected all communities in Massachusetts, for the Indian villages *were* New England towns. County and provincial courts played an increasing role in the life of individuals and villages, white and Indian. The disease, poverty, and death brought by the colonial wars devastated both colonists and Indians. Puritans as well as Indians experienced unease and community conflict over accepting acquisition and profit as positive values. Colonists and natives suffered from economic disruptions, such as the massive inflation of the 1740s and the growing gap between rich and poor, and many were forced to find land or their fortunes far from their homes. Indeed, the desire to earn a "competency" near one's relatives and community, a need felt by colonists as well as Indians, generated additional conflict between natives and newcomers. When rapid Anglo-American population growth caused an apparent shortage in land and wood, some colonists sought a solution to their problems by pasturing their cattle on Indian land, stealing wood from native enclaves, or maneuvering to obtain Indian land by manipulating debts and lawsuits.

The seizure or dominance of Indian villages by colonists did not thrust native families out of the area or destroy informal networks in the region. A community can exist on many levels, particularly when a group is bound by kinship and culture. First, a community can be a "body of people organized into a political, municipal, or social unity." Second, it is "those members of a civil community, who have certain circumstances of nativity, religion, or pursuit, common to them, but not shared by those among whom they live." Third, it can also be "common character, . . . identity . . . Social intercourse; fellowship, communion."[2] Indians in eastern Massachusetts moved from the first (identifiable Indian towns) to the second (enclaves) and then toward the third (an ethnic group) during the colonial period. By the time of the Revolution, only a few native villages remained in eastern Massachusetts, and most Indians lived in small neighborhoods or as isolated families, but the growth of their ethnic identity produced a lasting regional Indian community.

Fundamental continuities persisted in Indian society and culture despite the massive changes and traumas of eighteenth-century Massachusetts. Clans had dominated aboriginal societies, and throughout the colonial period family networks remained the essential substructure of native groups, initially bonding individuals to their parents' villages and later creating or renewing regional ties that facilitated Indian survival in the hostile environment. Native community organizations, some formally recognized within the provincial polity, separated Indians from their white neighbors. Indian culture also remained deliberately apart from the Anglo-American world. Surviving legends identified avarice and other evils with white intruders and stressed the importance of respecting the old ways. Most enclaves maintained communal landholding, favored subsistence economies, and emphasized sharing over individual advancement.

Some changes, as well as continuities, served to strengthen Indian communities against colonial pressures and demographic problems. Children of mixed marriages were brought up as members of their Indian community and clearly identified with village values and institutions, although those ties began to weaken as the region's African-American community grew in numbers and strength. Perhaps the most remarkable brace for Indian survival in Massachusetts was the church. While John Eliot and other English missionaries designed Indian churches to "reduce" Indians to "civility" and make them more like whites, native congregations and preachers actually operated to maintain social and cultural boundaries, and were crucial in forging the new Indian identity that began to emerge in the mid-eighteenth century.

This study focuses on eastern Massachusetts. The second chapter, which covers the period between 1676 and 1700, deals entirely with Indian communities in the old Bay Colony, while subsequent chapters include native groups in what were, before 1692, the separate colonies of Plymouth, Nantucket, and Martha's Vineyard. Of course, Indian social, political, and economic networks did not follow colonial borders, which were also uncertain and subject to dispute. Yet there are substantial reasons for the structure of this study. Colonial boundaries in southern New England were, to some extent, influenced by the larger native political groupings called tribes. New Plymouth, for example, got much of its land (through grants, fraud, or force) from the Wampanoags, and the Bay Colony took most of its territory and its name from the Massachusett Indians. In addition, the shocks of King Philip's War, along with the political and economic disruptions that followed the defeat of Metacom and his allies, curtailed or ended many of the old transcolony native networks, and "walled in" the remaining Indian communities. During the eighteenth century, many of those ties would be renewed and new ones created as a regional Indian community emerged, transcending old tribal divisions. Finally, a colony's laws and events clearly influenced Indians within its boundaries. Thus the structure of this study closely follows developments in the Indian communities of eastern Massachusetts.

)(

This study reveals the frontier that endured in eastern Massachusetts even after the colonists' Pyrrhic victory in King Philip's War. The subtlety of this cultural encounter is quite different from most Americans' perception of Indian-white relations along the frontier. Even enlightened late twentieth century children grow up with a cardboard cutout image of the Indian: the noble horseman who shoots buffalo with a bow and arrow on Monday, ambushes the wagon train or stagecoach on Tuesday, sees his family slaughtered by soldiers on Wednesday, makes a dignified speech full of wisdom and pathos on Thursday, and on Friday retires to a desolate reservation to spend the weekend dancing, drunk and indigent. The reality of the frontier encounter in eighteenth-century eastern Massachusetts, where Indians dealt as neighbors with and even married whites and African Americans, will still seem strange to many of us today.

The experiences of Indians in eighteenth-century eastern Massachusetts were similar to those of other native groups caught behind the westward-moving line of Anglo-American dominance. This period in North America has been pictured as the time of gestation for a new people and a new nation, as colonists and British officials pushed and pulled over issues of empire and local institutions. For Indian groups on the Atlantic seaboard, however, it was a time in which they struggled to maintain their families and communities. While individual circumstances varied, the threats were the same everywhere: pressures exerted by white settlers, internal crises brought on by demographic decline, and problems they faced in a changing economy. These shocks, however, did not destroy all Indian groups east of the Appalachians. From Maine to Georgia, a cultural frontier continued to separate Indian and Anglo-American societies as some Indians survived in enclaves on lands set aside in law for natives and others survived in informal networks of scattered families. Studies of Indian groups in South Carolina, Virginia, and along the lower Mississippi River echo the theme of this study: that by the beginning of the Revolution, isolated Indian households and shrinking native enclaves had developed new regional networks and a modern ethnic identity that laid the groundwork for group survival.[3]

CHAPTER I

"Gotten our land"

The natives of southern New England found their world reshaped by European exploration, trade, and colonization. Some of the most tragic aspects of the changes were unintentional, most dramatically the diseases that slaughtered thousands, brought by explorers to this "virgin soil" in 1616–17 — with many more to follow in 1633. Other alterations came with European traders in the first few decades of the century, for the village leader that controlled the trade within an area could enlarge his authority; the relationship between traders and sachems centralized native political power and sharpened conflicts in the region. The arrival of English immigrants after 1620, and their sometimes intimate, sometimes distant or even hostile relationships tugged and pulled at native communities. While the newcomers provided fresh sources of religious, economic, and political power, alterations to native society flowed through these connections. Military alliances with the English offered a means for one native group to dominate another, but such links also allowed colonial leaders to expand their authority in the region. The colonists also brought alien animals, different desires, and a strange view of how people used (owned) land. English political and economic demands threatened the natives' livelihoods and leaders, and in 1675 pushed Metacom (King Philip) into launching a revolt that reshaped the human landscape of southern New England.

But despite the changes wrought by English colonization and war, Indians in southern New England retained most of their aboriginal culture. Precolonial linguistic and political boundaries remained significant, and native leaders continued to derive their authority from clan connections and the ability to meet the needs of their people. Indians preferred their traditional economies and housing, even in the mission "praying towns" where the inhabitants adopted colonial dress, Puritan religious habits, and English gender roles. While Puritan leaders could legislate radical changes in native ways, they could only enforce such rules among individuals directly under their influence, such as servants and students within English towns. Indian communities near colonial settlements retained many connections to relatives who were far from Puritan laws and authority, and thus possessed an "escape valve" that could not be ignored by English authorities. Even the villages that accepted the English gospel did so largely on their own terms. Native societies demonstrated a remarkable ability to absorb changes, even the major disruptions of epidemics and wars, while maintaining key traditions — a tenacity that would continue to shape native communities after the colonists' victory in King Philip's War.

)(

New England was shaped by the cultures and desires of natives and newcomers. Indians were intimately tied to the land at a subsistence level, looked for the security in a stable, diversified economy, built sociopolitical networks through family connections, and sought religious and political power by giving and receiving knowledge and goods. Their communities were small, their hierarchies weak, their possessions few. While Europeans also built their polities on family networks, and their peasant communities cherished stability and security, after 1400 economic expansion in and imperial competition between western European nations caused them to develop strong governments and aggressive cultures. Just as aggressive were European animals, plants, and even viruses. The latter proved particularly merciless and effective at reshaping New England's human landscape.

Native society operated on three levels: clan, village, and tribe. The clan, an extended family that claimed a common ancestor, dominated an individual's life. Clans worked and held fields and hunting territories. The village, containing up to several hundred people from one or more clans, set field boundaries and organized the political and economic life. The tribe, the largest and least powerful grouping, connected villages and clans with a common dialect and culture, but lacked stable hierarchies and could be reshaped by outside influences or internal conflicts.

Gender roles and seasonal diversity shaped the native economy. At the village during the spring and summer, women cared for fields of corn, beans, and squash while men fished and hunted small animals. In the fall, women harvested the crops while men conducted diplomacy and war. In some areas in the late fall, villagers dispersed in clan groups for men to hunt big game, reassembled during the winter in sheltered, wooded valleys, and then returned to their homes in the spring for the women to plant again. Fields could be used for eight to ten years before declining in fertility and requiring fertilization with fish or the burning of woods to create new fields. This "slash and burn" agriculture created a wide range of habitats for a rich variety of game animals.

Native political and religious authority was spread throughout the community. Each clan was headed by its eldest member — if matrilineal, the oldest woman. Each village was headed by a sachem, who symbolically "owned" the land (much as a European monarch "owned" the nation) and assigned new planting fields to families. The sachem did not rule as a monarch, but depended upon village consensus, while a council of prestigious men (and sometimes women) provided counsel. The tribe was ruled by a council of sachems, with an individual occasionally recognized as a superior war or peace leader. The community and its members believed that all living and many inert things contained spiritual power, called manitou, and that the supernatural could be mobilized through rituals. Some rituals could be performed by individuals, while others required a communal setting and a qualified holy man or woman, called a powwow.

Natives of northeastern North America first made contact with Europeans in the early sixteenth century. In the Old World, in the wake of the

Crusades and recovery from the Great Plague of the fourteenth century, nationalism and the search for wealth in new places joined forces. Colonies provided key raw materials to the mother country that would have otherwise been purchased from competing nations, and created new markets for processed goods. The claims of Spain and Portugal in the Americas drove other European powers toward the northern part of that unknown hemisphere. France cultivated an extensive trade with native groups along the St. Lawrence, while the Dutch developed an equally impressive fur trade network along the Hudson River, east as far as Narragansett Bay, and north up the Connecticut River. For the region's natives the new sources of power became flashpoints for latent conflict. Iroquois fought French Indian allies for a piece of Quebec's fur trade and Mohawks battled Mahicans to control trading along the Hudson. The latter conflict held the greatest relevance for southern New England, as native groups in that region also fought with the Mohawks and became entangled in the Mahicans' battles.

The fur trade helped to reshape native societies as far east as the New England coast. Native networks adjusted to war and trade by becoming more centralized and powerful, extending clan and village connections to become more like a modern Indian tribe. The fur trapping and intensified warfare impinged on traditional seasonal activities. In some areas, villages dispersed into small hamlets for more efficient hunting, and in other places, small groups coalesced into larger settlements for better defense and to reinforce their sachem's authority. At the same time, the trade fit aspects of precontact culture. Indians sought goods that fulfilled traditional needs or concepts, from such strange items as mirrors (seen as reflectors of the soul, like a still pond) to ordinary objects such as blue beads (a sacred, hard to obtain color). The persistence of community values, in fact, encouraged certain changes; for example, the tenacity of the virtue of reciprocity made it easier for individuals able to dominate trade to create a higher level of personal authority. Throughout the region such "big men" (and some women) built stronger political structures through their "personal drive, magnetism, and the ability to manipulate resources, rather than from any ascribed right to leadership in their cultural systems." Yet these leaders were still not absolute rulers, and continued to depend on kinship connections and prestige to maintain authority.[1]

Europeans brought more than their goods and greed to the New World. Native Americans, long isolated from the pathogens of the Old World, lacked the antibodies to resist the impressive roster of contagious diseases to which whites had developed at least partial immunity. In this "virgin soil," diseases such as measles often raced ahead of direct contact with Europeans. In 1616–17 an epidemic decimated villages along the New England coast, killing 90 percent of the inhabitants in some places; those fortunate to survive became vulnerable to "imported" tuberculosis and pneumonia. These demographic catastrophes devastated sociopolitical relationships based on kinship and undermined traditional beliefs and practices. Natives continued to be vulnerable to European viruses long after English colonists conquered the region.

Colonists were driven across the dangerous sea by England's social, economic, and religious upheavals. Rapid population growth, bad harvests, disruptive economic changes, and political and religious conflicts tore at the fabric of society, undermining traditional relationships and putting new demands on individuals — who then sought a renewed stability in salvation. Puritanism emerged as the spearhead of the movement to reform the English church and to create a moral, godly, and disciplined society.

The first group of English colonists to arrive in the region was a particularly radical sect of reformers who fled the hopelessly corrupt church, first to the Netherlands and then in 1620 to Cape Cod and Plymouth Bay. After barely surviving their first New England winter, the Pilgrims managed with the aid of the fabled Squanto to establish relations with Massassoit, sachem of the neighboring Wampanoags (or Pokanokets). Weakened by an epidemic, the Wampanoags hoped that the newcomers would aid them against the Narragansetts, the strongest tribe in the area; the Pilgrims saw that these ties would help them survive in the new land and possibly open a profitable fur trade. Plymouth gained a number of advantages from the negotiations, including recognition of English legal preeminence: an Indian suspected of assaulting a colonist would be handed over to the Pilgrims for trial. Such twisted bargains became a consistent part of New England's first half century.

The Puritans' Great Migration soon eclipsed the Plymouth settlement. With the blessing of a royal charter to the region around Massachusetts Bay, between 1630 and 1633 approximately 3,000 devout English men, women, and children poured into the mushrooming settlements. The natives in the region, known as the Massachusett and Pawtucket tribes, had been devastated by the recent epidemic, and only about two hundred remained to greet the Puritans. As in New Plymouth, not only were the natives too weak to organize opposition, but they saw the colonists as protectors against their enemies — in this case Micmacs from the north and Mohawks from the west.

The English presence, however, soon proved disruptive. Native villages adjoining the Puritan and Pilgrim settlements were pressed to observe the colonists' laws. While trade and politics increased the power of the sachems, they were held responsible for any violations of English law committed by their people; thus their traditional role of maintaining harmony within the community was recast to reinforce colonial domination. Conflicts over resources also grew. Colonists and Indians frequently disagreed over the borders between their communities, English livestock often wandered into unfenced native fields and destroyed Indian crops, and feral pigs devoured clams needed by Indians. But in 1633, just as the increasing antagonism betokened war, a smallpox epidemic swept through the Indian villages of New England, again killing many Massachusetts and Pawtuckets, along with any incipient rebellion. The disease, in the words of the Bay Colony's governor, John Winthrop, "cleared our title to this place."[2]

Puritan leaders were determined to defend and strengthen that title. In 1633, the Pequot tribe invited the English to join the Dutch in establishing trading posts in the area, and one year later the Bay Colony wrangled from the Pequots the rights to the Connecticut River Valley (and a huge sum of wampum) for arranging a peace treaty with the Narragansetts. Three years later the Puritans, motivated by fear of internal dissent (the antinomian controversy), fear of Indian raids, and perhaps simple greed, put together an army with their Indian allies that destroyed the Pequot "capital," and then captured and killed the survivors. In the war's aftermath English settlers streamed into Pequot territory and established two separate colonies, Connecticut and New Haven, increasing from 800 to about 5,500 in 1643, while the white population in Massachusetts doubled to 13,000.[3]

The English not only wrought demographic, political, and social changes among the Indians of southern New England, but altered the very environment on which the natives depended. The growing number of colonists cut deeply into the forests; trees were felled for fuel, shelter, and export, and an increasing amount of land was taken for farms. The cows and pigs not only destroyed Indian crops and shellfish beds, but also consumed foods needed by deer and other native herbivores hunted by the natives. Cattle also required much more land than food crops, multiplying the colonists' demand for more territory. Plants and animals brought by the settlers crowded out native flora and fauna. A number of factors discouraged seasonal migrations: the development of wampum (made from shellfish available only at coastal sites) as a currency to buy furs farther inland, military threats from settlers and other native groups, and the demand by colonists for land. Centralization of settlements became common, resulting in increasing social tensions and more intensive land use near remaining villages. Sedentary life brought overfishing, overhunting, and weakened soil. Finally, when the fur-bearing animals that had fueled tribal power were gone, the "new" chiefs sold the only other resource desired by the colonists: their people's land.

The changes in the world of the natives provided a fertile ground for the Puritans' theological seed. Indians and Puritans similarly believed that God or gods acted in everyday occurrences. Therefore both groups saw recent events as evidence that Jehovah had overcome the native gods and that the natives' survival required adoption of the English God. John Eliot stepped into this psychic gap among the Massachusetts after learning the native language, preaching that Indians could find salvation only by shedding their heathenish ways and adopting Puritan disciplines in order to breath the rarefied air of Calvinist doctrine. Eliot has been depicted as everything from a saint to a land-hungry Machiavellian incompetent. The scholarly consensus is that Puritan missionaries were (by modern standards) inflexible and authoritarian, and immediately condemned cultural ways they could not understand. But the Puritans' criteria were high for anyone who wished to be among the ranks of the godly, regardless of skin color, education, or wealth.[4]

After Massachuset sachem Cutshamekin spurned Eliot, probably because the missionary's call for social reformation threatened his power, the minister approached Waban, head of the Massachuset village of Nonantum, northwest of Neponsett. Waban found the power of Eliot's God attractive. At this time Puritan rulers offered the carrot of secure land title for groups that accepted the missionary's message, and created a strong stick for Eliot by passing laws that promised death to anyone, "whether Christian or pagan . . . deniing the true God." Perhaps due to Waban's interest, Eliot's audiences at Nonantum grew. The missionary began traveling between several Indian communities in the area, gathering converts. Indian converts wore their hair like the English and forswore many old habits, from religious ceremonies to body greasing, to demonstrate their ability to walk the Christian path of righteousness. Waban, who led the converts, requested a tract of land on which the Christian Indians could build a new English-style town of their own. In 1651, he received a tract of two thousand acres straddling the Charles River, eighteen miles upriver from Boston and six miles from Dedham.[5]

The decision to embrace the Puritan message was made within the evolving Indian world view. When Eliot and Waban developed their symbiotic relationship, both gained prestige and authority. Those who joined Waban's community, which became Natick, enjoyed special status in their relations with colonial authorities. The missionary served as a conduit for material and spiritual power, and even brought the power of literacy. Yet this embrace of a new religion was not simply an expediency. Many of those most directly affected by the arrival of the newcomers may have converted because the aboriginal cosmos could not adequately explain or affect the technology, writing, sense of superiority, power, or disease brought by the Anglo-Americans. Christianity apparently offered answers to these challenges. But not all Indians were receptive to the new beliefs, as shown by Cutshamekin's rejection of Eliot. The sachem's loss, however, was Waban's gain. Nearly a decade after Natick's establishment, a group of Puritan visible saints approved the conversion experiences of a number of Indian converts, and a church sprouted in the town.[6]

Paradoxically, this apparently radical change presented the Indians with the opportunity to maintain many traditions. Natick became John Eliot's showpiece and the model for subsequent praying towns. Yet even this town contained a fascinating amalgam of English and aboriginal customs. The Indians built an English-style meetinghouse, fort, and arched footbridge across the Charles. House lots were laid out for nuclear families in the English tradition. Yet for the most part these families erected traditional housing instead of English clapboard. Massachusetts Bay Colony authorities appointed a superintendent of Indians, Daniel Gookin, to call the Indian magistrates to session and to monitor their decisions. The praying Indians adopted a legal code that forbade many traditional practices, from premarital sex to long hair and cracking lice between one's teeth. Eliot also established a Biblical polity by having the Indians choose "chiefs of . . . hundreds; fifties; and tens" (Exodus 18:21). Yet these new positions were filled by pre-mission community leaders, for the familiar elite gained importance in the sea of change. Those leaders, including Waban, enforced a traditional regard for community peace and stability. In addition, while the shape of this authority seemed to change as Puritan regulations cemented the status of rulers, individuals who violated community norms (by getting drunk or engaging in forbidden religious activities) could still be deposed.[7]

Old rivalries resulted in the establishment of a second praying town, Punkapoag. When Cutshamekin found his authority moving with his people to Waban, he joined Natick and became Eliot's first ruler of a hundred. After Cutshamekin's death, when Waban took his place in Natick,

Josiah Chickatabut, Cutshamekin's heir, rejected Waban's authority. Eliot therefore obtained six thousand acres from Dorchester, where he organized the Punkapoag settlement. The Punkapoags adopted English animal husbandry and made cedar shingles and clapboards to sell in Boston, Dorchester, and Dedham. By 1674, the community had shrunk to twelve families, as a number of "honest and able men" had died in the past decade, and others had "turned apostates" and left. Those who remained followed more aboriginal ways than their cousins in Natick, causing Gookin to lament that the "dispensations of God have greatly dampened the flourishing condition of this place."[8]

As the population and authority of the Bay Colony grew, John Eliot spread his message farther from Boston. Since a number of Nipmuc men from villages west of Natick were among Eliot's first converts, their relatives seemed particularly fertile ground, and while Nipmucs often came to Waban's village to hear Eliot, the Puritan missionary recognized the need to reach out to the inland tribe. The Nipmucs' territory between Connecticut and Massachusetts also had strategic importance, as both colonies recognized Indian allies as a means to extend sovereignty. Eliot founded the first Nipmuc praying town at Hassanamisset, thirty-eight miles from Boston along the Indian path to Connecticut. After carefully separating the converted from the rest of the village, in 1671 the Puritan missionary established the second (and last) Indian church at the "place of small stones." Three years later the Christian hamlet had sixty residents, including sixteen full church members and about thirty baptized persons. The new praying town seemed a promising foundation; Gookin noted that its four square miles "is capable to receive some hundreds. It produceth plenty of corn, grain, and fruit; for there are several good orchards in this place. It is an apt place for keeping of cattle and swine; in which respect this people are the best stored of any Indian town of their size."[9]

The Pawtuckets (or Pennacooks), whose territory stretched along the Merrimac River into southern New Hampshire, were another strategic group approached by Eliot. The Puritan missionary established the praying town of Wamesit at the confluence of the Concord and Merrimac, the northwest edge of the Bay Colony. The site met both the colony's ecclesiastical and secular needs, for during the fishing season "a great confluence of Indians" came from the north, providing an opportunity to extend Puritan influence and religion into a region rich in fur and timber. The Pennacooks also retained close ties to western Abenaki groups between New England and New France. The drawback, of course, was that the seventy-five Pennacooks who resided in Wamesit also socialized frequently with their unconverted and "rebellious" relatives.[10]

By the close of the 1660s Eliot and Gookin had created a network of seven praying towns—Natick, Hassanamisset, Punkapoag, and Wamesit, Okommakamesit (or Whipsuffrage), Nashoba, and Magunkaquag—that lay along the frontier of colonial settlement, and whose inhabitants maintained connections with unconverted relatives who spurned English law. The Puritan missionaries labored with their native allies to develop new networks that could operate independently of aboriginal kinship and political ties. Only Natick and Hassanamisset had churches, so the "elect" of other villages made weekly pilgrimages to the nearest meetinghouse. These two praying towns with churches served as training centers for Indian missionaries who were loyal to Waban, Eliot, and colonial authorities. Their influence reached beyond the praying towns. Sassamon, a Massachusett born near Punkapoag, taught at Natick before traveling to the Plymouth-Rhode Island border to work as a secretary and teacher for the Wampanoag sachems. In the early 1670s other missionaries began to take their Puritan message deep into Nipmuc territory, serving as teachers and preachers in seven villages west of Hassanamisset.[11]

This expansion of Puritan influence, even by Indian agents, was seen by both natives and colonists as an extension of English authority, threatening established Indian customs and leadership, and providing an opening for new land purchases. Thus Uncas, the Mohegan leader loyal to the English, warned Eliot not to enter Mohegan territory "to call his Indians to pray to God." While the missionary protested that "he did not meddle with civil right or jurisdiction," Nipmuc leaders were aware that the Indian preachers dispatched by the Bay Colony worked to supplant native authority.[12] The threat was territorial as well as political, for the Nipmucs were uncomfortably wedged between the growing population of Boston, Connecticut, and New Haven. As the English population around Boston increased, ambitious investors from Massachusetts, including Daniel Gookin and other influential men in the colony, sought to purchase "vacant" lands between the coast and the Connecticut River. In fact, when Gookin traveled with Eliot in 1674 to encourage the new Nipmuc praying towns, he was also able to attend to his personal finances by meeting with two Nipmuc leaders who gave him and his fellow investors a deed to the land that later became Worcester.[13] Despite such apparently amiable relations, the Nipmucs were increasingly apprehensive about the Bay Colony's expansion.

While Eliot and the Bay Colony built a string of praying towns, a very different missionary enterprise was under way on the independent island of Martha's Vineyard, where the natives vastly outnumbered the English settlers. The resulting Christian Indian community retained more autonomy than those under Eliot's authority. In 1642, twenty Puritans, including the Mayhew family, established a colony on the Vineyard. One year later, Hiacoomes, a Wampanoag of "mean descent," came to Thomas Mayhew Jr., the colonists' pastor, and expressed an interest in Christianity. Mayhew tutored the Indian, and Hiacoomes soon had his conversion experience. In marked contrast to Eliot, Mayhew did not require converts to abandon most of their customs, and aboriginal festivals persisted even as they acquired a Christian cast. In addition, Mayhew respected the existing leadership and property rights, paying rent to pagan Indian leaders and obtaining their consent to various projects involving the converted natives. Soon a strong Christian Indian network emerged on the Vineyard, with daily religious needs filled entirely by native pastors, church elders, catechists, and musicians. This fellowship soon spread to the neighboring island of Nantucket.

The people of Nantucket maintained close ties with other Wampanoags on the mainland and Martha's Vineyard. The twenty-five hundred natives of this island were perhaps the last Indians affected by New England, for although they accepted the Christianity brought by native missionaries from the Vineyard in the 1640s, few white families lived on Nantucket until the end of the century. But even before settlement the English generated political conflict on the island by purchasing the west side from two sachems, Wanachamak and Nickanoose, who had no authority in that area. Natives on the island were also influenced by the Wampanoag leadership on the mainland. In the 1660s, after the English began arriving in large numbers, Nickanoose, his father, and Wanachamak went to the Wampanoag "capital" at Mt. Hope to consult with Wamsutta and Metacom, and in 1665 Metacom visited the island. Throughout the subsequent century the Nantucket Indians would continue to be affected by their ties with Wampanoag leaders and groups on the mainland and Martha's Vineyard, as well as by relations with their English neighbors.[14]

When English families began to move to Nantucket in the 1660s, primarily from the crucible of religious and social dissent north of Boston, they came in search of new economic opportunities as well as to escape from the Puritan Commonwealth's increasingly tight restrictions. At that time the island, like its western neighbor Martha's Vineyard, was (under English law) owned by the Mayhews, and ten years later both islands were placed under New York's jurisdiction. Most of the English families settled on the west side of Nantucket. The separation of English settlements and native villages offered the opportunity to avoid future conflicts. The colonists had also obtained, however, half of the meadows and marshes and all of the grazing rights (following the Indians' harvest) throughout the island. The apparently inevitable battles over resources followed as English herds and feral cattle intruded on the marshes and other areas that Indians used for fishing and gathering herbs and raw materials for baskets and other goods.[15]

A few Wampanoag communities in New Plymouth were also approached by missionaries at midcentury. Richard Bourne, a farmer and town leader in Sandwich on the western edge of Cape Cod, began about 1660 to preach to nearby natives. Bourne followed the pattern set by Mayhew, permitting his converts to maintain traditions and manners officially not tolerated by Eliot's followers. The first community that responded to his message, on Sandwich's southeast border, became known as the Mashpee or "South Sea" Indians. In 1665 and 1666, with Bourne's assistance, the Mashpees obtained grants of land from the sachems of the region; the deeds were formally recognized by New Plymouth and barred the sale of the land by any member of the community without the consent of all. By 1674, a number of Wampanoag preachers under Bourne's authority spread the gospel throughout the Cape, creating seven groups of praying Indians and one "gathered church." At this time, John Cotton also tried to spread Christianity along the western edge of his colony. But his efforts bore little fruit, for he was treading on the home ground of the powerful Wampanoag sachem, Metacom (King Philip), who was increasingly at odds with Plymouth.[16]

Metacom became the symbol of resistance to the English after he inherited the sachemship from his older brother, Wamsutta. Wamsutta had become the Wampanoag sachem in 1663 following the death of their father Massassoit, the Pilgrims' angel of mercy during that first difficult winter. The elder brother tried to build good relations with Plymouth, including asking for English names for his younger brother and himself — which is how Metacom became Philip. But Wamsutta, renamed Alexander, made Plymouth colonists nervous by selling land claimed by the colony to Quakers and other Englishmen from Rhode Island and Providence. Wamsutta died after being taken prisoner by Plymouth soldiers, supposedly to answer rumors that he was planning a revolt, and Metacom suspected poison. The new sachem faced increasing pressure from Plymouth colonists to stop selling land to other English. Ironically, the Pilgrims were also upset by Metacom's adoption of one of the most distinctive aspects of English farming, raising pigs — not only because it undermined the chief colonial ideological justification for displacing Indians, but also because he undersold colonial farmers in the marketplace! Pig raising was not as radical a change in aboriginal culture as might appear at first, for swine were apt substitutes for the increasingly scarce deer: pigs needed little care, and when allowed to go feral fit within the traditional universe of gender roles distinguishing men (hunters) from women (farmers).[17]

Conflicts over land became acute in 1667, after Plymouth violated an agreement with Metacom by authorizing the purchase of land within his territory (from *any* Indian) to create the town of Swansea. War parties began to appear near the new village, possibly led by the sachem in an effort to intimidate the colonists. In 1671, Plymouth tried to bring the new Wampanoag sachem to heel, demanding at gunpoint payment of tribute, all of his people's muskets, and renunciation of past land sales to outsiders. Metacom sought the assistance of the Bay Colony, to whom he had sold land. The English closed ranks, however, and in September 1674 Metacom was compelled to recognize Plymouth's sovereignty. The Wampanoag sachem prepared for war, seeking the backing of other Wampanoag leaders and other Indian groups (such as the Nipmucs) who felt besieged by the colonists. The most difficult challenge was to establish an alliance with the Narragansetts, old enemies but the most powerful tribe in the region. Metacom was also forced to play a waiting game, attempting to keep his angry warriors from raiding colonial villages while developing an effective alliance. Rumors of his plans seemed confirmed when the bruised body of Sassamon, the Indian teacher who had kept Plymouth informed of Metacom's actions, was found in a frozen pond near Assawompsett, where he had settled on the edge of Wampanoag territory.

New Plymouth tried three Wampanoags for Sassamon's murder, including one of Metacom's counselors. The three were found guilty, entirely on the suspect testimony of another Indian, and on the scaffold one of the three supposedly confessed their sachem's guilt. Tensions increased. The colonists' worst fears seemed confirmed and the Wampanoags, angered by recent events, believed that the English planned to kill Metacom and take their land. In July 1675, Metacom's men again appeared outside Swansea, slaying cattle and convincing many colonists that an assault was immanent. After an English boy killed a warrior, they attacked the town, in turn killing several colonists. The uprising began, apparently touched off more by the rage of Metacom's people than by the sachem's plan. When a colonial army tried to besiege the sachem near his home on Mount Hope, he escaped with his warriors and their families. Metacom's warriors stunned the colonists with quick, effective raids against a number of border settlements.

The 1675 revolt spread to other Indian groups in southern New England upset by the colonists' growing power and arrogance. Indians in southern Maine and the Connecticut River valley raided English settlements, and most Nipmucs and Wampanoags joined Metacom's warriors. When Massachusetts and Connecticut sent troops into Rhode Island (the hotbed of heretics) against the Narragansett, to quickly eliminate the expected threat and perhaps win their rich lands, the warriors slipped away and joined Metacom's forces. The Indians were initially successful, raiding one town after another near Boston, and the English felt themselves in dire peril.

Native support for the war was not universal, however, for precolonial tribal bonds had been weakened by the new Christian networks and by political connections with the English. The Massachusetts, Pennacooks, and a number of Nipmucs and Wampanoags refused to join Metacom, and many men in the older Eliot-established praying towns asked to join colonial forces. But despite the loyalty of some Indians, most colonists blamed all natives for the revolt. In August 1675, as the war grew more intense, the Massachusetts Bay Colony confined all "friend" Indians to a few of the easterly praying towns. Gookin noted that "the clamours and animosity among the common people increased daily, not only against those Indians, but also all such English as were judged to be charitable to them." Colonists confiscated or destroyed property, including crops and tools, in the praying towns of Wamesit, Hassanamisset, Magunkaquag, and Chabanakongkomun.[18]

By October 1675, as the raids on English towns increased, the Bay Colony's authorities became more sympathetic to the "clamour and animosity" against the Indians. Okommakamesit inhabitants were arrested and marched to jail in Boston when Marlborough residents accused them of participating in Metacom's attacks; they were released after several days and sent to Natick after surviving an attempted lynching. When a haystack was burned in Chelmsford, the court ordered the arrest of Wamesit and Punkapoag men; the latter were released after a quick interrogation, but the Wamesits suffered a long period of imprisonment in Boston. The Pennacook sachem, Wannalancet, along with most of his remaining followers, avoided arrest by fleeing up the Merrimac River away from Massachusetts. After those imprisoned were released and returned to Wamesit, they were raided several times by colonists from a neighboring town who burned their homes and crops and killed many women, children, and elderly men. The survivors hurried to join Wannalancet, crying that "there is no safety for us" among the English. Finally, on October 30, when an old shack burned in Dedham, the neighboring Natick Indians were forced from their homes and interred on Deer Island in Boston Harbor.[19]

By February 1676, the incarcerated Indian population on the small island swelled to 550. The Punkapoags had been sent there in December and the Nashobas arrived in February after spending several months locked in a house in Concord. The inhabitants on the windswept bit of rock were "in want of all things almost, except clams, which food (as some conceived) did occasion fluxes and other diseases among them; besides, they were very mean for clothing, and the Island were bleak and cold with the sea winds in spring time, and the place afforded little fuel, and their wigwams were mean." Despite English hostility and abuse, Indian men on the island clamored to help in the war against Metacom, showing their deep loyalty to the Christian colony, an older dislike of the Wampanoags, or perhaps a strong desire to escape conditions on the island. When the General Court finally approved native enlistment, about one hundred Indian men contributed their critical scouting skills to the colonial victory. Those who remained on the island depended on the little food sent by the governor's council and brought by Eliot.[20]

The tide of battle soon turned in the colonists' favor. The previous December, short of food and in need of allies, Metacom sought support from the Mahicans at their capital north of Albany. Old and cherished hostilities that had developed before colonization remained between the Mohawks and more easterly Indian tribes, including the Mahicans and the Wampanoags, and it took little urging from the governor of New York for the Iroquois tribe to attack the Mahicans and their visitors. The Mohawks shattered Metacom's army and pursued the Wampanoags who fled east. Bands of warriors abandoned the region, while others surrendered to the colonists. The spring thaw and news of the Mohawks' success reached the colonists at the same time, and the militias (supported by Indian allies, some of whom had served with Metacom) began successful campaigns against the remnants.

The ultimate English victory became clear in the spring of 1676. In May, the Massachusetts General Court ordered the release of all of the Indians held on the islands in the Bay. Ironically, the "friend" Indians in Plymouth, the colony that had forced the conflict, were treated better than those in

Massachusetts; after declaring their neutrality they were confined to their reserves in Mashpee and Sandwich, but suffered no other misfortunes.

)(

By the outbreak of the great war, the world of the natives in eastern Massachusetts had been turned upside down. The European fur trade had helped increase the authority of certain sachems within the region, but English colonists then undermined that nascent power by increasing their demands on native leaders and backing challengers such as Waban. In large areas, native animals and plants had disappeared, replaced by strange creatures and crops — some adopted by Indians. In 1642, the Narragansett sachem, Miantonomo, mourned that "our fathers had plenty of deer and skins, our plains were full of deer, as also our woods, and of turkies, and our coves full of fish and fowl. But these English having gotten our land, they with scythes cut down the grass, and with axes fell the trees; their cows and horses eat the grass, and their hogs spoil our clam banks, and we shall all be starved."[21]

The Indians who tried to adopt English scythes and axes, along with the Puritan Bible, maintained a fair degree of autonomy, but when war erupted their English allies put them in a concentration camp. Metacom and others who tried to adjust to the colonists while maintaining their customs and sovereignty before finally turning to armed resistance were killed or burned out and starved to defeat. The most fortunate natives were those on Martha's Vineyard, Nantucket, and Cape Cod, who retained their local demographic and political dominance and were barely affected by the war or its aftermath. The Massachusetts and Nipmucs who survived imprisonment found themselves in a strange new world dominated by a colonial culture. Resettling after the war, the survivors would regain much of their autonomy. This "breathing space" would last, however, only a few decades.

CHAPTER 2

"Their proud & surly behavior"

The few Indians who remained in the Massachusetts Bay Colony after release from their island concentration camps soon resettled in the former praying towns of Natick and Punkapoag. The customs that emerged in these villages during the next generation, however, were very different from those inculcated by Eliot. Circumstances allowed or even compelled Indian communities to "reinvent" their culture during a generation in which they enjoyed virtual social and political autonomy along the frontier of English settlement. A migratory subsistence economy, along with a deerskin and beaver fur trade and aboriginal patterns of leadership and land management, reemerged among the Indian enclaves. At the same time they maintained religious and economic connections with the Puritan commonwealth. Neighboring preachers and deerskin traders visited frequently, Indian leaders met with provincial leaders to deal with land issues, and native men went to work for English farmers and served in the colonial militia. The postwar Indian culture in the Bay Colony featured a fascinating blend of aboriginal customs, characteristics that were part of the early fur trade period, and lifeways wrought by the long-term English presence.

The challenges that followed King Philip's War did not leave the Deer Island survivors unscarred. A number of natives were sold or forced into servitude in English households — as some had been before the war — and others resided in near-peonage among the colonists. The Indians initially resettled only two villages because of the continued threat of Mohawk attacks. Prewar divisions between native groups retained some of their power, the Punkapoags going their own way and Natick's heterogeneous community fracturing when Nipmuc families returned to Hassanamisset and Chabanakongkomun. The locations of these villages along and beyond the postwar frontier of English settlement led to continued tension with colonial authorities and neighbors. In addition, colonial demographic growth and political controversies would have long-term effects on native groups. Yet provincial authorities and white neighbors only occasionally intruded on the Indian enclaves before 1700. As a result, Indians in the Massachusetts Bay Colony emerged from the wartime crisis confident of the future, as distressed English neighbors acknowledged when they complained about the natives' "proud & surly behavior."[1]

)(

The "friend" Indians who survived the island in Boston harbor found no rest in the immediate aftermath of King Philip's War. Provincial officials did not allow the former praying Indians to return to their towns, but placed the survivors under the oversight of white guardians near Boston. The natives spent the following year working for English farmers, fishing, and gathering. In addition to settlers who might mistake them for hostiles, Indians outside English settlements faced the threat of Mohawk raiding parties that had played a key role in defeating Metacom. Many who tried to resettle in their praying towns met bitter opposition from English settlers who had seized their personal and real estate. As before the war, some individuals served as servants and apprentices to English families, in some cases involuntarily, while others found employment as laborers.

When the General Court released the Indians from their prison island in May 1676, the survivors divided into two groups following prewar factions. One group, with 252 people (75 men and 175 women and children) retained ties to Natick, Wamesit, Nashoba, and Hassanamisset or other Nipmuc towns west of Boston. The second group, with 35 men and 140 women and children, included those from Punkapoag who had spurned Waban's leadership (estimated at about 60 people in 1674) and others who were either alienated by Waban and his allies during their imprisonment or sought to be closer to relatives along the Massachusetts-Plymouth border. This community went southwest to work for English farmers in the towns near Punkapoag. The first group spent the summer in Cambridge where the land "was very commodious for situation . . . convenient for fishing, and where there was plenty of fuel," while some worked in nearby towns for English farmers. Five months later this group broke apart. The largest faction, led by Waban, split into four bands, each of which settled at or near Natick — including one at Waban's old village of Nonantum. Other bands returned to Concord (those originally from Nashoba) and Namkeake (near Wamesit). That winter Daniel Gookin and John Eliot, who remained the Indians' primary contacts, divided their weekends between the Punkapoags at Brush Hill and Waban's people at Nonantum. When spring replaced winter in 1677, the Punkapoags returned to their village and Waban's people fanned out to Natick, Hassanamisset, and Okommakamesit to plant their crops.[2]

Continuing Mohawk raids, however, forced the Indians to retreat to English population centers for several months. The Iroquois' war against New England Indians, triggered by long-standing hostilities, did not precisely match the colonists' conflict; Mohawk warriors hit both the enemies and allies of the colonists and refused to stop with Metacom's death. But news of an agreement between the English and the Mohawks provided sufficient encouragement for the "friend" Indians to resettle Natick and Punkapoag in September 1677. Yet this was not the end of the Iroquois threat, for raiding parties continued to make the edges of English settlement very hazardous, and indeed those in the two resettled praying towns built forts against future attacks. That fall Mohawks captured two elderly women when they went to Hassanamisset to make cider, and less than a year later warriors carried off twenty-two Natick Indians from cornfields in the adjoining praying town of Magunkaquog.[3] In July 1680, a group of Massachusetts living at Spy Pond in

Cambridge — only a few miles from where the General Court met — were attacked by Mohawks; two were killed and several others "carried away."[4]

The Indians seeking to resettle their towns faced more problems than the threat of Mohawk attacks. Despite the end of the war and the valuable military service performed by many native men, colonists continued to distrust and fear all Indians and to lust after their land. The Indians at Okommakamesit soon felt the desire of their English neighbors in Marlborough to gain "a fair tract of land." When the threat of Wampanoag or Nipmuc attacks declined, a number of white settlers stole fencing and fruit trees from the temporarily deserted plantation. When the praying Indians tried to return and plant crops, "some persons of that place expressly forbid them, and threatened them if they came there to oppose them, so that the poor Indians being put into fears returned, and dared not proceed."[5] Most Okommakamesit families moved to Natick, and for years wrangled with inhabitants of Marlborough and the General Court over claims to the former plantation.

The hostility and greed of colonists could even frustrate the province's strategic interests. With peace established, the Pennacook leader, Wannalancet, returned south to Wamesit, bringing about fifty relatives (most of whom were women), but they found their corn fields already appropriated by white settlers. He and his people were placed on a nearby island, and the selectmen of the neighboring town of Chelmsford took the opportunity to apprentice (or place in servitude) some of the children with English families. Less than a year later, in September 1677, a party of Indians, "that came from the French, [including] his kindred and relations," persuaded Wannalancet and all but two men to return north with them. Massachusetts authorities must have continued hoping that Wannalancet and his people could be persuaded to return, probably because they offered security against Abenaki and French attacks, for in 1681 the General Court named Wamesit as one of three reserves where Indians in the colony could live. Wannalancet and his people never returned, however, and between 1685 and 1686 the Pennacook sachem sold Wamesit's five hundred acres to English investors.[6]

Of course, strategic interests more often meshed with the desires of English settlers. At the outbreak of Metacom's revolt, Nipmucs from Wabbaquassett, one of the new Christian groups created by Eliot's native protégés, had moved south into Mohegan territory under Uncas's protection. Some returned to their homes after the war, but in 1693 the General Court forcibly removed these Indians from their village when it established the town of Oxford deep in the frontier region. Settled by Huguenot refugees, Oxford was one of only two colonial towns created in Nipmuc territory during the forty years following King Philip's War. The court moved the Wabbaquassetts south to Woodstock, along the border with Connecticut and just below the resettled Chabanakongkomun community. The Wabbaquassett community vanished from colonial records until 1774, when Connecticut created an Indian reserve in the northwest corner of the town, but members undoubtedly maintained close connections with the nearby Chabanakongkomun (or Dudley) enclave.7

While Natick or Punkapoag became the home of most of the Indians who survived Deer Island, some elected or were forced to make new lives among the colonists. These isolated individuals and families laid the foundations for a regional Indian network that later transcended surviving enclaves. David Munnanow, who lived at Hassanamisset before the war, moved to Marlborough, where he lived in a wigwam by a tavern alongside a lake until his death in 1740; a century later his grandchildren still lived in the town.8 In 1677, twenty-five Indians lived in Ipswich, an area once inhabited by Pennacooks, and fifty Nashoba Indians lived in Concord, where they worked for the colonists. Those who chose this path still felt the suspicion of their white neighbors, for the fifty in Concord were kept "under the inspection of the committee of militia and selectmen." The Nashobas later moved to Natick, but others remained among the English. Gookin noted in 1677 that about six native families lived scattered around Watertown and Cambridge "under English inspection."9 These households were largely invisible in provincial records, but occasionally emerged from the shadows when individuals moved to or claimed property in Indian enclaves. The survival of Indian families in white towns in the eighteenth century, and their occasional movement between these towns and Indian enclaves, points to a growing web of Indian connections invisible to the colonists' gaze.

Some Indians also lived among the English as servants in colonial households. Their numbers swelled after the war with the addition of many young captives, some made orphans by the execution of their parents. These children were to serve until the age of twenty-four in exchange for room, board, and instruction in a trade, English, and Christianity.10 At the turn of the century, Indian servants lived in the households of many of the Bay Colony's elite, including the chief justice (who was also secretary of the missionary New England Company), Daniel Gookin, Daniel Oliver, William Hutchison, and Samuel Sewall's daughter.11 Their numbers grew during the eighteenth century as children and adult males found themselves forced into involuntary servitude to repay debts or (supposedly) learn a trade. Native leaders complained that their people were unjustly bound for small debts and treated badly, and beginning in 1700 the General Court would try to regulate Indian indentures. Many colonists feared the "savages" in their midst and some towns tried to ban Indian servants or visitors.[12] Subsequent frontier warfare seemed to increase the danger. In the early morning of 14 September 1689, for example, as war flared between New England and New France and her Indian allies, Bostonian Samuel Sewall heard the alarm raised in Charlestown across the Charles River; later he found out that "the occasion was some Indians seen in their back fields. Run-away Servants they appear to be; by which means the Town was generally rais'd."[13]

The colonists' fear and suspicion led the General Court to regulate Indians in the colony. In May 1677, the court confined all Indians in the colony, except for servants and apprentices, to Natick, Punkapoag, Hassanamisset, and Wamesit.[14] Yet the province did not enforce the law, for the Pennacooks never returned to Wamesit, Hassanamisset was not reoccupied until the 1680s, and some Indians lived outside English households in Concord, Marlborough, Ipswich, and other communities. Four months later the court admitted the failure of its regulation, noting that a number of Indians "coming dayly to Boston upon their [the town's] occasions of Market & otherwise" were "drunken and disordered . . . to the Disturbance of ye town & Inhabitants." The legislature again tried to limit the residences of Indians in 1681, ordering all natives (again exempting servants and apprentices) "to come among & under Government of the Indian Rulers of Natick Punkapoag or Wamesit."[15] These laws had little effect, at least in part because the entire colony was, in a sense, an open frontier, and those who knew hidden paths and backwoods found no hindrance in laws they could not read. On 30 December 1685, after winter's onset, a native man was found dead on the Boston Neck — which connected the town with western villages — with a bottle of rum between his legs. Three years later, in the winter of 1688, "three Indian Children being alone in a Wigwam at Muddy-River [Brookline], the Wigwam fell on fire, and burn them so that they all died."[16] Clearly, even the Boston area was not yet fully "civilized," and the Indians within the province were hardly limited by its laws.

The vivid image of the derelict Indian man who perished in the cold winter, drowned in the bottle of his people's problems, conjures up a stereotype that was all too true. Nearly every white observer of Native Americans remarked on the Indians' thirst for liquor. For too many natives in late seventeenth-century New England, the taste for alcohol unfortunately became an addiction. Of course, this was also a growing problem among Anglo-Americans, but the Indians' long list of medical and social tribulations was particularly "sobering" — including not only crime, debt peonage, and poverty, but less resistance to European diseases and lower fertility rates.[17]

The aftermath of Metacom's revolt raised the Indians' use of liquor to a new level of desperation and bitterness. Drinking clearly became an addicting escape from a sense of dependence and helplessness. Initially, alcoholism seemed to be less of a problem in the native enclaves than among those scattered in English towns, but by 1720 Cotton Mather mourned that rum had become a "River of Death" for Indians in the region, and about the same time Experience Mayhew reported from Martha's Vineyard that liquor was a growing problem, affecting many church members and often leading to their excommunication. The expulsion of formerly dependable church members hints that hostility to the increasingly dominant colonial culture played a role in the use of alcohol.[18]

Of the "approved" postwar Indian enclaves in the Bay Colony, Natick became the largest and most prominent. Following resettlement, the village's population surpassed its prewar level until the 1740s, as most of the surviving residents of other praying towns moved to Eliot's former "capital." Gookin reported 267 "Natick Indians" among the four groups around Nonantum in the summer of 1677, and probably all resettled that village in September.[19] The enclave's population would decline over the next two decades to about two hundred by the end of the century, due at least in part to an epidemic in 1683–84 and emigration between 1682 and 1692 to resettle two Nipmuc villages.[20] Natick attracted most of the Deer Island survivors, first because it was the focal point of Eliot's missionary network, and second because it was closest to Nipmuc territory, where some would return when peace came to that war-torn region.

The Punkapoag community, like Natick, experienced a sudden population increase in the immediate aftermath of the war and then a gradual decrease following resettlement. While 12 families, about 60 people, lived there one year before the war, in May 1677 Gookin counted 35 men and 140 women and children.[21] But by 1706 only 8 men — perhaps 40 people in all — remained in the village, and two years later a minister who occasionally preached there had his stipend reduced "upon consideration of the fewness of the Indian families now residing at Punkapoag."[22] The reasons for these population shifts, particularly the precipitous decline after 1677, remain mysterious. Some families may have gone to Natick, to Plymouth, or completely left eastern Massachusetts when changes in the ecological, social, and political environments became too disruptive.

)(

The nature and structure of authority in the Indian towns after the war is difficult to determine, in large part because documents from this period are lacking: Punkapoag never kept records, and the few remaining from Natick began around 1700. In addition, the needs and pressures of the postwar period, particularly in heterogeneous Natick, shaped a fairly amorphous polity. While Eliot's Biblical structure seemed to vanish, many postwar native leaders were those "blessed" by the missionary as rulers, teachers, or ministers. Of course, most of the prominent Christian Indians had been village leaders before Eliot arrived on the scene, and that older pattern remained conspicuous. Indeed, aboriginal leadership patterns reemerged after resettlement, in part from the Indians' needs and desires, and in part because provincial officials (and their legal system) found sagamores, sachems, and their heirs useful in obtaining land in the region. At the same time, entirely new political forms emerged in response to the pressures of postwar circumstances, particularly in heterogeneous Natick, where factions sometimes struggled over land sales and other issues. While the Indians' polity remains somewhat enigmatic, a high degree of postwar political and even legal autonomy is clear.

This mixture of aboriginal and praying town characteristics is highlighted by postwar Punkapoag's leadership. By 1684, Charles Josiah, the grandson of Massachusett sachem Chickatabut, claimed that office. The sachem was not, however, the autocratic ruler that some colonial leaders wanted or expected in an Indian leader, and aboriginal limits on his powers remained. The year before, Josiah's counselors, "old Hahawton" (Ahauton), William Ahauton, and Robert Mamentag, contested an Englishman's claim to land supposedly granted by Charles Josiah. They told the court that "according to the Custom of Indian Sachims, they never sell any Land without ye Conse[n]t of their Counsil or wise men," which they denied ever giving. The three had advised first Chickatabut and then Wampatuck before Charles Josiah inherited the office. One of the Ahautons had also served as the leader of Christians in Punkapoag before the war, although the

Massachusett sachem had actually headed the community. When Charles Josiah died sometime later without leaving any heirs, the counselors, led by the Ahautons, became the town's rulers. Aboriginal and praying town leaderships merged in postwar Punkapoag.[23]

Natick also featured a mixture of native and Christian authority. Following resettlement, Waban, Piambow, and Thomas Tray led Natick. Waban was Nonantum's headman before Eliot arrived. After the establishment of Natick he served as the praying town's leader, and with the departure of Wampatuck rose to the top of Eliot's pyramidal hierarchy. Piambow, Eliot's second convert, had been prominent before the war as the deacon (and father of the minister) of the Hassanamisset church, as well as a "ruler of ten," and apparently gained authority on Deer Island. Thomas Tray's background is more mysterious, although the family was clearly prominent in the region. While the English called the three "rulers," they clearly served as more of a council or court than a hierarchy. As in both aboriginal and Puritan societies, all three derived some of their authority from their age. Also prominent in the community were three others whose titles were not given but who doubtless served as counselors: John Awassamog, Peter Ephraim, and "Daniel." Awassamog was an elderly sagamore who retained authority and land in the region, Ephraim represented Natick to the General Court after the war, and Daniel was probably Daniel Tokkohwompait, the "sober and pious young man of Natick" taken by Eliot and Gookin in 1674 to be the minister of the Nipmuc town of Quantisset, and who was trained by Eliot in the 1680s to become Natick's minister.[24]

These links to other villages also highlight the community's sensitivity to its heterogeneous population. In addition to their prewar roles in Natick and Hassanamisset, all three claimed connections, through marriage or unrecorded allegiances, to a number of praying towns, including Okommakamesit, Nashoba, and Wamesit. Also prominent in postwar Natick were John Wiser, from Quabaug; James the Printer, from Hassanamisset; James Rumneymarsh, from Essex County; the Wamsquam family, from Okommakamesit; Jethro, from Nashoba; "Black James," from Chabanakongkomun; and Joseph Trask, John Thomas, and Thomas Dublett, from Wamesit. While only men are listed in the petitions that highlight community leadership, they may have derived much of their authority from their mothers or wives; they clearly gained additional connections to other towns through these relationships. Thomas Waban, for example, held a connection to Nashoba's sachemship through his mother, and Thomas Dublett had a similar affiliation through his wife.[25] James Speen, of Natick, who had served as a teacher in a Nipmuc town before the war, also held a claim to Okommakamesit through his wife, and by 1702 claimed to be from Nashoba.[26]

One scholar has pointed to Natick's diversity as the roots of its ultimate failure in the middle of the next century, noting that it held "too many groups, with conflicting allegiances, and no traditional connection to the lands on which they settled."[27] The community's polity evolved to meet these needs, however, and the resettlement of two Nipmuc towns in the 1680s and 1690s relieved any incipient pressure.

The ranks of Natick's leaders expanded as the town's polity seemed to change following the death of Waban and Piambow about 1684, yet the connections between aboriginal and mission authority remained. In July 1685, Tray, John Magus, John Moquah, Thomas Waban, three Awassamogs (John, Thomas, and Samuel), and "old Speen" represented Natick in a major land trade (four thousand acres) with the neighboring town of Sherborn.[28] Before the war, Moquah had, like Tokkohwompait, been trained as a minister in Natick and served in a Nipmuc town, Maanexit.[29] Thomas Awassamog had gained his authority three months before the land deal when he inherited his father's sachemship, including the fealty of five "Principall men of Nataicke" — John and Samuel Awassamog, John Moquah, Peter Ephraim, and Eleazar Pegan.[30] The Speens had held the land on which Natick was established, and members of the family had served before the war as teachers in Natick and in Nipmuc towns.[31] Finally, Thomas Waban, as Waban's oldest son, inherited much of his father's authority, by both native and Puritan custom.

In the spring of 1685 several visitors came to Natick, including English traveler John Dunton, who was fascinated by Indians. After tying up their horses, they "were inform'd that the *Sachim*, or the Indian King, and his Queen, were there. The place, 'tis true, did not look like the Royal Residence; however we cou'd easily believe the Report, and went immediately to visit their King and Queen." The two were almost certainly Thomas Waban and either his wife Elizabeth or his mother Tohattawan. "The Sachim was very tall and well limb'd, but had no Beard, and a sort of a Horse Face. The Queen was well shap'd, and her Features might pass pretty well; she had Eyes as black as Jet, and Teeth as white as Ivory; her Hair was very black and long, and she was considerably up in Years." Natick Indians, not colonists, pointed out the sachem and "his queen" to the visitors, so we can be fairly sure that these offices continued to be recognized by the community.[32]

Thomas gained leadership in Natick only after losing a short but bitter contest over the degree of his authority. The uproar manifested the new forms of Natick polity — town meetings, or gatherings of large factions — that had emerged in response to postwar needs. In May 1684, Waban, James Rumneymarsh, and nine others sought to sell Okommakamesit to Marlborough proprietors, but Gookin and Eliot protested the arrangement, in part because the price was so absurd (forty pounds for the plantation's fifty-eight hundred acres) and in part because the "Drunken & debach[ed] indians" who had agreed to the deal had angered "other more sober indians." The two also pointed to an agreement made two years before by a meeting of the Indian leaders "that no indian or indians should sell any land belonging to ye towns without the unanimous consent of every proprietor." And indeed, one month later twenty-four men (including Natick's five "rulers": Tokkohwompait, Tray, Magus, Nehemiah, Moquah) asked the General Court to reject the sale because Waban and "Great James" had sold Okommakamesit without proper authority. The court agreed. The uproar showed that decisions over the community's land were so significant or controversial, particularly given Natick's heterogeneous population, that a broad consensus was required. This was a notable reduction of the powers usually granted a sachem.[33]

The controversy over Okommakamesit also shows that confusion erupted over authority within Natick as leaders of other villages made their homes there after the war. Certainly, Natick's neighbors noticed such disorder, as the selectmen of Dedham told the General Court in 1681 that they had "received diverse & some complaints about the manners and practices of ye Indians that have come in and dwelt among us or near us since the late wars." The selectmen complained about those Indians' "proud & surly behavior"; that they "rob us of our corn & other provisions out of our fields, That cattle in ye woods have been torn by their dogs," and that they "have affrighted some women to the great hazard of their lives." When the leaders of Dedham went to the Indian community to have their counterparts take care of the problems, however, the "antient and soberest Indians at Natick complaint [that] their young men are ruined by these Indians [that they] cannot govern or have any command of them." In response, the legislature (again) ordered all Indians in the province, except servants and apprentices, "to come among & under Government of the Indian Rulers of Natick Punkapoag or Wamesit." While Dedham's complaint is suspect, generally because of the white settlers' fear of Indians and particularly because of that town's continuing conflict with Natick over boundaries, it does point to divisions within the heterogeneous and still-unsettled community.[34]

Natick's mixed multitudes also generated conflict within the town's church. By 1683, Eliot had trained and ordained his successor, Tokkohwompait.[35] Thus an Indian led Eliot's sole surviving native congregation even before the Puritan missionary became ill and stopped visiting, dying in 1690. Tokkohwompait was not alone, however, for Daniel Gookin Jr., son of the Indian superintendent and the minister in neighboring Sherborne, preached once a month in Natick. Gookin's lectures were a gift of the New England Company, an English missionary society headed locally by prominent Boston ministers, merchants, and politicians.[36] There is no hint of how Tokkohwompait and his flock felt about this "hired gun," but their anger and his jealousy is easy to imagine, particularly when Gookin's lectures brought "many English, especially of Sherburn" into the Indian church.[37] Others in Natick, however, preferred Gookin to Tokkohwompait. In 1684, thirteen Indians asked the aging Eliot to raise Gookin's stipend so he would preach more often, for the visiting minister preached in English and attracted white families who "raised the tone of the services."[38] Elsewhere in the region, most notably on Martha's Vineyard and in Mashpee, Indian enclaves insisted on ministers who spoke their tongue and preferred those who shared their culture. Clearly, some in Natick disliked Tokkohwompait or his supporters, and hoped to undermine his authority within the community.

Puritan authorities supported Gookin, in part because they disliked Tokkohwompait's unspecified "Errata."[39] They were also worried, as Cotton Mather would mourn in 1702, that the late great Eliot's once-flourishing church was "much diminish'd and dwindl'd away."[40] Indeed, in 1698 visiting ministers Grindal Rawson and Samuel Danforth found only ten full church members, compared to forty to fifty "visible saints" three decades earlier.[41] Tokkohwompait's "Errata" may have involved the incorporation of aboriginal rituals in his church, like the pipe-sharing ritual later described at an Indian church on Nantucket. He may have also relaxed the church's membership requirements, for in 1711 Mather proposed an inquiry into the admission standards in Natick's church, noting he had heard that they had "degenerate[d] into a very lax Procedure."[42] What troubled the Natick congregation in 1699, however, was not the moral plight of their assembly but its "greatly deminished & impoverished" condition due to "the death of many and removall of others who during the time of the late wars have been sojouring among the English for their support, and are not yet returned to their plantatione."[43]

The Indians particularly bemoaned the unfortunate condition of their meetinghouse. That structure, built at the town's founding nearly half a century before, had collapsed. The Natick congregation told the General Court that they were unable to construct another, and therefore asked to give two hundred acres to an English carpenter to have him "build us a place for our comfortable meeting together." Their request, interestingly, casts doubt on the claims of Eliot and Gookin that the Indians had built the first meetinghouse in 1651 without English assistance. While the number of "visible saints" in the Natick church had declined, the institution did not seem to be in dire straits, for it remained the community's social and spiritual center. The hired carpenter soon built a new meetinghouse for the village.[44]

Far less is known about the state of religion in the colony's other Indian communities. The first group of Nipmucs to leave Natick, led southwest after 1682 by Black James (the prewar praying Indian constable), resettled Chabanakongkomun, far from English settlements, and the village did not reappear in colonial records until the 1720s. Hassanamisset, resettled by another group of Nipmucs in the 1690s, was also too far from any colonial towns to receive the attention given Natick, although James Printer, who had helped print religious tracts in the Massachusett language at Harvard College, taught and preached to the community. Printer died in 1712, leaving Hassanamisset without any obvious religious leader.[45] Punkapoag was somewhat similar to Natick, for the New England Company paid Peter Thatcher, Milton's minister, to preach to the neighboring Indians once a month — and the Punkapoags showed little regard for Thatcher.[46] In 1703, they ordained one of their headmen, William Ahauton, the community's teacher before King Philip's War, and seven years later gave land to a different English minister to "preach the work of God among us . . . [when] not scattered abroad at our hunting houses."[47]

)(

The manner in which the Punkapoags were frequently "scattered abroad" points to how the surviving Indian communities in the Bay Colony resumed their prewar economies, featuring mixed aboriginal and English traits both within and outside the colonial marketplace. The Indians apparently resurrected their aboriginal migratory economy, for in 1684 John Eliot noted that, in addition to worship services at the four "stated" reserves — Natick, Punkapoag, Wamesit, and Chabanakongkomun — they held "occasional" prayer meetings "at places of fishing, hunting, gathering chestnuts, in their seasons."[48] In part this was due to necessity: replacing confiscated farm tools and animals was prohibitively expensive, so many were compelled to hunt, fish, or gather food and plants. The Indians' economy was far more complex than Eliot's letter indicated, however, for Natick and Punkapoag had regular access to regional markets. Indeed, one year after Metacom's defeat the General Court moved to regulate the natives' frequently "drunken and disorderly" trips to the Boston marketplace. There is no record of the goods they sold, although surplus corn and beans and perhaps wild game would be the most obvious products. A demand also existed for Indian baskets, brooms, and wood crafts.49

Natick's economy also represented cultural change *and* continuity. Some Indian men lived and worked for farmers in the immediate aftermath of Metacom's revolt. Even during wartime restrictions (described below) many men continued their seasonal wage labor.50 Wage labor for others was not, of course, an aboriginal custom, and clearly linked the Indians to the colonial economy. At the same time, the temporary, seasonal, and migratory nature of this labor did form a link with native traditions. For the colonists, even the relatively few Indian laborers may have been an important resource, given the chronic labor shortage in rural New England — and the Indians apparently realized this advantage, since in 1681 Dedham selectmen complained that the Indians "refus[ed] to work for the English, except upon unreasonable terms."51

The Indians in the Bay Colony even managed to resurrect the fur trade and to create a new trade in deerskins. Historians have described the fur trade in southern New England as extinct by the mid-seventeenth century due to overhunting and ecological changes. But the destruction of both Indian and white settlements by King Philip's War in the center of the province provided the opportunity for animal populations to recover rapidly. Natick and Punkapoag lay along the eastern edge of this unsettled territory, with unobstructed access to excellent hunting and trapping, and (after 1684) the resettled Nipmuc towns of Hassanamisset and Chabanakongkomun were deep in that region, where the English rarely ventured. In October 1681, Dedham selectmen complained that the Natick Indians "spend almost all their time in hunting, to ye great damage of ye English, wastefully destroying the Deer which might be a great relief to many familys, for [they] take no care to save the flesh, but only get ye skins." The extent of the deerskin trade is difficult to reconstruct, but the Dedham officials reported their Indian neighbors "destroyed & wasted in this manner above an hundred deer in a year, & others of them sixty, fourty, or some such great number apiece."52

Two months later, six colonists traveled to Natick "to buy som[e] Dears Skins of ye Indian." Piambow and Thomas Tray, as well as one of the visitors, later testified that one of the white men believed that a Natick Indian, Job Nussutan, had stolen a beaver trap and an animal in it from another of his party. The accuser, Ciprian Stevens, went to Job's home, and when he found it vacant took a beaver skin "out of a paile of beaver skins [that] were in the wigwam." Stevens also got into a confrontation with James Wiser, told Wiser that his brother Anthony owed twenty fathoms of wampum to another colonist — and took James's gun from Thomas Tray's wigwam in payment, even after James told Stevens that the gun was his and that Anthony was in Nashaway (Lancaster, in Nipmuc country). This incident is a unique glimpse into the enduring frontier of eastern Massachusetts, a world that most historians assume ended with the war or existed only much farther to the west or north. We see a deerskin and beaver trade, traps, wampum, and wigwams. At the same time, we know about this incident because Job later charged Ciprian Stevens with the theft of the beaver skins — in the Middlesex County Court in Cambridge, a stone's throw from Harvard College. Natick lay along the line between colonial and aboriginal worlds.[53]

Natick's postwar material culture was clearly far more aboriginal than English. Visitors to Natick in the spring of 1686 found no houses or cabins, only wigwams and the ruins of two barns. Dunton carefully described the "peculiar" dress of the woman identified as the sachem's "queen."

> Sleeves of Moose Skin, very finely dress'd, and drawn with Lines of various Colours, in Asiatick Work, and her Buskins were of the same sort; her Mantle was of fine blew cloath, but very short, and ty'd about her Shoulders, and at the Middle with a Zone, curiously wrought with White and Blew Beads into pretty Figures; her Bracelets and her Necklace were of the same sort of Beads, and she had a little Tablet upon her Breast, very finely deck'd with Jewels and Precious Stones; her Hair was comb'd back and ty'd up with a Border, which was neatly work'd both with Gold and Silver.[54]

This was hardly the English clothing required by "praying Indian" rules before the war, and had far more in common with contemporary Iroquois costume than their colonial counterparts.

Punkapoag's economy was quite similar to Natick's, judging by the way they were often "scattered abroad at our hunting houses." Even in the middle of the next century the community traveled every summer to fish along the southern side of Massachusetts Bay.[55] The Punkapoags' hunting and gathering economy led the General Court to impose wartime restrictions on that enclave as well as on Natick, for their locations along the frontier fed the fears of their white neighbors. In 1690, after the eruption of King William's War with France and her Indian allies, the General Court admitted "the great danger and Inconvenience both English, and Friend Indians are exposed unto, during the present war with the Eastern Indians: It being very difficult to discern between Friends & Foes," and (once again) ordered all Indians in the Bay Colony to go to Natick or Punkapoag. This time the legislature also ordered "two meet persons to reside at Natick, and one at Punkapoag, who are to call over the Names of the Indians men & women every morning & evening." This measure was not designed to be particularly oppressive, for provincial authorities first consulted with representatives from the two villages (William Ahauton represented Punkapoag, and Peter Ephraim and James Rumneymarsh spoke for Natick[56]) to ensure that the restrictions would be "most expedient for the present settlement of the Friend Indians, so as may be for the safety of themselves and the English." In addition, while one or two guards sufficed to reassure white neighbors, such insufficient force could not actually control the Indians if they had revolted.[57]

The few documents from Chabanakongkomun and Hassanamisset indicate that villagers in the resettled communities almost certainly made their living as did Indians in Punkapoag and Natick, for these enclaves lay far from colonial markets and employment, deep in the "no man's land" of Nipmuc territory. In 1684, Chabanakongkomun was named by Eliot as one of the four surviving praying towns with widely scattered meetings "in their seasons," and when Black James sold all but one square mile of the reserve twenty-three years later, he carefully retained "the right to plant, hunt, and use such parts as would be necessary for their support."[58]

Wartime regulations also furnish evidence about their economies. The isolation of Chabanakongkomun, the westernmost Nipmuc town reestablished in the 1680s, is indicated by its absence from the 1690 restrictions. Hassanamisset's resettlement in the early 1690s, along with colonists' occasional alarm about strange Indians in the Nipmuc region, finally drew the attention of provincial authorities in 1696. In 1694, the General Court passed a measure aimed at "encouraging the prosecution of the Indian Enemy, and preserving such are Friends" by resettling all Indians east of the Boston-Rehoboth road with the exception of "Kekamoochuck near Woodstock" (Chabanakongkomun). One year later the legislature reconfirmed the restrictions for Hassanamisset and imposed the same on Chabanakongkomun.[59]

The Indians in eastern Massachusetts must also have renewed their aboriginal gender roles, for if the men left to hunt, trap, or work for English farmers, then the women must have been (once again) in charge of the community's fields. Although no women appeared among the ranks of community rulers in Massachusetts, at least one female sachem retained her authority in the neighboring Plymouth Colony.[60] Several deeds selling land in abandoned praying towns do, on the other hand, indicate that Indian women maintained some authority over communal territory.[61] This socioeconomic renascence was not stopped by the wartime restrictions, for when the General Court ordered watchmen for the native villages it also mandated that "Indian women & children be not hereby restrained from frequenting the Flats" — probably the now-filled tidal basin between Roxbury and Boston known as the Back Bay — "where they have been accustomed to get Clams."[62] Indian women gained even more responsibility during this period, for in 1689 and again in 1704 the colony sought out and recruited large numbers of their husbands and young men "to go forth with our Army" to Maine. The Bay Colony's effort to recruit Indian soldiers from Natick and Punkapoag is ironic, for the Puritan authorities who had once hoped to "civilize" (that is, make into good Englishmen) these Indians were unwittingly reinvigorating "savage" aboriginal gender roles.[63]

While many Indians in Natick found fulfillment in the revival of their native gender-ordered economy, others sought "improvements" aimed at allowing the community to function more like neighboring colonial towns. In 1684, the village traded four thousand acres in its northeast corner for an equal area owned by the town of Sherburn which was closer to the center of Indian settlement, consolidating its territory and gaining more accessible land. Sherborn also agreed to set aside land, to be chosen by Eliot, Gookin, and Natick's rulers, for a "free school" that English and Indian children would attend together.[64] One year later the Indian community gave fifty acres to an Englishman to build a grain mill in order to save the long trip of twenty (or more) miles to an existing mill.[65] In some ways these developments brought the Indians closer to their white neighbors: the school was to serve both white and native children, and an English miller came to Natick to build and run the mill. Those within Natick who advocated the efforts may not have approved of the aboriginal renascence, feelings also indicated by Dedham's note about the complaints of the "antient and soberest Indians." Or perhaps the village sought the improvements to supplement or diversify their frontier economy, as no doubt many realized that the fur and deerskin trade wouldn't last.

)(

Unfortunately, Natick's deepening connections with its neighbors also made the village vulnerable to those who sought to defraud the Indians. In 1682, the community sold two hundred acres of "remote and waste land" to Samuel How and Samuel Gookin (the son of Daniel Sr.), but the Englishmen somehow managed to lay out 1,700 acres of Natick land. The region's wartime insecurity showed in the Indians' protest in 1695, for their attorney (Thomas Sawin, of Sherborn) told the court that not only was this land grab "to ye great damage of sd indians," but also "to ye great griefe of many English in ye adjoining townes who look upon such dealings as highly injurious and most abhorred, especially at such a time when God is contesting with us by ye Eastern [Indians]." The court confirmed the land grant, but gave Natick one thousand acres alongside Sherborn, apparently from the Nipmuc lands.[66]

A more complicated controversy involved two farmers from nearby Sudbury. About 1680, John Grout bought fifty acres in Natick from two Indians ("without the townes privily, or consent"), and afterwards altered the deed to read *five hundred* acres. The village sued and won, but recovered only four hundred acres.[67] The acreage claimed by Grout lay far from the village center, surrounded by lands owned by Englishmen, so the community decided to sell most of it to another colonist, Matthew Rice.[68] Unfortunately, this only complicated the continued conflict with Grout. The dealings with Rice also turned sour, and in 1700 the village complained that he claimed to own some leased meadowland, and that "when some of us have discoursed with him about it he says wee are poore creatures & have noe money, & if you goo to Law & I [ar]rest you might goe to prison & there Lyue & rott."[69] The actions and the words of these frontier entrepreneurs highlighted the contempt that many colonists felt towards their "friend" Indians.

Fear and bitterness were also apparent in the hostile relationships between the Natick Indians and certain neighboring towns, although more mercenary motives are visible behind the often-angry words. The conflict with Dedham, for example, began with a border dispute at the birth of the praying town in 1651, and continued after King Philip's War. In 1698, the English town checked its border with Natick, and in the process (according to the Indians) stole 1,400 acres, including "forty orchards and forty cornfields old and new & upon where Indians doe dwell."[70] Similar enmity shaped relations with Marlborough, where, following the war, former residents of Okommakamesit were driven away when they tried to return to their neighboring village. A year later, a dozen men from Marlborough and other towns asked for Okommakamesit, telling the court that many Indians from that village had "proved very perfidious" in the past war. After the court rebuffed the request, "outsiders" began buying pieces of the abandoned praying town from various Indians, worrying Marlborough's leaders and leading to their (illegal) purchase from Thomas Waban and a few other Natick men. While the court commonly validated such deeds, the objections by Gookin and Eliot and the political problems faced by the colony swayed the assembly against the purchase — although the inhabitants of Marlborough later divided up Okommakamesit lands without any formal deed.[71]

The Indians were also aware that they had friends and allies among some of their neighbors. Two Englishmen testified to Ciprian Stevens's theft of beaver skins and a gun from a Natick Indian in 1681. The people of Sherborn seemed to have particularly amiable relations with Natick, trading land to the benefit of both towns and attending the Indians' church when their minister, Daniel Gookin Jr., preached in Natick. Indian rights could spark conflicts between colonists. Walter Shephard visited two friends in Sudbury as John Grout's Natick land claims were being fought in court. Shephard exclaimed that "before [Natick] would so part with ye land they would and should fight for it!" His host was horrified, telling the visitor that if he supported the Indians in such a fight "were you my own brother I would as soone shoot you down as I would a Dogg" — though the issue was moot since "surely the Indians would not fight in such a case." Shephard angrily replied that, yes, "they would fight for it & that speedily to[o]." These harsh words between friends not only showed a well of support for the natives' efforts to defend their territory, but also highlighted the colonists' general fear that their Christian Indian neighbors were, in some ways, still "wild."[72]

)(

The Indians' relative autonomy would soon be undermined by the sale and settlement of Nipmuc territory. The vacant lands in central Massachusetts initially acted as an "escape valve" for the natives, providing good hunting and a place to evade the English. While the valve would not actually close until the threat of French and Abenaki attacks ended with the Treaty of Utrecht in 1713, and colonial settlements quickly sprang up between Natick and the Connecticut River, the foundations for the change in autonomy were laid by the sale of the Nipmuc lands in the early 1680s.

Bargaining over Nipmuc territory was driven by regional issues and shaped by fractures within the Natick Indian community. Between 1660 and 1680, the Bay Colony grew in population, wealth, and political power, straining the Puritan commonwealth. The demographic growth was not matched, however, by the colony's geographic expansion. In the wake of King Philip's War, after the threat of Mohawk raids diminished, a new conflict erupted as colonists and "friend" Indians tried simultaneously to return to the few flat and cleared tracts in the region. In May 1681, twenty-two "inhabitants of Natick, Punkapoag, and Hassanamissett" (the latter still not resettled), pressed their claim to "a Natural Right to most of the Lands Lying in the Nipmuc Country."[73] Nipmuc Indians now sought to resettle their ancestral homes and profit from surplus territory, and others in Natick looked to gain from the transactions.

Provincial authorities were sensitive to Indian claims in the region. Many of them hoped for new riches and prestige by investing in the apparently vacant Nipmuc lands, and no doubt would have preferred to ignore the natives. But colonial politics made settlement of the Indian claims critical, for Connecticut and Plymouth pressed competing claims to land and sovereignty in the region, and the Crown's challenge to the Massachusetts Charter endangered unilateral grants made by the General Court. On May 13, the court appointed William Stoughton and Joseph Dudley "to Examine all claims and grants with the sd Country and that the remainder bee disposed some way for this Countrys benefit" in order to sort out the "several Indian claims and some already devised to some persons abroad and amongst ourselves utterly improbable to be of benefit to this Colony."[74] Dudley, chair of the United Colonies (a military council of Connecticut and Massachusetts) and one of New England's most ambitious politicians and land speculators, used the occasion to enrich first the colony and then himself.

Controversy among both Indians and whites created many claims to the Nipmuc lands. Around 1670, John Wampas, a Nipmuc, was chosen by the Natick Indians to "get sealed and recorded the Indians title & Right to those lands," primarily "because he spake English well & was agreeable to the English."[75] Instead he tried (and failed) to gain power by granting land to influential whites. In 1677, an Indian council at Nonantum denounced Wampas's claims; he was accused of selling land to buy liquor, and those present "forbid him to medle any more about those claims."[76] Nonetheless, he continued conveying deeds to Nipmuc land until his death in 1679, after which several Englishmen claimed the "rights" granted by Wampas.[77] In addition, in June 1681, when Stoughton and Dudley hosted a general meeting of Indians in Cambridge, they "found them willing enough to make claym to the whole [Nipmuc] Country but Litigious & Doubtfull amongst themselves."[78]

The "Litigious" conflict over the Nipmuc lands shows Natick riven by at least three factions that reflected prewar divisions between villages. During the summer, the factions resolved their disagreements, so Stoughton and Dudley asked "several of the principall Claymers" to join the party surveying Nipmuc territory. A group of Indians "Belonging to Natick and other towns Punkapoag & Wamesitt" and "ye Hassanamissett Men now resident at Natick" (including Waban, Piambow, John Awassamog, and the Trays) claimed the land between Natick and Hassanamisset. Another faction, including Peter Ephraim, Nehemiah, Elizar Pegan, Joseph Anins, and "several of their Kindred," claimed the section between Manchage (modern Oxford) and Pakachoog (Worcester), apparently including Hassanamisset. Black James, who had ruled Chabanakongkomun before the war, claimed the southern third of Nipmuc lands, including the former site of his village. A fourth section of territory, west of Hassanamisset and north to Nashaway (Lancaster), was claimed by both Hassanamissets and Black James at Natick. The separate demands made by different groups point to the persistence of prewar tribal, village, and clan divisions among Indians in the Bay Colony.[79]

The General Court decided to press the colony's rights to the lands but to pay "some compensation" to the claimants "to prevent future troubles & pretensions." By the following March, Black James and a number of other men had signed the deed that gave most of the Nipmuc territory to Stoughton and Dudley, acting on behalf of Massachusetts; in return, James and his "company" obtained twenty-five square miles in two tracts in the south, where they settled alongside Lake Chabanakongkomun. Claims by Natick and Hassanamisset Indians to the middle and northern sections were met by giving them the area between the two plantations that adjoined Medfield, Sherborn, Mendon, Marlborough, and Sudbury. The colony gained about one thousand square miles, and for their troubles Dudley and Stoughton kept two thousand acres.[80]

While the claims based on Wampas's deeds were scorned by Stoughton and Dudley as "very uncertain," the dead man's sins continued to reshape the former Nipmuc territory.[81] In 1683, Peter Ephraim, John Awassamog, and others from Natick complained that a group of colonists "make large pretences to the Land of Hassanamisset, by virtue as they say of a will of John Wampaus."[82] One year later, faced by another effort to press a Wampas deed, the General Court seemed to squash such claims when it ruled that "it knowes not of any land that Wampas, Indean, had any true or legall right unto."[83] Yet in 1704, Joseph Dudley — the same Dudley who in 1681 had called the Wampas deeds "very uncertain" — endorsed one of the deeds to sixty-four square miles around Hassanamisset.[84] What had changed? Dudley had become governor of Massachusetts, and probably saw the Wampas deed as a way to confirm the province's authority over an area. Perhaps more importantly, the land that the governor owned with Stoughton lay alongside the disputed tract. Early in the next century Joseph Dudley and his heirs would obtain additional Chabanakongkomun land from Black James, and during the following decade the General Court recognized additional claims based on Wampas deeds.[85]

All parties seemed satisfied by the Nipmuc country arrangements. By unambiguously gaining nearly all of the Nipmuc lands for the Bay Colony, Dudley and Stoughton prepared the region for colonial settlement. The Indians living in Natick recognized the Nipmuc territory as an important asset, but expressed little if any opposition to selling most of the land. Since Stoughton and Dudley were quite willing to acknowledge the specific (though modest) claims made by the three Indian groups, and to deny competing claims based on the Wampas deeds (in exchange for deeds to the rest of the territory), the Indians probably saw the arrangements as beneficial rather than harmful. They retained incontestable rights to the places that they wanted to resettle, and indeed over the next decade, groups left Natick to reestablish Chabanakongkomun and Hassanamisset. White settlers showed little interest in the rest of the Nipmuc territory and would stay out for another three decades, and the area continued to provide an escape valve and important resources for the Indians. The negotiations also showed that internal divisions based on prewar residences endured in Natick, but that the "mixed" Natick community could also work together to fight Wampas's deeds.

Unfortunately, the province's leaders recognized the potential of the area for English settlers, and maneuvered to monopolize or gain more Nipmuc land. Just one year after arranging the Nipmuc deeds and "pocketing" their payment of two thousand acres, Dudley and Stoughton purchased one of the two tracts reserved for Black James's people. Indian signatures — *any* Indian signatures — were a useful weapon for competing claims, and a number of the Indian deeds from this period retain a particularly dubious odor. For example, in December 1686, five Indians deeded twelve square miles to white investors for twenty-three pounds, including much of the middle portion of western Worcester County. Four of the five (Joseph Trask and Simon Piticum, of Wamesit, and Job, Sosawannow, and James Wiser, of Natick) lacked such authority, for only Wiser had previously signed any other deed, and none had ever appeared as a leader in their communities.[86]

The pressure on the natives to sell or give land increased under the Dominion of New England. Charles II repealed the Bay Colony's charter in 1684 and a year later his successor, James II, threw the region in political and legal chaos by uniting Massachusetts, Rhode Island, Connecticut, New Hampshire, and Plymouth into the Dominion, and by appointing Joseph Dudley to be the temporary governor. For nearly a year, until the arrival of the military governor, Sir Edmund Andros, Dudley and his cronies manipulated land and law to increase their fortunes. The repeal of the charter resulted in additional demands on Indian lands when the existing Puritan land grants were suddenly plunged into a limbo of legal uncertainty. Towns and provincial leaders went around arranging Indian deeds to back up more tenuous claims. While most of these deeds seem to concern land already occupied by the colonists, the situation created new opportunities for misunderstandings or fraud.[87]

Yet the Indians' relative autonomy was barely disturbed by these land deals. They were also hardly affected by the controversies rocking the colony between 1685 and 1692, although the fallout from these events would in the long run reshape their world. Andros shocked New Englanders by abolishing their legislatures, limiting their town meetings, and forcing toleration of Anglicans and other dissenters. When England's gentry overthrew James II in 1688, after the birth of his son promised another Catholic monarch for England, Boston joined in the Glorious Revolution by arresting Andros and his councilors in April 1689. Massachusetts' victory was mixed. While William and Mary let the Dominion die, they issued a new charter to Massachusetts in 1691 that kept the colony attached to the Crown, made property ownership the sole criterion for voting (instead of church membership), and mandated toleration of dissenters and Anglicans. On the other hand, the Bay Colony obtained New Plymouth, Martha's Vineyard, and Nantucket, and with these areas gained a large population of Indians, including large enclaves such as Gay Head and Mashpee. The combination of these colonies would, during the next century, facilitate the resurrection and expansion of native networks.

꩜

Indian groups in postwar Massachusetts melded aboriginal, praying town, and English habits in their relatively autonomous resettled communities. Leadership in the Indian villages reflected both traditional ways and praying town patterns. The frontier locations of Natick and Punkapoag provided access to the traditional subsistence economy as well as the colonial market, to English farmers as well as prime hunting grounds. Hassanamisset and Chabanakongkomun, deep in Nipmuc territory, were even more independent of colonial authority and the regional economy. The Indian communities' relative autonomy was aided by their social as well as geographic isolation. The two men who had encouraged and facilitated prewar ties accomplished little after the war; Daniel Gookin saw his people only occasionally at meetings in Cambridge before his death in 1685, and John Eliot made only infrequent visits to Natick until his death in 1690. While the New England Company paid ministers to preach every month at Natick and Punkapoag, it generally neglected the Indian communities until 1700, when new commissioners were appointed in Boston. If the Indians who survived Deer Island had not already been inclined to renew older ways, these conditions would certainly compel many in that direction.

Harvard's famous Indian College symbolized the trend of the colony's relations with its natives. The largest building at Harvard had been built in 1655, a few years following Natick's founding, to educate Indian scholars, and within five years also housed the Cambridge Press, which produced Eliot's famed Massachusett-language Bible. Before King Philip's War few Indian scholars survived Harvard, and after the war few (if any) tried to enter the college, so in May 1698, after receiving permission from the New England Company, Harvard pulled down the structure and used the bricks to construct the new Stoughton College.[88] Indian enclaves in the Bay Colony were so secluded that in the same year the commissioners of the New England Company dispatched two ministers to visit and report on conditions in the native communities.[89] The Indians' beneficial isolation would soon be destroyed, however, by the rapid expansion of colonial settlements.

CHAPTER 3

"Encouraged to a more Neighbourly, and fixed habitation"

Indian groups in eastern Massachusetts developed closer links to the province and New England's culture during the first two decades of the eighteenth century. Native villages discovered new conflicts with their white neighbors and formed new alliances with provincial authorities as the political, demographic, and economic tides shifted. Many of the changes were heralded in 1692, when Massachusetts increased its power and influence in the region by incorporating New Plymouth, Nantucket, and Martha's Vineyard—adding a large Indian population to the Bay Colony. The colonial population continued to grow rapidly, causing older settlements to expand and new ones to emerge, and putting new pressures on land and other resources held by Indian groups. Native workers also became a sought-after "commodity," particularly in the developing whaling industry. As their short period of autonomy declined, Indians began to take their protests against labor exploitation, border violations, trespass, and poaching to provincial authorities — moving deeper into the colonial web as they seemed to gain sympathetic ears. At the same time, the colonists' fear and dislike of Indians helped to reinforce the social and cultural boundaries between the two groups.

At the turn of the century, Indian groups in Massachusetts began to weave new native networks that cut across old boundaries between villages and clans. Native threads were, in part, forced to expand into this new pattern, for the pressure of colonial settlements drove many to larger enclaves, and service in the colonial militia or on whaling ships brought members of different communities together. And, of course, the Indians' relative powerlessness and the rise in white racism created common problems and needs. But connections were also created and expanded by native ministers who traveled between different enclaves and brought distant communities together in worship.

A common culture with English and aboriginal attributes emerged among many of the scattered groups. Christian religious services united many communities, but their worship included native music and cere-monies, and aboriginal folklore retained its prominence. Many Indians displayed their desire to live in "a more Neighbourly, and fixed habitation" as cattle became common and cabins began to replace wigwams.[1] At the same time, land was held in common, and individuals could not sell real estate to whites; several communities even overthrew sachems who violated that rule.

)(

Indians in the areas newly annexed to the Bay Colony had experienced relatively little colonial intrusion away from Plymouth Bay. Native families in the interior and along Cape Cod vastly outnumbered the few colonists in their neighborhoods, and maintained a majority on the islands of Martha's Vineyard and Nantucket. Only a few English villages existed between Plymouth and Buzzards bays and on the middle or outer sections of Cape Cod. Glacial ponds, cedar wetlands, and rivers provided unspoiled support for native villages and their traditional cultures. These conditions allowed

Indian communities in the region to remain far less compact or centralized than those in the old Bay Colony, even in the early eighteenth century, making it difficult for historians to reconstruct residence and leadership patterns, social networks, and economic conditions. Relations between natives and colonists were also very different: missionary efforts were barely backed by colonial political muscle and depended on native interest and leadership, and those who did not follow Metacom into war were treated far batter than their cousins in the Bay Colony.

Regional changes in the wake of incorporation brought new challenges to the Indians. The colony's newly consolidated political and economic framework facilitated English expansion and development. Existing settlements grew and colonists established new towns in areas that had been native refuges. Indian communities experienced increased pressure on their resources, including land claims made by colonists and backed by Massachusetts authorities. Such pressures caused families who formerly lived far apart to move closer together. Centrifugal influences also developed during this period, particularly men's service with the colonial militia in the northeast and participation in the developing whaling industry. But the trend was toward fewer or more compact settlements. Out of this process five distinct Indian "spheres" gradually emerged in the annexed territories: southeastern Massachusetts (the former seat of Metacom's power), lower Cape Cod, the upper and middle Cape, Nantucket, and Martha's Vineyard. The five were shaped by precontact political divisions based on watersheds and family and religious networks, and by colonial religious and political developments.

Massachusett remnants in the northern half of the former New Plymouth coalesced into two neighboring enclaves between 1680 and 1700. Missionary John Cotton reported in 1674 that when he preached at Mattakeesit, an Indian enclave alongside Pembroke Pond near Plymouth, listeners came from Assawemit (Assawompsett) and Ketchiquut (Teticut).[2] But the village at Pembroke rapidly shrank, from about sixty inhabitants in 1685 to around twenty in 1698.[3] A Pembroke legend describes how, following an epidemic and the disappearance of Hobomoc ("their evil spirit") from a pond in the town, all of the Indians but "Queen" Patience Keurp left their wigwams for "new hunting ground in the far valley of the sweetwater."[4] Indeed, many Mattakeesits moved to Assawompsett (also called Betty's Neck, from the English name for Assowetough, the daughter of John Sassamon) or Teticut, pushed out by Pembroke's expanding English population.[5] During the eighteenth century, Assawompsett and Teticut inhabitants would gradually form an amorphous group, often called the Middleborough Indians for the colonial town between the two groups. Close relations between the two were facilitated by blood ties, combined Christian prayer meetings, encounters along the path to the clamming beds at Buzzards Bay and, later, colonial pressure on their lands.[6]

After 1700, new ties developed between the two Massachusett groups and Wampanoag enclaves to the south, along the coastline between the uncertain border with Rhode Island and the west side of Cape Cod. Sakonnet and Cokesit were located on the west side of the long estuary called Pocasset (or Little Compton), which later became part of Rhode Island, and to the east, within the boundaries of Dartmouth, lay Nukkehkummees, Achushnet, and smaller, anonymous Indian villages. Old tribal ties and new Christian networks often brought these communities together. The Wampanoag minister William Simons first preached in the two villages in Dartmouth, and then from 1700–30 extended his ministry to all Indian assemblies in the region, becoming "sort of a Bishop among them, travelling every year to several of their settlements to preach & Administer the Sacraments among them." Simon's preaching forged clear connections between the Massachusett and Wampanoag areas, for his church at Nukkehkummees included a number of Assawompsett families.[7]

The development of a southeastern Indian sphere was also encouraged by military service in the colonial militia, for men from different villages in the region served in the same companies. These connections became most apparent when Massachusetts created a new reserve for its native soldiers. In 1701, the province gave 190 acres to an Indian company that had fought for the Bay Colony in King Philip's and King William's wars. The new reserve lay between Sakonnet and Assawompsett, and brought together twenty-five native families from Little Compton, Teticut, Tiverton, and other villages in the area.[8] Initially, the village was identified with Freetown, and later, perhaps after Fall River's establishment in 1803, called the Troy Indian reserve. The soldiers who founded the plantation either used their new home as a base to support or renew a migratory economy or soon moved elsewhere, for in 1763 visitors found only nine cultivated acres and seven houses.[9]

The next Indian sphere, lower Cape Cod, included the only Indian reserves set aside by New Plymouth's laws: Herring Pond and Mashpee. Herring Pond lay along the edge of Cape Cod, between Plymouth and Sandwich, where in 1685 about 120 Indians lived on about three thousand acres. Two other native hamlets lay nearby: Kitteaumut (also known as

Moniment ponds), within Plymouth, and Mannamett, within Sandwich. Christian assemblies tied these three Indian communities together. John Cotton preached throughout the area in the 1670s and 1680s, and in 1685 Plymouth's governor reported an Indian church at Mannamett, where 110 congregants — probably more than the number living in the village — were led by an Indian minister assisted by Captain Thomas Tupper, an unordained Englishman.[10] Three years later Samuel Sewall financed the construction of a new Indian meetinghouse at Mannamett.[11]

The meetinghouse attracted additional natives to the church and to Mannamett, for in 1693, the Indian leaders of the congregation reported 226 people above the age of ten, from at least four different villages, "that belong or owns the meeting house." At least 135 of the members lived in Mannamett. The native language remained dominant among the Indians in the area; not only did Tupper preach in Wampanoag, but those who attended the church had names such as Squaoppoban, Wunnanomuhkukogk, and Mahtoannmum, and they called the meetinghouse "Pomppashpissit."[12] Five years later, two visiting ministers found that the church had grown to 348 adults and adolescents, meeting in two assemblies led by Tupper and two Indian preachers. Relatively isolated from English settlements, Herring Pond, Kitteaumut, and Mannamett (and Tupper's church) vanished from the records for a half century.[13]

Mashpee, the largest Indian enclave in the region, lay only about ten miles southeast of Herring Pond in similarly isolated circumstances, for its core lay far from the colonial roads and was cloaked by hills from the main areas of English settlement. The reserve had been set aside for a group of Christian Indians by Wampanoag sachems in 1665 and 1666; their deeds, accepted as legally binding by the Plymouth General Court in 1685, mandated that the land could not be sold without the permission of the entire community.[14] Like the natives around Herring Pond, those within Mashpee lived in scattered hamlets; in 1674, Richard Bourne noted seven villages with about one hundred adults and adolescents in or near Mashpee, meeting in two Christian assemblies.[15]

Toward the end of the century, families from the villages around Mashpee began to move onto the large reserve. The movement may have been, in part, a result of the effort by Plymouth to restrict Indians in the area to Mashpee during King Philip's War. More important were the centipetal forces of Christian Indian meetings and the pressure exerted by colonial growth. In 1685, Plymouth's governor reported 264 Indian adults and adolescents attending the three churches, and only eight years later Sandwich's minister,

Rowland Cotton, noted but one native assembly, almost certainly Mashpee, with 214 adult "praying" Indians from three contiguous villages (Mashpee, Sanctuit, and Cotuit) — instead of the eleven settlements identified two decades earlier.[16] In 1698, two visiting ministers reported slightly more people in Mashpee (263 in 57 families) than Cotton had found in the three villages — almost the same number reported by Hinckley in the three Christian congregations fourteen years before — and did not note the existence of Sanctuit and Cotuit.[17] The two villages did survive as distinct neighborhoods, but Mashpee was clearly becoming more of a unified community than a series of discrete villages.

Native families were drawn to Mashpee's resources and church. Even in 1794 the reserve was still particularly "adapt to an Indian town. . . . In the two salt water bays are very great plenty of fish of every description; and in the rivers are trout, herring, &c. And in the woods till lately have been a variety of wild game, consisting of deer &c."[18] Mashpee's church was led by Simon Popmonit, who was highly respected by both Indians and colonists. The son of the Mashpee sachem and brother of one of the town's four rulers, Popmonit maintained both his family's authority and the Wampanoag language within the community. When he died in 1720, a large number of Mashpee residents could not or would not understand English.[19]

The Indian communities on the middle and upper Cape were similarly reconfigured toward the end of the century. In 1674, Bourne reported four Indian assemblies in the region with 313 adults and adolescents, drawing from ten villages, five of which lay in or near the English town of Eastham.[20] Within a decade the enclaves around Eastham shrank to three, with 264 inhabitants above the age of ten.[21] Throughout the area, the number of villages apparently shrank as the Indian population grew, for in 1693 Eastham's minister, Samuel Treat, reported only four native villages with about 500 inhabitants in the region: Sahquatucket, Potawaumacut, Monomoy, and Billingsgate.[22]

The Bay Colony's annexation of New Plymouth signaled an upheaval within these Indian communities. Cotton and Treat represented New Plymouth's interests as well as orthodox Calvinism, and the political change cast their authority into doubt. In September 1694, two native leaders representing villages on the middle and upper Cape told the Massachusetts General Court that since the new charter, "the young men of sd Indians have imbibed an opinion that their former Lawes are vacated, and so will yield no obedience thereto but every one acts according to his own will observing no manner of Religion amongst them as they were accustomed, but prophanes the Sabbath and run into many other vices as drunkeness and the like."[23] Clearly, Puritan strictures were not yet cemented among the Indians on the Cape, perhaps because there were few English colonists in the area, or because many that had settled there were religious dissidents and social deviants.[24] But this unique complaint invites further speculation. Perhaps a powwow had emerged to rally support for the "old religion," subverting village leaders who had built much of their authority on a close relationship with English ministers. Indeed, nine years later, village representatives again asked for "the revival of our former methods of civil order," for not only did "immoralityes grow audacious," but they feared "ancient idolatry." Yet no colonist noted religious, political, or social unrest among Indians in the area, so if a revitalization movement did arise, it remained a "domestic" concern that left few tracks in the records.[25]

Between 1700 and 1720, the number of Indian enclaves in the middle and lower Cape shrank farther, as previously "unorganized" areas of Cape Cod became more densely settled by the colonists and new English towns emerged. The Billingsgate community disappeared, probably moving to Potawaumacut by 1703. The Monomoys sold their land about 1714, and most moved north to Potawaumacut or west to Sahquatucket.[26] Sahquatucket also disappeared at about the same time, and its inhabitants may have moved to or become part of the "Indiantown" created by Yarmouth in 1713 (discussed later). The growth of the English population in the region was no doubt the major factor reshaping Indian settlement patterns. The political and social upheaval hinted at by the 1694 and 1703 petitions may have also helped shatter Monomoy and Sahquatucket.

The pattern of Indian settlement on Nantucket was also shifting at the turn of the century, although on this small island the economic changes wrought by the English had far more significance than the influence of native churches. Colonists had begun settling on the west side of the island in the 1660s, although when Massachusetts annexed Nantucket, Indians still outnumbered colonists. The natives also retained over half of the land on the island, and much of their autonomy and traditional ways. At the end of the century, four primary areas of Indian settlement remained: Squam, Polpis, and Gibbs Pond on the east side of the island, where few English lived, and Miacomet, south of Sherburne, the growing colonial town at Nantucket harbor.[27] Sherburne and Miacomet both expanded as the English built an international whaling trade on Indian knowledge and skills.[28]

By 1720, a new economic cycle was established in which many Indian men worked as mariners for colonial shipmasters in the spring and summer. Just as the whaling industry's importance brought a growing number of English families to Sherburne, the need for employment pulled many Indians to Miacomet. The new conditions coincided with a rapid decline of the Indian population on the island, from 800 in 1700 (and only 150 whites) to 358 in 1763; a result of disease and men drawn off to the sea and colonial wars. These circumstances led to a surplus of Indian land, which was rapidly sold by native sachems to the English. By 1725, Indians were a minority that owned only a quarter of Nantucket, and a growing percentage (if not a majority) lived throughout the year in Miacomet.[29]

Native settlement patterns on Martha's Vineyard were reshaped by the same centripetal forces at work elsewhere, as colonial growth and religious connections caused the Indian population to coalesce into a few core villages. Disease soon decimated the natives. While around three thousand natives lived on the Vineyard at midcentury, visitors in 1698 found only 956 Indians on the island.[30] Yet despite their decline the native population continued, as on Nantucket, to outnumber the colonists until the 1720s. In the last quarter of the seventeenth century, the Vineyard held eight distinct Indian villages, in addition to scattered native hamlets, but by 1730 only three consolidated settlements remained. Those that vanished lay within the growing centers of English habitation: Nashanekammuck (one of the largest native villages in 1698, with 231 residents) and Seconchqut (one of the smallest, with only 35) were within Chilmark, and Nunnepoag (84 people), Sahnchecontuckquet (136), and Nashamoiess were located within Edgartown, the first English town.[31]

Chappaquiddick, Gay Head, and Christiantown became the three centers of Indian settlement on the Vineyard in the eighteenth century. An islet separated by a narrow strait, Chappaquiddick included 138 natives in 1698 and grew as it became a refuge for many Indians from Edgartown. When Chappaquiddick's last minister, Jonathan Amos, died in 1706, it became the only Indian community on the Vineyard without a church. In 1727, Experience Mayhew wrote that the island "being thus unchurched, was filled with Drunkards instead of the Good People who had before inhabited it."[32]

At the other end of the Vineyard, connected by a narrow peninsula, lay Gay Head. Perhaps because of its distance from Edgartown, Gay Head became the last native community to accept Christianity (in the 1660s) and remained more insular than other Indian communities in the province.

Gay Head was also the only native community to suffer a religious schism: around 1700, when the village's church was led by Hannit, about thirty Gay Headers withdrew to form a Baptist society that would gradually swell during the century.[33]

The third settlement, Okohammeh or Christiantown, lay in a deep valley shielded by wooded hills from colonists and the shore's storms. In 1660, the one-square-mile village was, like Mashpee, reserved by the local sachem to "remain forever in the possesion of the praying men, that is thus: — that, if the inhabitants turn from God his wayes, other Praying Indians of Takemmy will have their land." The sachem of Takemmeh also promised to enlarge the reserve when twenty families settled in the town, and by 1698 the community contained seventy-two praying Indians.[34] Like Mashpee later, in the 1710s Christiantown insisted on an Indian minister, resisting the New England Company's efforts to replace Japheth Hannit, the renowned native minister, with Experience Mayhew.[35]

Christian Indian preachers helped reorder the Vineyard's Indian enclaves by creating new networks between villages and lending their authority to particular towns. Tackanash, one of the first converts to Christianity, preached in various Indian congregations before his death in 1684. Jonathan Amos of Chappaquiddick became deacon of an Indian church in Chilmark in 1698, before being called five years later to head the church in his hometown.[36] Native ministers also brought people from scattered hamlets to attend services, and many stayed to live in the village with the meetinghouse. Japheth Hannit moved between Indian churches in Nashanekammuck (Chilmark), Gay Head, and finally Christiantown at the turn of the century. While he soon left to preach among the Pequots, Narragansetts, and Mohegans, it may not be a coincidence that Nashanekammuck "disappeared" around 1730 while Hannit's last home on the island, the once-smaller Christiantown, survived into the twentieth century.[37]

Northwest of the Vineyard, emerging from the southwestern edge of the Cape, lay a chain of small islands known today as the Elizabeth Islands. Indians from the Vineyard and the mainland along Buzzard's Bay frequently visited or lived on the islands. Visitors to the islands in 1698 found that the community on Major Winthrop's Island, the largest piece of land, had recently suffered a devastating epidemic that cut their numbers in half, to only thirty people in nine families. While both a white and an Indian preached to an assembly on the island, which often included three families from Sakonnet, most belonged to Japheth Hannit's Nashanekammuck church—no doubt later moving with him to Christiantown. Slocum's and Sandford's islands also hosted a small number of Indian families. Native communities on the Elizabeth Islands were cultural and political extensions of Vineyard enclaves, with members traveling to the Vineyard for important religious festivals and hosting visiting ministers and teachers from the larger island.[38]

Within the old Bay Colony, two spheres of Indian settlement had formed by 1700, one around Natick and the Nipmuc region, and the other at Punkapoag. While the two Nipmuc towns (Chabanakongkomun and Hassanamisset) were isolated from English authority until the 1720s, family networks continued to bind these "traditional" Indians to their "reformed" brethren in Natick. The Hassanamisset leader, James Printer, occasionally traveled to Boston to help translate and print Algonquian-language publications, no doubt staying in Natick along the way.[39] The Indians in Punkapoag, the other surviving Massachusett settlement in the old Bay Colony, never redeveloped close ties with their cousins to the west. Instead, after 1700, older tribal connections reemerged, particularly between families such as the Ahautons and Mamentaugs, with members in Punkapoag and in Mattakeesit and Teticut, along the border with New Plymouth.[40]

Indians in the enlarged province were clearly not helpless remnants. The degree to which native groups shaped their fate is perhaps best seen in the resistance of the former Eliot praying towns to the provincial authorities' clumsy efforts to reorder Indian settlement in the region. In 1706, the New England Company's commissioners, unhappy with the persistence of aboriginal culture in Natick, ordered an inquiry into the state of affairs in the village.[41] Three years later they suggested that "an Essay be made of laying out distinct Lots at Natick, in order to Establishing a more Constant, & Numerous Cohabitation," and two years later sent another investigator to report on "what Course may be taken for the Reformation of what is amiss among them."[42] Since the Indians had made no complaints about conditions in the village, no doubt they saw nothing "amiss among them" and resented such interference. The commissioners decided, in their July 1712 meeting, that "the miserable Condition of the Indians at Natick" could best be solved "by suitable Encouragement to endeavour to bring the Indians from Punkapog, and Hassanamisco, and such other near adjacent places as may have Scattering Indians in them; unto a Cohabitation at Natick."[43]

This "Cohabitation" was not unlike the process under way in south-eastern Massachusetts, but here provincial authorities sought to force changes. Combining the communities would, of course, make it easier to supervise their reformation. The commissioners, including Cotton Mather and Samuel Sewall, decided to meet with Indian leaders on 22 July in Natick to offer their "Encouragement" for the enclave's "Reformation" and to persuade the Punkapoags and Hassanamissets to immigrate. The natives must have gently but firmly refused the company's ideas, for the colonial authorities made no record of the meeting and organized no changes.[44] In February 1713, the commissioners discussed developing a plan to combine the three towns, but again nothing transpired. Clearly, the Indian communities had no interest in being reformed by outsiders.[45]

Provincial authorities did facilitate some connections between Indians in older parts of the Bay Colony and those annexed in 1692. In 1708, New England Company commissioners took Peter and Caleb Brand, two of the grandsons of the Mattakeesit sachem, and paid to have them boarded and educated in Roxbury, just north of Punkapoag.[46] Later, Peter moved to Natick, where he became a famous physician, and Caleb returned to Mattakeesit.[47] Company officials brought John Neesnumin, the renowned Sandwich Indian minister, to preach in Natick, and in July 1717, after Daniel Tokkohwompait's death, representatives of the community asked the company to obtain Neesnumin's services.[48] Company officials even paid Neesnumin's debts on Cape Cod so he could take the post.[49] Unfortunately, the new minister, considered "the most accomplished person, possibly, in the Province, for understanding the English and Indian Languages, and Speaking them," followed his predecessor into paradise two years later.[50] But while the development of an Indian network may have been facilitated by colonial interests, the initiative and interest was shaped more by Indian needs than English goals.

While new ties developed between Indian enclaves, some local distinctions persisted. Coastal and inland groups had slightly different economies: Natick and Nipmuc Indians hunted on land while those on the Vineyard and Nantucket hunted on the ocean, and, as already noted, inland laborers worked for English farmers, and those on the coast sailed for colonial sea captains. More notable was the tenacity of different Algonquian dialects. In 1710, Sewall urged the New England Company to spread English literacy instead of teaching the native language, in large part because of the linguistic differences between Indians in various regions within Massachusetts — and, of course, because Indians could "scarce retain their Language, without a Tincture of other Salvage Inclinations." Yet the peculiarities of local dialects would decline over the century, as Indians moved between communities and the books published by Eliot and his successors created a more uniform language in the region — and paved the way for the eventual dominance of the English tongue. Indeed, this process was already under way, as Sewall observed that "their Language is also continually changing; old words wearing out and new ones coming on."[51] By 1722, Experience Mayhew could boast that, since the Vineyard Indians had adopted the Natick-dialect Eliot Bible, "most of the little differences that were betwixt them, have been happily Lost, and our Indians Speak, but especially write much as those of Natick do."[52]

)(

Christian Indian assemblies wove new ties among native communities, particularly in southeastern Massachusetts and the islands. The situation was replete with irony, for the religion introduced by English invaders now acted as a cement for native enclaves, and the transformation of Indian groups was in part facilitated by the faith that offered social and psychological stability in the sea of change. A number of Indian preachers traveled throughout the region, fulfilling their Christian desire to encompass the larger tribe of God's children within the community of believers. In the 1680s, Rachel, the daughter of the first Vineyard sachem to convert to Christianity, and her husband Jonathan Amos, who became deacon in one of the Indian churches in Chilmark in 1698 and later preached in the Chappaquiddick Indian church, lived in one of the Indian communities in the Dartmouth area.[53] Neesnumin, of course, traveled from Sandwich to Natick. Japheth Hannit often visited Pocasset and other native communities in southeastern Massachusetts, before he left the Vineyard to preach to "unsaved" Indian groups in Connecticut and Rhode Island. Hannit's success was no doubt aided by the network created by William Simons, the Indian minister in Nukkehkummees, who preached throughout the area and whose church included natives from various towns in the region.[54] The religious networks between the mainland and the islands played a major role in creating a new regional ethnic community through shared language and religious rituals. By the late 1760s, Indian enclaves in the region would assemble each summer to worship as a community.[55]

Key distinctions set native congregations apart from their English neighbors, despite a similar stress in their rituals on sermons, prayer, and Biblical verses. Native languages dominated Indian church services; this, along with English scorn for these tongues, reinforced the Indians' sense of a common, separate identity.[56] Many Indian congregations insisted on a public confession and conversion narrative from prospective members; while this custom seemed quite "primitive" (and admirable) to Puritan visitors, its persistence drew strength from roots in the aboriginal oral culture.[57] Other important Indian rituals also survived in the new Christian context. Even in the late eighteenth century tobacco retained its sacred nature, at least among the Nantucket Indians, who passed around pipes after their religious meetings: "And when the meeting was done, they would take their tinder-box and strike fire and light their pipes, and, may be, would draw three or four whifs and swallow the smoke, and then blow it out of their noses, and so hand their pipes to their next neighbor. And one pipe of tobacco would serve ten or a dozen of them. And they would say 'tawpoot,' which is, 'I thank ye.' It seemed to be done in a way of kindness to each other."[58]

The persistence of aboriginal culture can be seen in the continued importance of folk beliefs and stories. A number of creation stories retained their authority, particularly those of Maushop, the giant who lived on the Vineyard before the Indians, and who created Nantucket and the other islands in the region. Witchcraft accusations, considered legitimate among both natives and Europeans, remained prominent in the Vineyard communities as a way to solidify community boundaries against internal and external (English) disruptions. The belief in *manitou* and various spirits, including the Indian "devil" Cheepi, also remained strong, though kept hidden from the English, who scorned and tried to crush such pagan remnants. Sacred places retained their importance, for Christian Indians continued to respect "sacrifice rocks," special sites often marked by cairns where visitors and passersby leave tokens of respect.[59] Even Christiantown's location showed the tenacity of native sacred places, for aboriginal religious ceremonies had been celebrated on its "Dancing Field" and the village was initially called Mannitwattootan (or *manitou* town) — a place of spiritual power.[60]

)(

The Indians' economy at the turn of the century similarly mixed aboriginal and English habits. The precontact ethos, that people could claim only the products of the land, not the land itself, remained strong in most enclaves, although toward the middle of the eighteenth century this tenure began to change, rapidly and significantly in some, slowly and slightly in others. Enclaves that survived into the following century retained their land in common; while families claimed and worked distinct plots that the children could inherit, ultimate title remained with the community and abandoned land could be claimed by others. Many Indians in New England, like the Natick men who resumed trapping and trading fur after the war, continued to gain their subsistence in traditional ways. At the turn of the century, for example, "several straglers that have no settled place" often attended the Mashpee church.[61] In 1700, the New England Company budgeted fifty shillings for the Punkapoags to plough their fields "so they may be Encouraged to a more Neighbourly, and fixed habitation," but a quarter century later the Indians were still often "scaterd abroad at our hunting houses."[62] Old technologies also remained useful, such as the fish weir that the Mattakeesits maintained in Herring Brook during the early eighteenth century.[63]

While Indians maintained many habits with aboriginal roots, they also adopted an increasing number of English ways, in large part because of their familiarity with and long-standing preference for colonial goods, but also because of the environmental alterations caused by the increasing colonial population. Although wigwams dominated native villages from Natick to Gay Head into the middle of the century, by 1700, Indians were "handsomely clothed in English apparel" — at least for colonial visitors. Traditional gender roles eroded as men increasingly planted English crops and raised cattle, sheep, and horses, and women spun thread and wove cloth for their English-style clothing. Visiting Gay Head in 1702, Samuel Sewall voiced his delight at the contents of the headman's wigwam, "especially the Furniture, demonstrating his Industry, viz, Two great Spinning Wheels, one small one for Linnen, and a Loom to weave it." When his Indian host returned from sowing English wheat, Sewall was given the very English beverage of "good Milke and Water." He also noted, on his way back to Chilmark, "four good Oxen which belong'd to one Indian."[64] Six years later, Experience Mayhew told Cotton Mather that "there are yet but a few Indians on Martha's Vineyard that have Houses of the English fashion, tho' the number of these is of late increased; but in respect of their Apparel, they are generally cloathed as the English are, & they by degrees learn the English way of Husbandry: Several of them have good Teams of Oxen, with which they Plough and Cart, for themselves & Neighbours, as the English do. Many of them have also Horses, Cows, Sheep & Swine."[65]

Men who did not work their land often obtained employment, usually as farm laborers or sailors. A few native men learned new trades: Mayhew noted that on the Vineyard there were "several Weavers, One or two house Carpenters, One Wheel wright, who is so good a Work man, as to be frequently employed by his English neighbours. There are several

Tailors, & one if not more Shoe makers, and one Black Smith . . . and one Cooper."[66] Vineyard Indians, particularly those from Chappaquiddick, also spearheaded the whaling trade from the island, although their relative isolation and economic autonomy kept debt peonage at bay until the middle of the century.[67]

Indian communities in early eighteenth-century southern New England did not simply "pick and choose" among aspects of aboriginal and English cultures. More often the two ways blended into a new path, visible in their economies as well as their worship. We have already seen how, in Natick during the 1680s and 1690s, hunting and horticulture were intertwined with the regional market. Similarly, natives on Nantucket frequently exchanged garden produce, deer, and fish (in addition to their labor and land) for colonial cloth, fishing and hunting supplies, and liquor. Changes in the regional economy could, ironically, even revive precontact ways: as Nantucket Indian men left on long whaling voyages, native women (as in Natick) gained authority and renewed their dominance of agriculture.[68] Women also developed a trade in native crafts, making baskets, brooms, and mats to sell to the English. The lack of a clear distinction between Indian and English ways at this time is illuminated by the first sight that greeted Samuel Sewall when he landed near Gay Head in 1714: "a Lame Indian, on Horseback with his Net on his shoulder, to catch Fish by Night." The fishing technology and the horse were English devices that improved the lives of the handicapped Indian and his community; the time and place chosen, however, as well as the diet that the fish represented, were native.[69] All native enclaves during this period shared this amalgam of aboriginal and English customs.

>(

Traditional lines of leadership remained surprisingly constant despite the deepening regional ties between villages, and the deliberately disruptive effects of Puritan missionaries. The new religion could actually help maintain cultural and social continuity, for many Christian Indian preachers and teachers, like Simon Popmonit of Mashpee, came from powerful families that produced sachems and other leaders.[70] Nantucket sachem Daniel Spotso, for example, preached to an Indian assembly on the island, and no doubt the aboriginal foundation for his authority helped to ensure that his congregation would be attentive to every sermon.[71] After Punkapoag's sachem died in 1703 without an heir, the community proclaimed William Ahauton, a descendant of one of the late sachem's counselors, to be their minister.[72] Even leaders who did not find salvation, such as Samuel Coomes of Martha's Vineyard, retained much of their authority, demonstrated their public spirit, and redistributed wealth by hosting important community celebrations — including Christian rituals.[73]

Indian groups on Nantucket were particularly conservative, for sachems continued to lead their people, although their authority was now tempered by native preachers and judges instead of powwows and counselors. These men conveyed land and resources, including grazing and stranded whale rights, to other Indians as well as whites, in return receiving payments and/or tribute. Natives also continued to show respect for their sachems by working for or giving goods to English merchants as a form of tribute; the sachems then drew on this credit for goods.[74] On their side, sachems no doubt continued to fulfill their traditional responsibilities of redistributing these goods by hosting poorer families, travelers, and community events.

But gradually, the polity of Indian communities began to reflect that of their colonial neighbors. By 1698, Nukkehkummees in southeastern Massachusetts chose their four rulers each year, just as colonists in New England town meetings did.[75] Most Indian enclaves had one or more judges or justices of the peace, who wielded the same quasi-judicial powers as English JPs, and like their white counterparts came from a village's leading families — probably the same ones that provided sachems and preachers. Judges were chosen each year by their people, and held the power to decide cases involving up to forty shillings, although their decisions could be appealed to English courts.[76] The power of these new offices grew with the decline in the authority of many sachems, as English goods and ideas "warped" their traditional powers and responsibilities. A chasm began to open between the needs of Indian communities and the actions of their sachems.

The nascent conflict between traditional authority and the evolving Indian communities emerged first in Christiantown and Gay Head on the Vineyard. Christiantown, or Okohammeh, was set aside for Christian Indians by the Takemmeh sachem, Keteanummin. Keteanummin never converted to Christianity, and later tried to sell the land to Tisbury farmers when the village failed to pay tribute. After his death, his son Alexander claimed the sachemship in 1700 and deeded all of his rights to one of Tisbury's richest men, Simon Athearn.[77] In response, the Takemmehs, including those in Okohammeh, met and rejected Alexander's claim, recognizing instead Keteanummin's eldest son, Zachariah Peeskin, as the Takemmeh sachem.[78] The Mayhew family intervened in favor of Peeskin, probably because they opposed Athearn, and, in August 1702, Peeskin confirmed the Okohammeh grant and passed almost all of his sachem's rights to the praying town. One year later the General Court rejected Athearn's deed and endorsed the Okohammeh reservation. In the wake of this affair the community assumed ownership of the sachemship and its lands — inside and outside Okohammeh.[79]

Although the Takemmeh sachemship suddenly belonged to Christiantown, consensus on the meaning or extent of its powers was eroded by the rapid socioeconomic changes on the Vineyard. Members of the enclave clearly felt free to use or sell to colonists unused Takemmeh lands, generating new conflicts with the neighboring town of Tisbury and within the Christiantown community. Tisbury complained to the General Court in 1704 that "several Indians have, and do yet, by force, possess and improve the land belonging to the English, (pretending that they are a part of their township)."[80] Ten years later, Samuel Sewall found many in the village angered that Isaac Ompany, their ruling elder, minister, and magistrate, "lives in the Town's English House [the meetinghouse] Rent-free." According to native custom, Ompany, as sachem and minister of Christiantown, would have been entitled to use the village's most prestigious building. Some in the enclave, however, clearly desired a new order. Sewall backed the "rebels" and ordered Ompany to pay twelve shillings rent each year.[81]

Even greater controversy embroiled Gay Head's sachems. Mittaark, the famous Christian sachem of Gay Head, was succeeded by his son, Joseph (or Josiah) Mittaark, who in 1687 deeded the area (and the Elizabeth Islands) to the governor of New York, Thomas Donegan.[82] The Gay Head enclave, outraged at this arrangement and threatened by the loss of their land, challenged the Mittaark deed. In August 1703, at a hearing on Cape Cod, the Gay Headers produced a document showing that in September 1681 Mittaark and his counselors promised that their land was "forever your possession." This contract spelled out the relationship between the community, its leaders, and their land. First, anyone selling Gay Head land would lose all of their communal privileges. Second, Mittaark promised that "if any of these sons of mine protects my sachemship, he shall forever be a sachem. But if [any of] my sons does not protect my sachemship and sells it, he shall fall forever." His counselors made an identical promise about their heirs. When the committee questioned the document, Hossueit, the Baptist minister, testified that "he wrote that writing long since Mattack's death [in 1683]." While this contract was almost certainly, like many other native documents in Massachusett, a valid oral agreement later recorded by Hossueit, the court's committee took the opportunity to declare the agreement a forgery and to uphold the deed to Donegan.[83]

While the Indian enclaves annexed to the Bay Colony adjusted gradually to English dominance and expansion, the inland Indian "capital" of Natick experimented with more radical modifications during the first two decades of the century. Natick was the only Indian enclave to leave written records, a unique legacy that betokened, facilitated, and documented the village's rapid transformation and decline. The village's records were kept by Thomas Waban, the son of Eliot's famous first convert, who was literate in both English and the written form of Massachuset developed by Eliot.[84]

At the start of the century, the town was led by three men, called rulers or judges, who combined judicial and legislative functions — as in many other Indian communities. But by 1707, Natick was holding annual elections of town officers — selectmen, constables, tithingmen, and others — just like its English neighbors and unlike any other Indian enclave in eastern Massachusetts. The records, which are quite spotty, provide no explanation for this radical change. Perhaps community leaders wanted to demonstrate their sophistication and stability to the New England Company officials who had suddenly become interested in reforming Natick.[85] At the same time, Natick managed this change in polity without actually altering leadership patterns, just as they had half a century before. The same individuals and families who had led the community under the older system were generally elected to serve as selectmen or constables. Other alterations in the village at this time would provide openings for even more substantive changes later in the century.[86]

Natick's landholding system at the turn of the century similarly mingled native and colonial customs. As among the English, heads of households were assigned shares or parcels of common land by the community's leaders, property was held in perpetuity, sons inherited from fathers, and men dominated landholding in the town — at least on paper. By the beginning of the century, as Natick families claimed, held, and inherited land in the village, a division gradually emerged between older men with long-term ties to the community and higher status, and those who were newcomers, younger, or less valuable to the community. Yet major landholding differences between them and their English neighbors remained. Some women inherited and held property, and the community sometimes interfered with land ownership and use.[87] Perhaps most importantly, land was not treated as a commodity and was rarely sold to outsiders, leaving the core of the community so intact that in 1703 a provincial official could report that the plantation "hath had but little Incroachment made upon it by the English Neighborhood."[88]

But after 1713, Natick's world changed rapidly. The 1713 Treaty of Utrecht ended Abenaki and French raids in the region, and along with them, the frontier status that had sustained the villagers' autonomy. Anglo-Americans quickly moved into the once-dangerous region between the Charles and Connecticut rivers. By 1715, the community felt compelled to ban the sale of timber to Englishmen, no doubt because of the region's rapidly swelling white population as well as Natick's deepening ties to the market economy and the growing demand for wood in Boston.[89]

This was also a turbulent time for Natick's church. Daniel Tokkohwompait died in 1716, and his replacement, John Neesnumin of Sandwich died only three years later.[90] After Neesnumin's death, the schoolteacher, town clerk, and selectman Thomas Waban led the congregation.[91] The loss of two highly respected native ministers left the Indian congregation despondent. In addition, their church was again in poor physical (as well as spiritual) condition. "[I]t is in danger of falling down; the Boards shattered & falling off, & the Windows broken down, & so open that the Rain & Snow drives all over the House, so that the Seats & Floors are much damnified."[92] The building was soon repaired, and not long afterward a new spiritual "carpenter," Oliver Peabody, an Englishman, arrived to rebuild the Natick congregation.

)(

As Indian communities in eastern Massachusetts adjusted to the post-war world, new pressures reshaped their relationships with the English. The whites' large families and long lives created land shortages in many Massachusetts towns. As colonial expansion brought Indian and white settlements close together, the fear and dislike of natives held by New Englanders looked increasingly like modern racism. The colonists' emerging racism facilitated (or vindicated) aggression against their Indian neighbors, as farmers coped with dwindling resources by trespassing on native lands and poaching Indian wood and fish. Provincial authorities reacted to the disorder by defending Indian rights and resources (at least verbally) against the intruders, creating a tripartite relationship between Indians, their white neighbors, and officials in Boston. Ironically, the willingness of the governor and the General Court to consider native complaints drew Indian groups deeper into the colonial culture as they tried to defend the lands and resources that preserved the remaining vestiges of their autonomy.

Provincial officials were initially, at least in part, anxious to preserve good relations between colonists and the "friend" Indians because their resettled villages helped guard the English frontier. Of course, the Indians' location also meant that their hunting parties could easily meet with Mohawks, Pennacooks, or Abenakis and their French contacts — a possibility that unsettled officials in Boston. In March 1700, the governor of Massachusetts reported "credible Information" that some "evil minded and wicked Emissaries" intended to provoke war by telling the Indians living in the remaining plantations that the King "designed to cut off and utterly extirpate them — By which lying spirits many of the sd Indians have been abused and put in fear and are said to have enterd into a Combination and Confederacy and to be drawn together in considerable numbers threatening a general Insurrection and in a hostile manner to fall upon his Majs Subjects ye English." In response, the governor demanded that His Majesty's subjects "inform them of the utter falsehood and untruth of any such reports," to avoid any provocations of or quarrels with the natives, and to "be very careful & vigilant in observing the behaviour and motions of the Indians."[93]

Four years later the frontier erupted as Abenakis, Caughnawagas, and their French allies surprised and destroyed the western town of Deerfield. Provincial officials felt compelled to address the alarm of colonists along the edge of settlements who complained about the "insolent manner" of Indians in the region who alarmingly "pass through the Towns & Travaile into the Woods without Licence from authority . . . by which their Liberty opportunity is given them that are so minded to Convey Intelligence to our enemies." Again the General Court restricted Indians in Natick, Punkapoag, and Hassanamisset "to prevent the sd Indians from travelling or hunting beyond the bounds and Limits then set them."[94] Of course, under these limitations the inhabitants of the three plantations soon ran low on food, so in 1706 the court began giving money to Leverett to buy supplies for the Indians.[95] In 1708, the court ordered better enforcement of the restrictions, "being Informed That the friend Indians Do still Presume to Travel into the Woods, & amongst the Frontier Towns, contrary to the Order of this Court, whereby her Majties Subjects are put in Terror, & the Lives of the sd Indians Endangered."[96]

The General Court created the wartime restrictions to quiet the fears of the Indians' white neighbors; only one guard was assigned to each native village. And the colonists' wartime "terror" no doubt helped inspire the New England Company commissioners' efforts to reform Natick and bring other Indians to the larger village. The Indians' useful loyalty was not an issue, for provincial authorities made special efforts to enlist Indian men to help fight the colony's battles. In 1704, "several parties" of Indians from Punkapoag and Natick were "drawn for her Majsty's service" by special recruiting parties sent by Indian superintendent John Leverett.[97] Six years later the court ordered additional companies of both English and Indians enlisted for another expedition against Port Royal in Nova Scotia, and one year later paid Captain Charles Church for raising seven companies of Indians for the Quebec expedition.[98] Military service was widespread, and after the war, Indians from Natick, Scituate (on the old border with the former Plymouth Colony), and Mashpee sought assistance because of wounds or illnesses. Compared to enlistment in later wars, however, their service created few problems for the Indian communities; no petitions were filed during or after the war to sell land in order to support widows or orphans.[99]

During the eighteenth century, the colonists' "Terror" began to develop into a racism that combined prejudice against darker skins with traditions of frontier danger (preserved in popular captivity narratives) and contempt for a people seen as inherently drunken and lazy. In December 1705, the General Court debated a bill to punish sex and marriage between whites and blacks or Indians "with extraordinary penalties." Not all of the province's elite favored such discrimination; some feared this would "be an Oppression provoking to God," and had the reference to Indians removed from the law.[100] But in any case the law was hardly necessary, for few of the colonists would have considered such a match. Natick's minister in the second half of the century, Stephen Badger, noted that the Indians "are generally considered by white people, and placed, as if by common consent, in an inferior and degraded condition, and treated accordingly."[101] A Pequot raised among whites in eastern Connecticut found that his people "were represented as having no souls to save, or to lose, but as partridges upon the mountains. All these degrading titles were heaped upon us. . . . prejudice stung the heart of every white man, from the oldest to the youngest, to the very center of the heart."[102]

The scorn that colonists felt toward natives in Massachusetts had three far-reaching and substantial effects. First, white racism reshaped and reinforced the frontier between native and colonial villages even as the line of English settlement drove west to the Ohio Valley and north into distant New Hampshire and Maine. Anglo-American towns and neighboring Indian villages maintained deep cultural and social boundaries even as the regional economy and many leaders of the province sought to assimilate native villages. In fact, the creation of higher racial barriers by the English allowed those walled in by them to take on additional aspects of the outside culture during the century without the risk of losing their distinctiveness.

Second, the cultural and socioeconomic gaps between Indian groups narrowed as members of scattered enclaves saw that they faced common problems. Ties between groups thickened, the social expectations and cultures of distant villages became more alike, and access to common resources became an increasingly significant community "marker" as Indians found themselves besieged by aggressive colonists. Provincial authorities unconsciously helped strengthen ties between villages by gradually fashioning common policies for all native enclaves in the province, including the right of Indian groups to manage resources as they desired.

The third effect of racism was to justify whites in exploiting Indian labor or native land and resources. Badger condemned the English settlers who felt free to take "every advantage of [the Indians] that they could, under colour of legal authority, and without incurring its censure, to dishearten and depress them." Yet even those colonists who wanted to help the Indians assigned part of the blame to the natives' passivity, abuse of alcohol, and "backwardness." Badger expressed his dismay that the natives "became more indolent and remiss in their attention to the improvement of their lands."[103] While the manipulation of debts and outright fraud and poaching later became a terrible plague, in the first two decades of the century some Indian communities were already on the defensive against the fraud and trespass of their white neighbors.

The abuse of economic and legal powers by whites in the region may, in fact, have been among the forces causing scattered Indian villages to coalesce into larger communities. In 1700, Simon Popmonit and two other leaders of Mashpee "and places adjacent to the town of Sandwich" complained to the General Court about their white neighbors' fraudulent labor practices. Whites made small loans to the Indians or threatened lawsuits for real or imagined damages, and then forced the natives to "bind themselves or [their] Children [as] apprentices or Servants for an unreasonable term, on pretences of or to make Satisfaction" for the debts. The General Court was clearly sensitive to this violation of equity and past laws, for they not only agreed to the Indians' request to have two justices of the peace approve future indentures, but also empowered the officers to act on any complaints against existing contracts.[104] Mashpee, the largest Indian reserve on Cape Cod, became the center for natives in the region during this period. Larger numbers, more concentrated settlements, and the abundant resources within Mashpee provided political autonomy and clout unavailable to scattered hamlets. Within two decades there would be no Indian "places adjacent to the town of Sandwich" other than Mashpee.

A worse situation existed on Nantucket, where many Indian men were forced into whaling vessels by the county's legal machinery, owned, operated, and often greased with rum by the merchant families who held the Indians' debts. In 1716, the Indians complained to the General Court about the "great Injustice and Oppression that they suffer from some of their English Neighbours," including fraudulent whaling contracts, and asked to have the island put in another county so their legal conflicts with whites would be heard elsewhere. The court responded by requiring judges from the mainland to hear the disputes. Two years later, in 1718, the legislature passed another law to prevent the "great wrong and injury" done when whites forced Indians into "unreasonable" debts "when they are in drink and out of capacity for trade" and then sued the natives for such high damages that "they have no way to pay the same but by servitude." Thereafter such contracts could only be made with the approval of two local justices of the peace. Of course, since those on the island were often from the leading merchant families, the law simply created a formal procedure for binding Indian laborers. Indeed, a few months later the Indians complained that "if [they] sue the English, the Judges, Jury, Sheriff & Clerk are the Defendants." While the General Court may have tried to solve the Indians' problems, on Nantucket as elsewhere it relied on the local elite — some of whom may have been involved in similar affairs, and many of whom supported their friends over "drunken lazy Indians," or at the least were reluctant to take action against neighbors.[105]

Indian groups increasingly took their problems to the governor and General Court, in part because they had no alternative, and in part because provincial officials showed a growing sympathy and readiness to intervene. Samuel Sewall initially puzzled over whether the "need" to reform Indian villages would be better served by ending the natives' distinct legal status or having the province "reserve entire, and untouch'd the Indian Plantation of Natick" and other lands.[106] But he and other Massachusetts leaders decided that justice and the colony's needs would best be served by interceding on behalf of native groups who sought to protect lands and resources. Their decision may have been inspired in part by competition with France at the opposite end of the province, in Maine. Abenakis who had already accepted Jesuit priests rejected Puritan missionaries at least partially because of the infamous hunger of English colonists for land. In 1701, the head of the

New England Company in London wrote to Sewall that the company "very much approve[s] of the proposition you mention of fixing sufficient boundaries to prevent the English Incroachments upon those poor people, which we think is not only just and Equitable in all civil respects, but may be of use for propagating the Gospel amongst them by removing of those Prejudices which they may entertain against us for Depriving them of their Lands."[107] More importantly, as the frontier disappeared in Massachusetts, the aggressive actions of settlers became a threat to the province's social and legal order. Encroachments thus posed both moral and political problems, so the protection of land reserved for Indians became an important goal.

At the turn of the century, the leaders of the Bay Colony faced the need to bring people in the newly incorporated areas into line with the legal standards of Massachusetts. Indians were an important part of this process, for they had already begun to bring conflicts with their neighbors to provincial authorities. In 1701, as the General Court began to receive their petitions, the legislature extended the Bay Colony's restrictions on the purchase of Indian land to the former New Plymouth, and voided any past transactions made without the approval of Plymouth authorities.[108] Four years later, the province published and sent to all Indian villages a book of laws in both the Massachusett and English languages, no doubt to ensure that the natives understood the new regime. In 1708, as part of the effort to bring native communities *and* their white neighbors into the colony's legal mainstream, the General Court ruled on a number of long-standing Indian claims. While the Indians lost most of their cases, the court's rulings provided a new stamp of legal legitimacy to the remaining native reserves.

Two of the cases decided by the General Court involved disputes between Teticut and the neighboring colonial town of Bridgewater over claimed grants by Massachusett sachems. In May 1699, Abigail of Teticut, the "only daughter and Heiress" of Josiah, the late Massachusett sachem who had lived in Punkapoag, complained that men from Bridgewater had taken a tract of Teticut land "without any grant from ye said Josiah."[109] At about the same time, the entire native community went to the General Court to complain that "their English neighbours of Bridgewater did some years past disturb them by laying Claim to their Town or a Considerable part thereof under pretence of some grant or purchase."[110] The Indians claimed three miles on each side of the Teticut River. Bridgewater, on the other hand, had a deed from Chickatabut that gave the colonists first claim to six square miles, after which the Indians could lay out their three square miles.

In 1708, after several hearings and long delays, the General Court ruled in favor of Bridgewater's claim.[111]

A similar dispute between Assawompsett and Bridgewater concerned a recorded will. Since no Assawompsett reserve existed in colonial law, the land on which the community lived belonged (according to the law) to a number of Indians, most of whom were descendants of John Sassamon, whose death had helped trigger King Philip's War. His granddaughter, Betty Sassamon, charged a number of Bridgewater settlers with trespass, and produced as evidence a will recorded after her ancestor's death. A witness told the court's committee that the document had been written "many years since" the person died. The committee therefore clearly doubted the Sassamon claim, but decided the conflict was moot since "the English do not Molest" her or her relatives on their eighty-five acres. The will was almost certainly given orally and written down after Sassamon's death, like the better-documented Gay Head will.[112]

The Assawompsetts brought an internal controversy to the court's attention at the same time. Betty Sassamon's late husband, Felix, who died without a will, had also been married to another Indian, Abigail, and the two women could not agree on who held the rights to Felix's land. While there are no additional details, the strife almost certainly involved a conflict between colonial and native customs of inheritance and ownership. The court's committee referred the issue to the county's probate judge "to Settle those Lands according to the [English] Law" — just as they did with their English neighbors.[113]

Several other cases decided in 1708 focused on the validity of oral memories put onto paper after the speaker's death. Two cases on Martha's Vineyard involved the conflict between Mittaark's agreement with the Gay Head community and deeds from his son Joseph giving the same land to the New York governor. The court's committee ruled that Mittaark's covenant on Gay Head, described earlier, "was forged & not true." The Indians also contested the sale of Nashawaquinssee Neck, which connected Gay Head to the main island, to John Mayhew. The committee did not repeat its assertion that Mittaark's agreement was fraudulent, but noted that by helping maintain a fence for many years between the Neck and Gay Head the Indians had demonstrated that they had accepted the transaction.[114]

Finally, in the contest over resources on Nantucket (detailed below), the English presented deeds showing they had purchased grazing rights from deceased sachems, and the Indians produced a document "to prove the former Conveyance of it to them by their Sachems." The committee found that the scribe and other witnesses of the Indians' deed "did not Agree neither to the time nor place [that] it was writt . . . w[hi]ch gives us Cause to believe that they were not true but forged & false."[115] Semiliterate Indians in the region often recorded land transactions and other verbal exchanges years after the event, and there is little doubt that the agreements rejected by the General Court were oral agreements between the sachems and their people, later committed to paper.[116]

Not all Indian objections to English deeds were scorned. As noted earlier, Simon Athearn's claim to Christiantown, sold to him by Alexander, was rejected by the court's committee in favor of an agreement made between Keteanummin, Alexander's father, and the Indian community that was quite similar to Mittaark's arrangement with Gay Head. But, of course, Keteanummin's deed was written, dated, witnessed, and agreed to by the English before Alexander sold the same area to Athearn.[117]

New England authorities thus generally ruled against the native's oral records but accepted grants by long-dead sachems. Not surprisingly, these legal standards led the General Court to rule against most of the Indian claims, although the same criteria also led them to reject some English claims. They also referred the only internal Indian conflict to the "proper" colonial forum, thus demonstrating that natives were expected to participate in the same institutions and to follow the same procedures as their English neighbors. Such expectations clearly put the Indians at a disadvantage, particularly since many did not even speak enough English to communicate their cases to the authorities. Much of the Indians' testimony in 1703 was "Interpreted to us, by persons well knowing of ye Indian Tongue."[118] Nor was language the only barrier, for, as the Teticuts later told the court, they had lacked "a true Understanding of the English Laws" when they pressed their case against Bridgewater.[119]

The Teticuts also found that the court's ruling against their case provided a large loophole for ambitious colonists. Seven years later, Isaac Woono and Joshua Ahauton complained that Edward Mitchell of Bridgewater "gives us Trouble at Law" in his effort "to claim the best part of our said Indian Town."[120] While the court seemed to give the Indians a large tract of land, the ambiguous law and lack of clear boundaries gave Mitchell an opening to claim land in the heart of Teticut. The court took no action, for Mitchell lost his claim in the Plymouth County court, appealed to the Superior Court, and then died before gaining a ruling. But because Mitchell's claim remained unresolved, it would provide leverage for his relatives to claim Teticut land in the late 1730s.[121]

Indian groups in the Bay Colony frequently found their borders challenged by white neighbors. Poor maps and aggressive settlers proved a potent threat to native resources. Natick and Dedham had, of course, sparred over their boundaries since the establishment of the Indian town. In 1710, Mashpee complained that the town of Barnstable was claiming "a considerable part of the[ir] Lands," and that whites had already built two houses in the disputed area.[122] The court sent a committee to review the boundaries between the two towns, but it was apparently unable to resolve the issue. Eight years later, three Barnstable men living in the disputed territory petitioned the legislature to settle the controversy, for they were "unwilling to contend with the said Indians in the Common Law by Reason of the Poverty of the said Indians." While the General Court settled this particular battle, conflict between Barnstable and Mashpee, like the bad feelings between Natick and Dedham, never really ended.[123]

Indian enclaves also increasingly suffered from trespass and poaching. Native communities held their fields, woods, streams, wetlands, and other areas in common, which, combined with poorly marked boundaries and the colonists' growing numbers and racism, made Indian resources tempting targets. In 1714, the Potawaumacuts complained that English neighbors rejected their long-standing rights to cut wood (for fuel and fencing) and gather plants in the undivided commons.[124] Additional battles over public resources, most notably whaling rights, would emerge there later in the century. Conflicts over valuable grazing rights also worsened on Nantucket. In 1695, natives were fined for exercising their rights to graze cattle and horses on and take timber from the commons.[125] Twenty-three years later, the Indians complained that "their English Neighbors . . . have pulled down the indian Houses & built on their Land, that they plow across the Indians & plant in their Land, & take away their Horses & Cattle to prevent their Plowing." Nantucket colonists denied the existence of any problems, and the General Court took no action.[126]

Gay Head and Chappaquiddick also faced problems with white neighbors over grazing rights. There were no wolves on Gay Head, so English herdsmen allowed their "Flocks of Sheeps & Goats [to] go at large without a keeper rambling over the Island. And if any sheep be stolen and killed, the English Owner is ready to be jealous the Indians did it."[127] During the same period a similar "very great controversy" erupted between Indians and the growing number of English on Chappaquiddick. Both groups agreed to have the conflict arbitrated by the governor of Massachusetts, and in 1715 his council gave white settlers part of the small island while guaranteeing that the Indians "shall forever hereafter jointly hold, possess, and enjoy the Soil of Chapaquidic aforesaid, to be never alienated sold or conveyed away in whole or in Part" without the General Court's approval.[128]

The agreement also upheld many native rights. The English were given exclusive access to salt hay on the commons, but the upland and "Wabsquau" grass were reserved for the Indians, the former for their horses and the latter for mats and other crafts. The island's winter grazing land was to be shared in common, but the English were required to pay the Indians for each head of cattle brought to that land. Both English and Indians were limited to a hundred "great cattle" or their equivalent in horses, sheep, or goats — further confirmation that the natives were actively involved in raising English stock, including horses. The sachem was given the governor's authority to choose someone each year to count the number of English cattle in the common grazing areas. Finally, the scarce timber on the island was reserved for the Indians' use. The Indians were satisfied with these decisions, but the English settlers were "of another Mind," and soon "broke thro said Settlement," generating renewed conflict forty-five years later.

)(

While some Indian enclaves were pressed to fend off the quickening desire of their white neighbors for land and resources, others gained new protection against such pressure. Between 1700 and 1725, four new Indian reserves were created: two by the General Court, one by a missionary society, and even one by a colonial town. While indigenous communities already existed in all but one of the locations (Freetown), legal recognition of their existence and boundaries were necessary for survival in the new century. The province's creation of the Freetown-Troy Indian reserve has already been discussed. In 1724, as part of the border settlement between Bridgewater and Teticut, the General Court created a one-hundred-acre Teticut reserve "on that Spot where the Indians had Improved from Time to Time."[129] After the court accepted Donegan's deed to Gay Head, in 1711 Boston commissioners of the New England Company persuaded the organization to buy the peninsula to make it "sure to the Indian aboriginal inhabitants . . . and promote peace."[130] Two years later, the town of Yarmouth on Cape Cod, when dividing up the last of their common lands where many Indians lived, decided to avoid conflicts and the governor's attention and set aside a reserve "for the native Indians of this town . . . for their use forever to live upon, and for planting and fire wood." Significantly, the natives were not only barred from selling or leasing the reserve or its wood, but also forbidden "to receive any other town's Indians to live thereon."[131] "Indiantown" in Yarmouth must have become the new home of natives who had left Monomoy and other enclaves on the cape.

The creation of native reserves was not, however, always motivated by a desire to preserve Indian rights. Instead of returning Gay Head to the natives, the New England Company retained ownership and charged the Indian families an "Acknowledgment" in order to finance their "civilization," hoping that "the consideration of their paying it to themselves in upholding the schools, will Sweeten the Exercise, and make the yoke easy to them; being brought on gently and gradually."[132] The Gay Headers resisted this arrangement: one man, for example, admitted to a New England Company commissioner that he had failed to pay his rent, "yet he expects to hold the Land, because his House is there" — and apparently he was not ejected.[133] The New England Company also planned to rent out "unused" portions to colonists. When Samuel Sewall visited Gay Head on behalf of the company in 1714, he "spake to them Endeavouring to persuade them how great Benefit & Security they had by the Company's Costly Purchase, and of our sincere Intentions," but "they could not be made willing that the Neck should be lotted out." In light of their hostility, Sewall advised the company in London that he "judged it best to proceed gently, and could not find it convenient as yet, to Lett out any part to Englishmen."[134] But Sewall's words were either disingenuous or ignored by others, for soon after his return to the mainland the company leased six hundred acres for ten years to Ebenezer Allen — Sewall's host during his visit to Gay Head. While the rent was to be used for the Indian community, the New England Company controlled the purse strings and evicted a number of native families from the area. The company's actions outraged Gay Headers, and in the 1720s the Indians would (with some success) fight the threat of additional leases.

The New England Company carried out a similar project on the mainland, with somewhat less opposition. In September 1715, company commissioners asked the Natick Indians to sell to them the apparently abandoned praying town of Magunkaquog; the company would then rent out the land to white settlers and dole out the rent money to Natick families. But many in the community still grew crops or retained deep emotional connections there. Magunkaquag meant "a place of giant Trees," and Samuel Sewall described in awe the many "great White Oak, and Chestnut Trees here, and much Champion Land very fit for tillage." He should not have been surprised that the Indians "at present shew some Indisposition to part with it."[135]

But the Natick Indians rethought their "Indisposition," and eighteen days after rejecting the company's offer, a committee from Natick came to Boston to meet with Sewall, and he was able to record in his diary that he had "Accomplish[ed] the Bargain for Magunkaquog Land, and paid Fourteen pounds in part. *Laus Deo.*" On October 11, he went to Natick with Daniel and Thomas Oliver, Harvard president John Leverett, and John Cotton to obtain the Magunkaquog deed — and as part of the deal paid each Indian proprietor three pounds. The next morning, a messenger from Natick told the shocked Englishmen that Isaac Nehemiah, one of the Indian signatories, had committed suicide during the night by hanging himself with his belt.[136] Sewall did not comment on the obvious parallel between Nehemiah's fate and the story of Judas's betrayal and suicide. Such actions were not uncommon among Indians, who killed themselves if they felt emotionally abused or dishonored. Nehemiah's suicide highlighted how some Indians "passively" resisted the sale of their lands to colonists, as well as the emotional attachment that many Natick Indians still held to Magunkaquog.

On the other hand, at least one Indian community, Punkapoag, backed their white neighbors against the "support" of provincial authorities. In 1703, Massachusetts Indian superintendent John Leverett found that, contrary to provincial law, seventeen white farmers had settled in Punkapoag "upon Leases taken of the Indians."[137] He challenged their right to live at Punkapoag without the General Court's permission and, after a few years of delay (and additional threats by Leverett), the superintendent submitted their leases to the governor and noted that "they are ready to come under a regulator." By that time the settlers had rented about half of the Indian reserve, at terms that averaged 153-year leases, eight pounds for a down payment and annual rents that ranged from peppercorns to a shilling.[138] The leases generated a fierce jurisdictional conflict between the governor and the General Court — which supported the settlers.[139]

The Punkapoags supported the settlers (and the legislature).

We have hiarde out to some of our English nighbors some of our Lande to settle upon amongst us because we hade more than we could improve it was with and by ye free consente of Dorchester . . . now your petetioners humbly pray they may still injoy ye same under Dorchester as formerly and that our english nighbors may still continue with us and peacably injoy those Lands which we have hired to them according to their Leases: for they are a benifite and a suchar to us many ways.[140]

The Punkapoags had a number of reasons to welcome the settlers. The colonists offered useful skills (such as carpentry) and assistance (such as food). Neighbors of Indians often commented (or complained) that natives sought food or shelter when conditions were bad, and unrecorded agreements may have been struck on such occasions. While none of the Punkapoag deeds survive, no doubt the community kept the right to gather plants and hunt animals on the lands leased to the settlers. The leases were finally allowed to stand, although the General Court took charge of administering the terms. In 1724, the legislature gave the settlers permission to buy their land outright, and by 1725 the Indians retained only a fourth of their original reserve.[141]

The Punkapoags felt that their shrinking community left surplus land that was best used to obtain new friends, for the land they retained was "more than we and our children can or shall improve."[142] Indeed, the Punkapoag population was rapidly declining. Two years later, the New England Company noted "the Fewness of the Indian families" in the enclave, and a decade after that, between 1717 and 1718, the community was devastated by "measles, feaver and ague."[143] Seven years after the epidemic, a group of English residents near Punkapoag asked to buy a third of the Indians' remaining fifteen hundred acres, which they claimed were "much more than ever they are likely to Improve, being very few & decreasing in Number."[144] Five Punkapoag men signed a petition supporting the sale, telling the court that "they are so few in number they are not able to settle more than a thousand Acres."[145] Unfortunately, the conflict between the settlers and provincial authorities in Massachusetts, glimpsed in Punkapoag and other Indian enclaves, would widen over the next few decades — just as relations worsened between the Indians and their neighbors, in Punkapoag as elsewhere in the colony.

By 1720, the patterns of Indian life in eighteenth-century eastern Massachusetts had taken on a clear outline. Fewer native villages existed than in 1700, and those that survived the first two decades would still be there at the Revolution. Internal religious networks and external pressures by white settlers brought Indians from many small hamlets to the larger communities whose common lands were protected by provincial law. Seven distinct spheres of Indian settlements emerged by this movement: Nipmuc-Natick, Punkapoag, southeast, lower and middle Cape, outer Cape, Nantucket, and Martha's Vineyard. Subsequent decades would see the ephemeral lines between these regions increasingly blurred as natives took on more elements of the dominant culture and moved between Indian enclaves.

At the same time, a new, even more rigid frontier emerged between Indian and colonial villages even as the wave of English settlement swamped native enclaves and moved far beyond them. Trespass, fraud, and poaching were not new. What *was* new was the increasing number of white neighbors, their growing desperation for resources, and their racism (or at the least the intensification of their ethnocentrism) that made the Indians even more vulnerable. On the Indian side of that frontier, the hostility of white neighbors helped to reshape and reinforce the cultural boundaries that native enclaves needed as they grew closer to provincial authorities and the dominant economy. Indians were uncertain how to deal with the challenges of belligerent white neighbors; neither leaving the region nor military resistance were viable options. Many groups went to provincial authorities for protection against the aggressive settlers — receiving moral support but little real relief. Problems with trespassers and poachers would only increase during the next two decades. The regional Indian community thus developed with the economic, demographic, and political pressures of the mid–eighteenth century.

CHAPTER 4

"To Live more like my Christian English neighbors"

In the second quarter of the eighteenth century, regional events and internal problems generated ever more rapid changes in Indian communities in eastern Massachusetts. Native groups found it harder to resist the pressures generated by expanding colonial settlements. The decline of the Indians' protective seclusion became even more apparent as all native groups were forced to confront the growing problem of trespass, fraudulent land sales, and poaching. Those in isolated hamlets or farms were drawn to the larger, more autonomous reserves. Connections between distant Indian families and groups deepened as more men from many communities came together in companies to serve on the Maine frontier, and often went to other enclaves to find wives or new homes. Demographic problems also reshaped Indian groups: the vulnerability of children and the elderly to disease led the survivors of small groups to move to larger communities, and debts and poverty from medical problems led an increasing number to sell land to English settlers. The movement of Indians from one village to another and colonial political and economic forces continued to erode old boundaries between native groups.

Indians picked two different socioeconomic paths in their efforts to cope with the colonists' economic and legal pressures. Some groups chose "to Live more like [their] Christian English neighbours."[1] They embraced landholding in severalty, English ministers, English consumer goods, and colonial neighbors — although they also maintained common and exclusive use of some woodlots and fishing ponds. Other Indian enclaves maintained communal landholding and a higher degree of cultural autonomy. Yet the more traditional groups also recreated their systems of resource management, for they increasingly faced the threat of land and wood sales by individuals desiring English homes and goods. They overthrew discredited sachems, allowed families to mark off and pass cultivated plots to their children, and limited the access of newcomers to communal resources. A group thus *created* "traditional" rules to preserve common resources.

Paradoxically, whether their path was "radical" or "traditional," Indian groups systematized and limited access to resources *because* of the developing ties between native groups, for social norms governing behavior eroded as people moved between communities. Native enclaves sought the assistance of provincial authorities in their efforts to defend community resources, in part against discredited sachems but primarily against the growing trespass and poaching by their white neighbors. Colonial farmers lacking costly land and wood saw the Indians as fair game, and the Indians fought back using provincial law. Thus a frontier between Indians and English survived in southern New England even after the colonists gained political, economic, and demographic dominance.

)(

Massachusetts developed rapidly in the second quarter of the century. Land shortages already troubled some towns at the turn of the century, as the Puritans' remarkably high birth and low death rates left insufficient land for their offspring. But after the Treaty of Utrecht ended the threat of

Indian and French attacks north and west of Boston, colonists felt secure to establish new towns in the former "no man's land." Native enclaves suddenly faced a horde of land speculators and settlers. This expansion extended to the economy of southern New England, as businessmen expanded trade with England and the Indies, creating a complex, commercial, consumer-oriented economy that led to growing inequalities. While some Indian enclaves tried to minimize their dependence on the unstable and disruptive colonial economy, none could completely resist the changes. Colonial expansion exacerbated by the Indians' low fertility and high mortality rates forced changes in settlement and economic patterns, undermining the control of resources that had helped maintain communal boundaries.

In southeastern Massachusetts, the Indians' sale of marginal or border lands showed that many native farms had become isolated islands within the expanding sea of the colonial population. As Indian families sold those lands, Teticut became the center of native population in the region. In 1736, Thomas Felix told the General Court that he wanted to sell his small farm in Assawompsett because it was surrounded by white settlers, and planned to buy land in Teticut.[2] Three years later, Samuel Thomas asked to sell his farm, which lay "four miles or more distant from any other Indian Plantation," so that he could resettle in the large Indian village, "where he may be near the meeting[house] & have many other conveniences which he is now destitute of." Fortunately, there was "good Land enough at Teticut" for Felix to buy and Thomas to "take up & improve."[3]

Teticut also drew Indians from farther north who retained blood ties to its residents. For example, Job Ahauton, from a leading Punkapoag family, moved there in the 1730s to care for his grandmother, Leah Shuntun, and her vast lands — nearly four hundred acres — some of which were held in common with Thomas Hunter, another Punkapoag Indian. Ahauton soon bought Hunter's shares, and by 1742 had amassed about four hundred acres in Teticut — ironically, more than half the size of the remaining Punkapoag reserve that he left behind.[4] By 1741, about half of the supposed Teticuts signing a complaint about trespassing actually "belong to other Remote places," claimed the three Englishmen who had trespassed on the native reserve. Only one of the signatories, they told the court, actually lived in Teticut in the late 1710s; the rest had only recently moved to the Indian town.[5]

This movement began to blur social boundaries between Assawompsett and Teticut, giving rise to the "Middleborough Indians." By 1736, Thomas Felix was referred to as a "Middleborough Indian" when he sought to move from Assawompsett to Teticut. In the late 1720s, Joseph and Jane Abel, from Little Compton, bought land in Assawompsett and later moved to Bridgewater, alongside Teticut.[6] Later in the century, references to Assawompsett and Teticut would largely disappear from provincial records. Of course, old distinctions between the two communities may not have vanished so easily in actuality, but boundaries between groups were clearly breaking down. Even wider and deeper tribal boundaries were crumbling, for Little Compton was deep in the Wampanoag "homeland," and Teticut had been part of Massachusett territory before King Philip's War. In fact, Indians soon disappeared from Little Compton altogether. The final trace of the community vanished in 1735, when two men and a woman decided to leave and sell their remaining ten acres — because their small farm was now surrounded by English farms.[7]

Similar dynamics were at work in and near Natick, the largest inland Indian enclave. While there are few descriptions of emigration, the village's detailed vital records, unique for an Indian community, point to many newcomers. Since the Natick Indian population remained fairly stable until the late 1750s, despite extremely high mortality and low birth rates, the community must have continued to attract other Indians during the first half of the eighteenth century. In fact, about 30 percent of native marriages between 1720 and 1740 paired members of established Natick families with individuals whose family names did not appear earlier in town records. The connections between Natick, other Indian enclaves, and isolated families in the region provided new blood for the community. Beginning in the 1720s, a new generation of Natick leadership included newcomers such as Jacob Chalcom and Nathaniel Coochuck, who brought fresh influences as well as new blood to the community.[8]

Ties between Natick and Hassanamisco made it particularly easy to move between the two villages. Mary Poignet left Natick at the turn of the century to marry Moses Printer, who became a Hassanamisco leader in the 1720s; in 1738, their daughter Mary returned to Natick to marry Zacharias Tom, and nine years later Mary and her sister Bethia joined the Natick church.[9] Economic as well as social ties connected the two groups. Many in Natick shared in the proceeds from the sale of Nipmuc lands to the province, and when the Hassanamiscos obtained offers in the 1720s for their land and millrights, Natick proprietors claimed a right to part of the payments.[10] Some Natick Indians later rented land belonging to Hassanamiscos, or claimed an inheritance in the community's land and monies.[11] In at least one case, a Hassanamisco and a Natick man jointly owned land in both enclaves.[12] Indeed, even after Mary Printer became Mary Tom, she continued to draw from Hassanamisco resources.[13] Of course, pre- and postwar connections also allowed the human tide to flow west. Samuel Pegan, for example, left Natick to join his Chabanakongkomun relatives (in fact, the entire community became known as the Pegan Indians) in the 1720s.[14] The Pegans even extended their influence into Connecticut, for in 1733 the New England Company dispatched Thomas Pegan from Natick as a teacher to the Mohegans.[15] While the early part of the century saw a population rise in Natick due to immigration, by the 1740s the flow of Indians would be largely away from that town (see chapter 5).

More hidden were the persistent ties between the two Nipmuc enclaves of Hassanamisco and Chabanakongkomun, even though the two were located only twelve miles apart. One incident spotlights the connections between the two groups. In 1733, the colonists in the new town of Dudley, which was created around the small Chabanakongkomun reserve, invited several ministers to ordain their new pastor, including "the Rev. Mr. Printer of Hassanamisco" — Sarah Printer's father.[16] The invitation not only reveals ties between the two Nipmuc groups, but is our only hint that one of the Hassanamiscos was an ordained minister. It also points to the hidden influence of the Chabanakongkomun Indians on the English town, for why else would the colonists have invited a native minister living several towns away?

Any analysis of changing Indian settlement patterns must acknowledge the uncertainties of colonial records. Some patterns are clear. For example, an October 1924 list of seventy-six Dartmouth Indian men in southeastern Massachusetts indicated nearly twice as many families as Rawson and Danforth found only a quarter of a century earlier. Given the Indians' high mortality and low birth rates, this rapid growth must have come from immigration — the two men listed with the last name of "Pequot" point to some of the newcomers' origins. The Dartmouth list also demonstrates that villages in the area, as elsewhere in the region, had coalesced, for English missionaries in 1698 had identified *two* Indian enclaves within the Dartmouth township, Nukkehkummees and Achushnet.[17]

Yet whites living in the area during this period later remembered visiting scattered native bands. The notable dearth of petitions or other records from the Dartmouth Indians also hint at a loose network of extended families scattered throughout the town. More traditional settlement patterns would have been facilitated by the lack of a legal reserve in Dartmouth, rich resources in the area, and the many sections of the huge township that lacked colonial settlements. A similar situation existed in Chabanakongkomun, for there are few letters or records from this community, and the reserve's rich diversity — including a cedar swamp, dense woodlands, and a good-sized lake — would have supported aboriginal settlement patterns.[18]

Regional networks and coalescing settlements were not, of course, mutually exclusive. This was particularly apparent on Cape Cod. As the number of villages on the Cape shrank, Mashpee grew, to the point that, in 1720, seventy Indian families (at least 280 individuals) made it the largest native enclave in Massachusetts.[19] At the same time, family connections extended throughout the territory. A Connecticut visitor recalled that a wedding at Potawaumacut in the mid-1720s, drew "seven score Indians" — far more than were ever noted by visitors to the town, and, since Puritan observers rarely counted children, probably many more than 140 natives attended the celebration. Indians must have come from all parts of the region to the celebration, clear evidence of developing ties between different Indian groups in the region. The extraordinary turnout at Potawaumacut also suggests the persistence of Indian clans, for a wedding would have been the most likely occasion for members of the bride's and groom's clans to gather from distant communities.[20]

The Indians' amalgamation and developing regional ties were furthered by their enthusiastic participation in the colony's militia. Military service brought men from distant villages together in the ranks to fight far from their homes. Between 1722 and 1727 the province waged war against the Eastern Abenakis, who continued to fight English expansion along the Kennebec River, and many Wampanoags helped defend English towns in Maine or joined in attacks against Abenaki villages. In 1724 and 1725, Richard Bourne recruited at least one hundred Indian men from Plymouth, Barnstable, and Dukes counties for service in Maine. Bourne discovered that aboriginal rules of etiquette retained their influence, for he was obliged to "treat the Indians with their Numerous Relations & Friends."[21] At about the same time, John Holman traveled to Cape Cod to enlist additional Indian soldiers, and the General Court authorized Thomas Church to offer a bounty of twenty shillings for every "able-bodied effective Indian" from Bristol County (including villages in Dartmouth, Freetown, and Little Compton) and by June about thirty men had enlisted with Church.[22] Two lists of Massachusetts militia raised in the 1720s show many Indian names, some recognizable as those of men from Natick (Benjamin Speen), Freetown (John Church), Mashpee (Joshua Wicket), and villages around Middleborough.[23] Service together in the colonial militia extended and strengthened the growing regional ties between Indian communities in eastern Massachusetts, dissolving the turn-of-the-century "spheres."

While outside pressures such as military service and expanding colonial settlements helped reshape Indian groups, their continuing demographic problems were probably the strongest agents of change. Indians shared certain demographic traits with their white neighbors. The only vital records of an Indian enclave come from Natick, and these show, between 1726 and 1785, an average age at marriage of 24.8 for men and 23.7 for women, only slightly lower than that for Anglo-Americans in the colony during the same period. Epidemics descended upon Natick in fifteen-year cycles (1725–30, 1740–45, and 1755–60), apparently corresponding to epidemics in other towns. In both Anglo-American and Indian villages, pestilence was often brought back by soldiers who survived the disease-ridden military. But the epidemics that scourged native enclaves (as in the previous century) caused far less devastation among colonists. Such epidemics probably increased in frequency and severity among Indians in eastern Massachusetts as the number and density of their English neighbors grew after 1710. While natives in the region were never completely isolated from the colonists, pestilence could spread faster and farther in an Indian community forced by the expansion of the colonial population to settle into a permanent, compact, densely settled village.[24]

Also contributing to the Indians' demographic predicament was their extraordinarily low fertility rate, particularly compared to that of Anglo-American colonists. A number of English observers were baffled by the constant decrease in the Indians' population. John Sergeant, minister of the Stockbridge (Housatonic) Indian community in western Massachusetts, noted in March 1740 that deaths had outnumbered births among his flock "ever since I have been acquainted with these Indians."[25] His friend from the Connecticut River Valley, Samuel Hopkins, added his view that "this perhaps is the case of the Indians in general who live bordering upon and among the English." Hopkins blamed the problem on "their intemperance . . . great irregularity in diet . . . [and] when they are sick they take little or no care of themselves or of one another."[26]

Some of the same diseases that killed so many mature natives, most notably smallpox and tuberculosis, also prevented conception, and alcohol addiction wreaked similar havoc on reproduction.[27] Many of the children were probably born underweight and thus particularly vulnerable to childhood mortality, reducing the size of subsequent generations. In addition, military service took many young men away, especially at midcentury, just as they reached the prime age for fatherhood. The combination of a low birth (or infant survival) rate and terrible epidemics proved overwhelming. This decline is best documented (as so much else) in Natick, where the Indians' high mortality rate outpaced their low birth rate throughout the eighteenth century, and proved a major factor in the decline of that community. In the average Natick family, 2.5 children survived to adulthood, compared to 5 for neighboring Dedham and 5.3 for more distant Andover in the same period.[28] The dwindling of other Indian enclaves can be glimpsed in Natick's statistics.

Sudden political and economic alterations joined with long-term demographic decline to reshape Indian communities on the mainland. The greatest transformations appeared in Natick and Hassanamisco, where the Indians embraced allotment of their formerly communal lands and accepted English ministers and neighbors. The reasons for their decisions are not clear, although the expanding colonial population was one known motivation. The growth of nearby towns discouraged hunting and gathering expeditions, and the expanding English population's extensive agriculture eliminated forest cover and forage for game. Regardless of their preferences, Indians in the region were certainly forced to rely more on crops when the catches from hunting and fishing decreased.[29] Finally, events and trends over previous decades may have made landholding in severalty seem the best way to stabilize the community.

Natick took the first dramatic step in 1719, when the villagers in a meeting decided to copy other New England towns by creating a proprietorship — the corporate entity that governed land allotments and met separately from the town. The villagers chose twenty proprietors, nineteen men and one woman, apparently the heads of long-established and prestigious families. The twenty then met separately and began dividing Natick's land among themselves; each initially took a sixty-acre plot and a share in the income from the 1715 sale of Magunkaquot. In addition, twenty-five men and two women were each given thirty to sixty acres but no stake in the Magunkaquot rents, no vote in the proprietors' meetings, and no guarantee of future allotments. The Indians probably saw the proprietorship, which provided secure land titles and boundaries under colonial law, as a useful institution in the face of outside pressures, including the disruptive immigration of other Indians. They were also influenced by their English neighbors' belief that ownership in severalty was essential for economic development. But the Natick proprietorship undermined the native community by severing landholding from the town polity and bringing the native community into a closer orbit to the province's legal and economic systems. It also reduced opportunities for those not granted proprietorship status, and unwittingly opened the village to an "invasion" of colonists who could now purchase land from individual Indians.[30]

Hassanamisco was also quickly affected by the frontier peace. The General Court sought to turn Nipmuc paths into roads that encouraged commerce and settlement, and in 1718 licensed Elisha Johnson to buy land from the Hassanamiscos if he would build two bridges across the Blackstone River "for travelers and drovers." The Indians were as eager as provincial leaders for improved travel and commerce, perhaps hoping to compete with their Natick cousins, and five years later helped survey a road through their reserve to connect Johnson's bridges.[31] They also negotiated with a miller who sought land for a mill and a home.[32] The Hassanamiscos seemed to welcome the new opportunities offered by a gristmill and better roads to connect them and their produce with eastern and southern markets.

As Hassanamisco closed its deal with the miller, they contemplated a far more radical change. In 1724, the Indians were visited by a legislative committee with an offer by a group of investors (from towns west of Boston) to buy their 7,500-acre reserve.[33] While the Hassanamiscos' reaction was not recorded, a year later the legislature approved the sale, and two years after that the governor gave his consent. The General Court required investors to pay sixteen hundred pounds (soon raised to twenty-five hundred pounds) within three months into an account managed by trustees for the Indians, settle forty families in the township within three years, build a "decent meetinghouse" and a school within three years, and reserve land for and to pay the salaries of a schoolmaster and a minister. The new town, to be named Grafton, was envisioned by both the Hassanamiscos and provincial authorities as an integrated community: Indian and white children would learn together in the new schoolhouse, their parents would be given "an equal dividend in fair land," and all would socialize in the meetinghouse where the Indians would receive pews.[34]

The Hassanamiscos probably felt they gained far more than they lost by selling the reserve. Their autonomy was diminishing rapidly as the surrounding countryside sprouted English households and roads penetrated the reserve. The seven Indian families, totaling only thirty-two individuals, resided in scattered farms instead of a compact settlement. They or their parents had lived in Natick for many years, had gained an intimate knowledge of English agriculture and material culture, and, judging by their reaction to the proposed roads and mills, were quite interested in increasing their ties to the colonial economy. These conditions allowed the Hassanamiscos, like their cousins in Natick, to easily accept landholding in severalty. The lack of a strong central settlement and their small population also made the sale of the reserve less threatening. Each Indian family, like the English settlers, received an allotment of approximately eighty acres of upland and eight of meadowland, apparently more than the families had farmed before the sale, and future shortages seemed unlikely.[35] The Indians would also get, gratis, a meetinghouse, schoolhouse, minister, and teacher.

The Hassanamiscos also gained a large pool of capital from the sale of their reserve. The fund was administered by overseers, prominent colonists who loaned the money to whites (providing an important source of capital for regional development) and divided the annual interest payments among the Indian proprietors. Each Hassanamisco family initially received one-seventh of the annual interest. Over time, of course, the division became more complex as individuals married, died, and passed their shares onto their children. These annual payments were supposed to finance agricultural improvements, and, as described below, some families clearly used the money to develop English-style farms.[36]

The Hassanamisco system would be enshrined by the United States government in the Dawes Act exactly 160 years later. The act directed government agents to divide tribal lands into family-owned plots and to pay portions of accounts and mineral royalties directly to Indian families and individuals. But in Hassanamisco the allotted lands and fund were to be indefinitely "reserved for the Indian proprietors and their heirs," while the Dawes Act provided a twenty-five-year trust period for the owners' "adjustment" to white civilization. In addition, Hassanamisco shares were owned by both women and men, and the husband of a shareholder had access to his spouse's interest payments only while the marriage lasted — contrary to Anglo-American property law, which the Dawes Act would try to force upon Indians. The two measures did share one effect, unforeseen in the Hassanamisco's new arrangement but which became the Dawes Act's primary goal: the trust fund undermined the Hassanamisco community by becoming their only material and legal tie. The Indians increasingly dealt with their white neighbors and the provincial government as families instead of as a larger group.[37]

A very different proprietorship was created in Mashpee in the early 1720s. Like their English neighbors and the Natick Indians, Mashpee proprietors had regular meetings and elected various officers, including a clerk to keep records (none of which survive). And like Natick, Mashpee may have created a proprietorship to better manage resources as more Indians on the Cape moved to Mashpee, and in order to better manage conflicts with white neighbors over land. But Mashpee shaped its proprietorship in a very different manner from Natick and Hassanamisco. Every family in the enclave received an equal share, but the land itself was not surveyed and divided. Instead, as before the proprietorship, families marked off plots of planting and pasture land. Children could inherit this land and the improvements on it, but if there were no direct heirs or if the land passed out of use, it would revert to the community. Thus the Mashpee proprietorship, supported by the conditions that the sachems had set forth in deeds that created the reserve, served to protect the community's autonomy. As a result, unlike other native groups on the Cape and Nantucket, the Mashpees for decades "kept our young men at home to work so that we live[d] pretty well."[38]

At about the same time, Teticut developed a landholding system that combined aspects of the Mashpee and Natick proprietorships. Like those villages, Teticut had been swollen by migration in the first quarter of the century. As in Natick, families within the reserve laid out land for themselves, but, as in Mashpee, the community did not record their allotments and continued to regulate access to resources. In the summer of 1734, three Teticut men, apparently community leaders, complained to the General Court that an outsider, Stephen David, had married a member of their tribe, Jemima, and was now "pretending" to have a right to Teticut land. Jemima had died without children, after which David had obtained the court's license to sell a "considerable quantity of land." The Teticuts told the court that David's connection to the community came through Jemima, and that the tie and his right to communal resources had dissolved when she died. Under their rules, Jemima's husband could have sold land only if they had children, since the land (and the children) were part of the community. Like the Mashpees, the Teticuts may have recently developed the rule that a "foreigner" who married into the community did not gain any transferable rights to its resources. Unlike Mashpee, however, and like Natick, Teticut in the 1730s and 1740s ruled that individuals who met the enclave's norms were allowed to sell pieces of their allotments without the approval of others (discussed in more detail later).[39]

Landholding systems similar to Mashpee's emerged at about the same time on Martha's Vineyard. Petitions from Indian groups on the island stressed communal landownership. At the end of the century the Chappaquiddicks told the General Court that "Your honours cannot be unacquainted of the manner that the Indians in General improve their Lands, being always considered as tenants in common which is the present tenure."[40] The Christiantown Indians added the detail that though they "hold as joint Tenants in common," families could claim and hold plots "so long as the Individuals, thereof remain thereon, beyond the memory of Man to the contrary."[41] Gay Head's headman told a state investigator that "the land that we hold in severalty which come by heirship or purchase inclose or taken in the rough and cleared is ours according to all indian customs in severelty." Later he would add that "we the proprietors on gayhead wish to conduct our own business separate from the foreigners & strangers we never have alowd them any pole right on gayhead therefore they have not any in our Land but work on their wifes portion of land. . . . When we set out our planting fields we do not set out any to the foreigner but to his wife if she is a proprietor." The emerging tie between land and Indian identity was particularly clear on Gay Head, for the enclave *did* give full rights to "other Indians that come from other tribes or settlements & settle with us."[42]

Indians in Mashpee, Teticut, and on the Vineyard adapted native land tenure to English law. Aboriginal land tenure had been entirely communal, the villages or clans holding and working tracts of land in common. Newcomers became part of this system. Before the English came along, individuals and nuclear families had no reason to take land away from the community, and even after the colonists arrived only the sachems could alienate land—and then only when representing (at least officially) the community. The native versions of English proprietorship represented a shift away from aboriginal customs in order to serve the more significant need of strengthening community ownership.

Under this "revised" landholding system, members of the community, called "proprietors" to satisfy the colonists, could claim land from the reserve's commons. Once worked, that land could be inherited by the "owner's" children. Outsiders who married into the enclave could not gain these privileges, in part to protect against individuals, such as Stephen David, who might seek to sell the community's land. The offspring of the "foreigner," however, who was born in the community and raised (presumably) within its value system, would be sufficiently acculturated to be trusted with proprietorship rights inherited through a native parent. These controls were particularly effective when, as in Mashpee and Gay Head, treaties recognized by colonial authorities barred the sale of land to whites without the approval of the whole enclave. The "Indian-style" proprietorship rules were, however, clearly contrary to English law, which gave a husband possession of his wife's property. Indeed, the General Court proved unwilling to apply Teticut rules to Stephen David's transgressions, and several years later allowed him to sell even more land.[43]

><

The Natick Indians' embrace of a New England-style proprietorship was a far more radical experiment, for many sought to plunge into the colonial economy by expanding or intensifying their agricultural operations. The sale of their land to whites, which needed the General Court's permission, was often required to finance the change. In fact, the first extant land sale request from Natick came in 1722 from the three brothers of the late Simon Ephraim. They asked to sell the lot where Simon had begun building a house, in order to buy cattle "& other Things Necessary."[44] Most of those selling land emphasized their need for cattle, husbandry tools, and even barns.[45] Three men even swapped land with colonists in Sherborn or Needham in order to consolidate their holdings and obtain farmland closer to their homes.[46] These sales and trades foreshadowed the transfer of land to whites living in nearby towns. It also highlights the trend, common in colonial New England, of farmers consolidating their holdings and moving away from the center of communal settlement to their fields.

The changing fortunes of some Natick families can be glimpsed in their land sale requests. Jacob Chalcom was not a Natick resident in 1719, and never became a proprietor, but did play an active role in the economic transformation of the village. In 1729, Chalcom asked to sell thirty-two acres for "building him a Dwelling house after the English manner for his more comfortable Living."[47] Two years later he told the court that he had incurred debts to buy land in Natick, plus a "very good house," a horse, oxen, and a cow. Those debts, however, were greater than Chalcom could manage, and he still needed a barn and additional tools, so he asked to sell thirty-seven acres "lying at a great distance from his house."[48] In 1739, still facing debts, and still "in great need of a small barn, for the better security of his corn, hay, Cattle &tc.," he asked to sell twenty-five distant acres. Chalcom also hoped to purchase a nearby twenty-acre lot.[49] The barn was still not built two years later when Chalcom asked to sell thirty-five outlying acres.[50] Six months later he wrote that he had paid all his debts and raised the frame to his barn, but needed to sell another ten acres in order to finish the building to store his hay.[51] Clearly, despite Chalcom's initiative and energy, he, like many other Natick Indian men, had problems "making it" in the colonial economy.

As their community changed in the 1720s, many Natick Indians decided to build English-style houses. Samuel Abraham, a member of one of Natick's leading families, asked in December 1726 to sell land to a white settler in order to build a house. Ecological alterations to the region had joined socioeconomic changes to give Abraham, like other Natick Indians, "a great desire to Live more like my Christian English neighbors"

> being weary of Living in a Wigwam, it being also now very difficult getting materials anywhere, near us, where with to build wigwams so often as we were obliged to do it, one lasting but a few years, which put me under a great difficulty as to living here at Natick, which is surrounded with English Towns, & whereas I have a great desire to continue under the Gospel, which I hope I should be able to do with more Comfort & Satisfaction, if by any means I could be able to build such an house, as sd English live in (as well as some of my Indian neighbors).[52]

Vacant land was Abraham's only commodity and he received permission from the General Court to sell twenty-two acres in order to build his house and buy "household stuff or stock or other things." In fact, more than half of the fifteen land-sale petitions from individuals in the first decade of the Natick proprietorship noted their desire for "a Dwelling house after the English manner."[53] Yet not all of the village's inhabitants were sure that they wanted or could afford wood-framed homes: in 1739 John Wamsquam sold twenty-two acres to build either a small house or a "convenient wigwam."[54]

Natickites also purchased English consumer goods for their new houses. They were not alone, for a prominent feature of the New England economy in the mid-eighteenth century was the gradual increase in the ownership of consumer goods, such as pictures and ceramics, even by the rural poor. The developing English consumer culture had a growing influence in Natick households. Between 1720 and 1740, English-style homes and barns increasingly replaced those of native design and materials, and Indians acquired farm and consumer items of English design. Inventories from the 1740s include beds and bedding, chests, chairs, tables, iron and brass kitchenware, pewterware, and even mirrors.[55]

One can rarely tease out the intertwined strands of culture and class, but certain patterns are clear from a comparison of the possessions of Natick's Indians and their neighbors. Clocks, wigs, and pictures were rare in both native and poor white households, suggesting common tastes, class lines, limitations on spending, or the rarity of such items in the rural colonial economy. Ownership of books, on the other hand, no doubt mostly Bibles and other religious literature, was widespread among both Indians and poor whites. However, certain goods fairly common among the English, such as salt, forks, and mirrors, rarely appeared in Natick Indian estates, showing how culture determined consumer preferences.[56] North American natives only slowly gained a taste for salt, and there is no indication that they ever enjoyed imported spices, beverages, or sugars. Similarly, forks were European introductions without parallel in native culture. Mirrors were a special case, for although during the early period of contact these objects were charged with power and meaning, only three appeared in Natick probate records.[57] The persistence of many other native cultural traits makes it more likely that the objects were treated with a special deference that precluded inclusion in probate records.

Unfortunately, few Natick Indians were successful in the colonial economy. In fact, the community was much poorer than other rural New England towns. For example, the Indians had much smaller personal estates than did the inhabitants of Andover, a farming community not far from abandoned Wamesit, and a far larger percentage lived in poverty (as the English saw it). Over 60 percent of the Indians' estates fell within the range of Andover's poorest third.[58] One source of the Indians' difficulties was the ecological improverishment of the region. Uncultivated resources, such as materials for building wigwams, were disappearing. Even the seemingly eternal supply of fish was threatened during this period. In 1738, the Indians complained (along with five neighboring towns) that a mill dam on the Charles River, recently raised in Watertown, "prevented [them] from the use of their privilege of taking Alwives and other fish."[59] Natick's economic changes made matters worse, for although the first few harvests with the new methods and materials were probably rich ones, the thin New England soil could be quickly exhausted.

Natick's poverty, relative to the region as a whole, needs further explaining, however, for southern New England generally had thin, rocky soil, and by the 1720s other towns in the area had used English farming techniques (ironically, tempered by methods learned from the Indians) for several generations. Were Indians culturally unprepared to handle English-style farming, as colonial observers felt? The biggest differences between native and colonial agriculture seem to have been the more intensive cultivation (symbolized by the use of the plow instead of hoes), barns to store crop surpluses, and manure from domesticated cattle. At least some Natick

Indians were aware of these differences, for plows and other English farm tools appear in a number of probate records, and the land sale petitions often mentioned the desire to build barns and buy cattle. While individuals and families had to learn to use the tools, care for the cattle, and store the surpluses, those who worked for white farmers at the turn of the century could have easily gained this knowledge.

We have no data on the Natick Indian farms besides the probate records, although one piece of anecdotal evidence suggests that at least some Indian farmers were initially successful in their effort to adopt English agriculture. Stephen Badger, the English minister who arrived in the town in the 1750s and expressed considerable sympathy for the Indians, noted later that "at the beginning of the present century" the Indians "were in a state of civil society . . . and in some measure [stimulated] to conform to the manners of their English neighbours." But the natives were too easily influenced by the bad behavior of their aggressive white neighbors, for "their examples of irregularities and excesses had (it is to be apprehended) too great, and even a predominant effect upon them." The persistence of aboriginal ways also caused problems, for the irregularities "in conjunction with that strange propensity, in their constitutions, to excess, brought them into some degree of disrepute."[60] While some Natick Indians succeeded, according to Badger, not all embraced New England's path to virtue, and those who maintained the old ways, including the sins of "irregularities and excesses," dragged down the righteous.

Indeed, not everyone in Natick moved toward the Anglo-American path. Sarah, a Pennacook from Wamesit, was born in Natick around 1702, when her family was traveling from the Merrimac River Valley to the Nipmuc community in Woodstock, south of Dudley. Seven years later she was bound to the household of John Braddish in Cambridge — perhaps because her parents died or could no longer support her, or because she saw this as her best opportunity in the changing world. When Sarah's service ended at the age of eighteen, she found work in the household of a Boston doctor, but soon married Thomas Lawrence, an Indian apparently from Cape Cod, and moved with him to Natick where they had two children before he died in 1730. Two years later in Weston, the widow married Solomon Wamsquam of Natick and the two had six children (a large family for Indians) before he died in Sherborn of tuberculosis in 1755. The family is an early example of the "wandering Indians" later described by Stephen Badger, as Sarah told the General Court in 1767 that she had not lived a whole year in any one place since leaving Boston. Like the Lawrences and the Wamsquams, many Indian families connected with Natick spurned or failed to achieve the English path of respectability and continued their aboriginal lifeways — and therefore left few if any documents of their achievements and possessions. That lack of records, of course, makes it impossible to determine precisely how many natives refused or tried to live like their Christian English neighbors.[61]

Badger's ministerial disapproval of "irregularities and excesses" hints at the survival of the aboriginal emphasis on communal sharing. Indeed, the almost universal Native American emphasis on sharing, frequently condemned and even outlawed by missionaries and government agents, persists in the late twentieth century, in urban neighborhoods as well as on reservations. But the probate records show a growing gap between the wealthiest and poorest Natick Indians, indicating that the traditional emphasis on sharing did break down toward midcentury. In fact, by the 1750s the share of all probated wealth held by the wealthiest 10 percent — a common measure of equality — was far higher among Natick Indians (56 percent) than in neighboring rural Suffolk County (31–38 percent).[62] Any social tensions generated by a growing economic inequality were not voiced, for other problems were more palpable, including developing conflicts with white settlers and terrible casualties from the colonial wars, but internal strife may have contributed to the exodus from Natick after midcentury

Far more critical to the Indians' economic fate than any persistence of sharing or "irregularities and excesses" were fluctuations in the Massachusetts economy. Natick inhabitants lacked tools and domesticated animals; those who wanted "to conform to the manners of their English neighbours" therefore depended on land sales to finance agricultural reforms as well as the purchase of consumer goods. Unfortunately, their situation made them particularly vulnerable to the region's economic problems. Within the province during the 1730s, the price of land and crops decreased relative to the cost of cattle and tools.[63] Indians were thus hit twice as hard as white farmers: not only did crops raised with the new tools and cattle garner less, but more land had to be sold in order to buy the expensive technologies that the colonists inherited or borrowed from their neighbors. This situation was made even worse by inflation that hit the Bay Colony in the 1730s and peaked in 1749; the capital that might have been garnered by selling some land or a good harvest quickly lost its value, perhaps before the farmer had time to buy tools, cattle, or building materials. Timing as well as circumstances were against Indian groups forced to bank on land sales.

Changes in Natick's material culture rippled out to other Indian villages in the area. After Samuel Pegan moved to Chabanakongkomun, for example, he sold land in Natick "to build a comfortable House after the English Fashion for the Convenience of him self & his Family."[64] Joseph Ephraim Jr. of Natick and Andrew Abraham of Hassanamisco decided to sell forty-four acres owned jointly in Natick in order to finance the "Building and finishing Comfortable Houses for the pet[itione]rs and purchasing of Cattle and Utensils for Husbandry & Improvement of their Lands."[65] In 1738, Abraham sold additional acreage along the Blackstone River "for building a house after the English manner for his comfort."[66] The Hassanamiscos seemed particularly eager to join Natick's experiment, for their few extant probate records show many of the material trappings of rural New England. Joshua Misco's will, filed in 1737, left his estate, including "all of my stock of catle and swine and other Creatures," to his wife Deborah.[67] However, as in Natick, most of the Hassanamisco wealth was in land; thus, few Indians were able or wanted to buy many English household goods. Ami Printer, for example, who died in July 1741 after being "badly froze" nine months before, left personal estate valued at slightly more than two pounds, but held real estate worth nearly £259.[68] The astonishing difference between Printer's real and personal estate was typical for even comparatively well-off Indian planters in the eighteenth century.

Initially, the Hassanamisco proprietors seemed to manage well under the new system, farming some of their sizable allotments and renting out the remainder to whites from nearby towns. They also had an important source of capital in the annual interest payments on money loaned from their fund by court-appointed overseers to whites. Unfortunately, these funds proved inadequate, particularly when medical problems and their costs crushed the fiscal health of the Indian families. While the 1727 Hassanamisco covenant required Indian holdings to remain in Indian hands, this measure, like the trusteeship period in the Dawes Act, proved meaningless. In the 1730s, Hassanamisco families began to lease, sell, and will their holdings to Englishmen in order to build houses and repay white friends. Loan defaults, and occasional fraud and embezzlement by white overseers (see chapter 5) caused the Indians' fund to shrink toward midcentury. Finally, medical problems generated by the Indians' lower fertility and high mortality rates, and by their participation in the colonial wars, created debts that could be met only by selling land.[69]

)(

High mortality, low birth rates, injuries, and illness forced a growing number of natives to sell land to white settlers. An increasing number of Natick Indians suffered from debts due to medical care and incapacitation. Disease and farm accidents forced only three families in the (late) 1720s to sell land, but in the following decade nine men sold parts of their children's inheritances to pay medical debts.[70] Debtor's prison, in fact, soon became a major threat. In 1737, for example, Thomas Pegan Jr. sold land to pay medical debts, but two years later his father was forced to sell some of *his* land to get Thomas out of the Charlestown jail — where he had been placed for failure to pay those debts.[71] During the 1730s, debts created by medical needs, from sickness or accidents, were already beginning to reshape Natick, foreshadowing the following two decades, when wars and epidemics would completely disrupt the Indian community.

Indian enclaves in southeastern Massachusetts similarly suffered growing poverty and indebtedness. In 1724, Benjamin Wannoe, a Teticut living in Bridgewater, sold forty acres to pay various debts.[72] One year later, Joseph and Bethia Peters, "Indians of Middleborough," asked to sell the twenty acres Bethia inherited from her father as they had "fallen into Poverty & run much into Debt for their necessary support."[73] As in Natick, medical assistance and care proved an exceptional burden, particularly as the Teticut community aged. In 1729, Charles and Alice Watnam, Teticut siblings, received permission to sell twenty acres to meet debts arising from their long illness.[74] Six years later, Jeremiah and Esther Anthony sold half of their one hundred "light Barren" acres in Assawompsett, owned in Esther's name, to pay debts of twenty pounds due to their illnesses. They noted that they were old, lacked children, and had no relations nearby to help.[75] In 1740, Samuel Thomas received permission to sell fourteen "worn out" acres in Middleborough, in part to pay his debts and in part because he was "old and feeble and in no wise able to get a livelihood of the above sd Land."[76]

As Indian communities in the region became more intertwined with the colonial economy, illness all too easily joined with the desire for "improvements" to increase the debts of Indian families. Jacob Chalcom of Natick, who sold thirty-seven acres in 1730 to pay medical bills, also needed to pay debts incurred to expand his farm.[77] Two years later, Thomas Pegan, from the same village, asked to sell land to cover medical debts and to buy cattle and farm tools.[78] In the southeast at the same time, David Poquechus asked to sell about twelve "distant" acres in order to pay for thirty acres closer to his home in Assawompsett.[79] Alas, his efforts to improve his farm came to naught, and he may have already been ill when he had made the request, for two years later the executor of Poquechus's estate sold most of the Indian's land in order to pay debts from his long illness.[80]

A particularly tragic but not unique chain of events destroyed the Teticut family headed by the unfortunate Stephen David, whom community leaders had tried to disown in 1734. In 1731, Jemima and Stephen sold some of her father's "Considerable Estate" (totaling about five hundred acres) for "Building a House after the English fashion, & buying necessary furniture Cattle &c" — and to pay debts from a long illness.[81] Nine years later, Stephen told a woeful story when he asked to sell another fifty acres. He had been thrown in jail in Rhode Island for medical debts and was, like so many Nantucket men, "Obliged to take a Vessel to Sea." During the year of his service, Jemima suffered from "a Large & Tedious fit of Sickness wch Continued for more than half a year for wch she was obliged to Several English for Credit to Support her & all his children but one Dyed." When Stephen returned he "found his wife in a miserable state of health & himself then not able & for a year afterwards not able to work for his Support by reason of Bodily Infirmities & sickness so that by the Providence of God he is much reduced & in Debt," to the immense sum of two hundred pounds.[82]

The enthusiastic participation of Indian men in the colonial militia created additional economic hardships. Even during the thirty years of peace between New England and New France following the Treaty of Utrecht, Abenakis continued to raid Maine settlements. Many of the defenders were Indians. While some doubtless failed to return, we do know the unfortunate fate of two who made it home. After David Job came back to Pembroke in 1725, following service at the fort along St. George's River in Maine, he found shelter in a barn on a hay mow — but fell off "and was very hurt and died." The General Court considered this "dying in the Service of the Province," and paid for Job's doctor bills and funeral.[83] William Jeffry, "a Harwich [Potawaumacut] Indian," was also at St. George's River when he was badly wounded. A bullet smashed the bones in his wrist, leaving him lame and dependent on annual assistance from the province for the next two decades. Clearly, the military recruiters had not been particularly choosy, because only four years after returning, Jeffry described himself as "an aged Indigent."[84] Militia wages may have been helpful to many native families, and the province at least tried to pay for the needs of Job and Jeffrey — and when Jeffry complained in 1741 that he had not received his five pounds per year pension for five years, the province quickly responded with the missing money.[85] But, doubtless, many received no assistance, and the loss of their men's labor probably forced many Indian families to sell land to buy food and pay bills.

)(

Social and political tensions increased within Indian communities as they developed closer orbits to the New England economy. The efforts of the Natick Indians to "conform to the manners of their English neighbours," for example, almost certainly created new conflicts as the gap grew between rich and poor; even in more "traditional" enclaves old bonds weakened as the marketplace drove a wedge between long-standing privileges and responsibilities.[86] New opportunities and Anglo-American concepts of property encouraged sachems to see the resources that they controlled for the community as theirs to use as they wished. Their people were outraged, of course, at the betrayal of their trust and the way in which the sachems' actions endangered the community's resources. As described in chapter 3, such conflict first erupted in 1701, when Christiantown rejected Alexander after he deeded their land to an Englishman. But toward midcentury the problem became more widespread, affecting Punkapoag, Mattakeesit, Nantucket, and the Vineyard in the 1730s.

Indian enclaves in eighteenth-century Massachusetts, like those before English colonization, acknowledged the authority of an individual based on prestige, ability, and family connections. But an individual's prestige and ability was easily destroyed by alcoholism and other problems that plagued many Indians. Amos Ahauton had inherited the mantle of religious and political authority in Punkapoag from William Ahauton, who had been ordained minister of the Indian community in 1703. But by the late 1730s, Amos was abusing both alcohol and his position of power, and had fallen from the community's grace. In 1741, the white trustee of Punkapoag funds complained that Ahauton had built a larger house than needed, "pretending as if the House was made to accomodate all the indians that would meet together in it on the Sabbath for Religious worship."[87] Yet when the house was built just a few years before, neither he nor any Indians complained, for Ahauton's actions did not violate community norms. But by 1741, the trustee reported, many in the Indian community were telling him that "Amos had of late given himself to Excessive drinking, and that they would not like him any more as a Minister." Ahauton's prestige was also hurt by his frequent absence from the native enclave, for after taking to the bottle he and his family "have ever since Dwelt longer in other Towns than in the Town of Stoughton" in which the Punkapoag reserve lay.[88] One gets the sense from this incident that Amos had the building erected on the hope that he would overcome his addiction and recapture the hearts and minds of his people. Unfortunately, Ahauton was never able to throw the bottle away, perhaps in part because his unfortunate medical and economic circumstances barred that door: he and his wife were "Aged & Infirm," and their only son was "Consumptive and often Lame and in a weak state of health," so the entire family depended on the community's funds.[89]

More revealing of the social pressures exerted by the region's economy was the fierce conflict that tore apart Mattakeesit. In 1735, John Quiksite and John Thomas complained to the General Court on behalf of the community, that "one Patience [Keurp], called their Queen Sachem, grandaughter to late King Josiah [Chickatabut], has made waste and strip of land given them by late King Josiah." The court's investigators reported that the petitioners "did not make out their Right to the said Land before the Committee, Yet the said Patience Makes great Destruction on the said Land, by Disposing of the Wood and Timber for little or Nothing." The petitioners lacked a deed from Chickatabut, and the committee considered their memory of an oral grant inadequate.[90] Four years later, Keurp asked the legislature for the right to sell some of her "very considerable lands in Pembroke" in order to repay debts to various Englishmen and to support her in the future. She noted that she was elderly, widowed, the only surviving descendant of Chickatabut, and unable to earn a living. The legislature agreed to consider her petition and, although there is no record of the result, the white debtors were almost certainly paid with the sale of Mattakesett land.[91] The conflict originated in part because of Mattakeesit's location along the former borders between the Massachusett and Wampanoag tribes and the Plymouth and Massachusetts colonies, creating confusion over ultimate control of resources. But the overriding problem arose from the series of conflicts generated within native ways by colonists, particularly when driven by the imperatives of the market economy.

Indeed, changing norms within New England Indian groups shaped the strife over authority and resources. Newcomers to Mattakeesit had obtained their lands from Chickatabut sometime in the mid-seventeenth century. Native standards of ownership at the time are not absolutely clear today, and no doubt were already changing in response to the strange English standards, but apparently the land was supposed to be theirs subject to continual use and the approval of the sachem and his or her descendants, the community's guardians. Thus Keurp had the moral authority under aboriginal standards to terminate the newcomers' holdings if they violated community norms or if her people needed the land. But few Indians in the area acknowledged Keurp's leadership, other than a few surviving relatives, and instead of regaining land for her people she was selling its resources to Englishmen, creating "great Destruction on the said Land, by Disposing of the Wood and Timber for little or Nothing." Thus conflict developed between the traditional right of the sachem to manage the community's land and her traditional responsibility for the community's welfare. The General Court tried to manage the Mattakeesit strife by appointing two white men to supervise the Indians' lands, but conflicts deepened even after Keurp died — in large part because of English intervention — and in two decades would again reach the legislature (see chapter 5).[92]

The needs of the community and the rights of sachems also collided on Nantucket. Sachems retained their role and authority on the island, granting land and whaling rights to both natives and Englishmen and expecting tribute from their people. They even used this aboriginal system to gain English consumer goods, as Indians gave labor or goods to English merchants as credit for their sachem's purchases.[93] Some of their labor, tragically, was probably given in the form of the deadly whaling voyages from which many did not return. But as in Christiantown three decades earlier, the transfer of leadership to one who had grown up within the island's changing economic system dramatically pointed to the problems created by the merging of aboriginal social and colonial market structures. Sometime around 1731, Benjamin Abel became a sachem of the community around Gibbs Pond, the Indian settlement on the island's east side. Over the following ten years, Abel took advantage of his traditional privileges by selling and leasing the Indian community's resources to English settlers, spurning his people's objections. The community became increasingly upset about the loss of their land, which represented not only a large part of their livelihoods but also their little surviving independence, and in 1741 they met and "all Greed as one to Put down the aforesaid Benjamin Abel not to be sachem over us any more . . . from doing that [which] he should not [have] done."[94]

The actions taken by these rebels point to the fascinating joining of Indian and colonial worlds. After deciding to depose Abel, the meeting turned to "all our Elders," who told them that "we may Put down Benjamin Abel from being Sachim in our Place and we may Chose another man to be Sachim over us" — which was certainly in keeping with aboriginal polity. The community then sent representatives to Boston and New York City to obtain the governors' approval, who supposedly told the delegations that they had this right "because this Benjamin Abel had no other Power but only what he had from us." In Abel's place they "Chose this man John Quaap to be for our helpe and sachim In our Town and Place and over us." Provincial officials later recognized Abel's authority.[95]

During this period, Gay Head and Christiantown found new conflicts between their needs and the archaic claims and privileges of Vineyard sachems and their descendants. The most active or prominent "pretender" seems to have been Elisha Amos, the great grandson of Mittaark, who tried over several decades to rebuild his ancestor's sachemdom, or create his own.[96] Amos was unable to gain authority in Gay Head, Mittaark's old community, even after he persuaded the English to appoint him as the enclave's justice of the peace. The Indians charged that he "had robbed us of our gardens and also our fresh meadows and our land . . . we would be much more miserable because of this Elisha Amos," and quoted Job 34:30, "let not the hypocrite rule."[97]

Christiantown, which had gained the Takemmeh sachem's rights (to land, stranded whales, and other resources) in 1703, offered a more hopeful beginning to the ambitious Amos. In 1735, he took into his home Jonathan Sumannan, an infirm member of the community, in an obvious demonstration of his responsibility and fitness for authority. Afterwards the town asked Amos to take care of Sumannan in exchange for forty acres, almost all of Sumannan's fields (which lay within Amos's own lands), the right to cut and sell wood, and, perhaps most importantly, Sumannan's share of the community's sachem rights.[98] Four months later, Christiantown preacher Hoseah Manhud and his wife sold Amos all of their land and sachem rights in Takemmeh in exchange for fifty pounds and the right "to stay in your house . . . as long as we both live."[99] Even Christiantown, however, soon rejected Amos, complaining to the General Court that he was "using divers fraudulent Practices for alienating their Estates from them."[100] An example of Amos's "Practices" reached the assembly on the same day as the complaint, when another Vineyard Indian, Amos Janosco, charged that Amos and a white justice of the peace had tricked him into signing a deed giving away his whole estate.[101] Sumannan's troubles pointed to the fraying of family and social ties among Indians. He was compelled to find refuge in Amos's home when relatives proved unwilling to provide care or support.

Similar problems appeared elsewhere on the Vineyard at the same time. A number of Indian families remained on unreserved lands at Nashowakem-muck, within the town of Chilmark. In the 1730s, Jane Nahoman, one of the group's leaders, suffered from some of the social effects of the new colonial economy. In 1735, she complained to the General Court that her son-in-law, Simon Coomes, had, with the help of two Englishmen, gotten her so drunk that she had signed all of her lands to Coomes "Contrary to her Mind when she was Sober, & in the Exercise of her Reason."[102] The records do not comment on the mistreatment of a native matriarch by her son-in-law, but such behavior would have been unthinkable a few decades earlier. Two years later, Nahoman was imprisoned for debt by one of the two men who had aided Coomes; old, sick, and poor, she was obviously not being supported by her relatives.[103]

)(

The emerging conflicts within Indian communities over rights and responsibilities derived, in large measure, from the "faceless" pressures of the market economy. But human events are never really faceless. The troubles of Indian communities came largely from their closer relations with the growing population of white neighbors. Changes in landholding opened the gates in some villages (most notably Natick and Hassanamisco) to a flood of Anglo-American settlers. In addition, to portray human concerns as purely economic is misleading. The forces that acted as a reagent in many Indian communities emerged from the wide range of cultural differences that persisted between Indians and Anglo-Americans. These differences are visible in the social boundaries maintained by the two groups — boundaries that created friction when individuals from both lived closely together. The most conspicuous tensions came in the churches, for colonial New England churches were the clearest manifestation of a community's cultural, social, and political order — or lack thereof.

In Natick, a new minister created new tensions within the Indian community and helped lower the village's barriers against white settlers. Oliver Peabody began preaching in the Indian village in July 1721, only two years after the community embraced English-style landholding.[104] It is not surprising, considering the socioeconomic transformations signified by the proprietorship, that Natick became the first Indian town to accept an English minister ignorant of the native language. Peabody, an impoverished Harvard College student, came to Natick in response to the New England Company offer of forty-five pounds to ministerial candidates who would "enter the indian service."[105] Natick may have accepted Peabody because frequent visits by white preachers had prepared the enclave for an English minister, or (more likely) because, after John Neesnumin died in 1716, the village could find no other qualified candidates. In addition, some in the community may have seen the newcomer as an important connection to the power and support of the province's elite. Unlike the Mashpees, who resisted the commissioners' appointment of a white minister (discussed later), the Natick Indians did not insist that Peabody be proficient in their language. In February 1723, Harvard agreed to pay Peabody forty pounds annually to become the town's minister, and when the Indians granted him a proprietary right, he became one of the first whites to settle in Natick.[106]

But strains in the church developed rapidly. Peabody "delighted much in theological investigations," and may not have been happy with his new assembly of uneducated natives; in turn, his listeners may have been more bewildered than enlightened by his sermons, or more impressed by his erudition than his message.[107] The cultural gap that separated minister and congregation soon loomed large, and Peabody sought to bring more whites into the church. In 1723 and 1724, sections of Sudbury and Needham asked to be made part of Natick in order to attend the closer Indian church.[108] Peabody may have seen this as an opportunity to create an English congregation, for he asked the New England Company to decide whether his church was "to Consist only of Indians, or only of English."[109] The minister's feelings became clear in 1726 when he supported an Indian's request to sell land, "in as much as it is very lonesome, uncomfortable and disadvantageous to be at such a distance from Neighbours as I am from any English (ye nearest English family being about a mile distant & no more within near two Miles) & if I might have two or three near me, it would (I believe) render my Life much more pleasant & Easy."[110] Peabody's manifest desire for more English neighbors created fissures within the Indian community, for although seven of Natick's leading citizens endorsed Peabody's request, most of the community soon demonstrated their lack of enthusiasm.

Three years later, provincial officials inspecting Peabody's work were disappointed to find that, out of thirty Indian families, only sixteen adults and twelve children were baptized. This was a noticeable decline from 1699, when nineteen men, representing additional women and children, called themselves "the remainder of the church of christ" at Natick. By 1729, as many whites as Indians attended Peabody's church: eight white families lived in Natick, and another thirteen from neighboring towns, primarily western Dedham, attended services at the Indian church. The visiting committee noted that the Indians "generally attend the publick worship but some are too careless and negligent — That they generally uphold the worship of God in their Familys praying and reading the Scriptures." While the Indians told the commissioners that "they understand & are all satisfied in Mr. Peabody's preaching," some were more comfortable worshiping privately than among the English. The visitors also reported "some difficulty" during the service when Peabody asked a white man to read a Psalm. The commissioners' report indicates that many Indians resented the growing presence of the English.[111]

Peabody's actions also precipitated a split along generational lines. The visitors noted that, when they discussed Peabody with the Indian congregation, "Younger persons" seemed particularly enthusiastic.[112] This implies that the younger generation (probably those between ages eighteen and thirty) was more interested in English culture, as personified by a minister who could not speak their language. The older Natick Indians, by comparison, were far more reticent about such changes. Two decades earlier, Samuel Sewall had described a similar split among the Vineyard Indians: "though some of their aged men are tenacious enough of Indianisme (which is not at all to be wondered at) Others of them as earnestly wish that their people may be made English as fast as they can."[113] Colonial religious leaders hoped that the younger generations of Indians would, as older people died off, lead their people to enlightenment. The elders' conservative influence in native communities (like their colonial counterparts) could not be ignored or eliminated, and in Natick their (at minimum) reticence was certainly justified.

Peabody's activities clearly made Natick more attractive to white settlers. The minister may have had that as a goal, or perhaps he sought to "civilize" the Indians; in any case, the outcome was the same. Peabody devoted his ministry "to rais[ing] the moral, cultural, and economic standards of his red parishioners," which of course included preaching in English.[114] Although many Indians responded by building houses and barns and adopting Anglo-American agricultural methods, his message attracted more colonists than natives. Those drawn to Natick and its church were responding to economic as well as religious interests, for the salary of the preacher in an Indian town (like Natick) was paid by the New England Company, allowing the village's residents to escape the annual ministerial levy. When Peabody was ordained in November 1729, five whites and three Indians joined the church. Fewer than a dozen Indians normally attended services. In all, 32 Indians (compared to 126 whites) joined the church before Peabody's death twenty-three years later. Peak Indian membership in his church reached only 15 percent of the native residents, compared to 29 percent of whites.[115] In all fairness, it must be noted that English congregants did not immediately seek to dominate the church, for an Indian, Joseph Ephraim, was unanimously chosen to be the congregation's first deacon. But as the visitors to Natick found in 1729, white churchgoers created new conflicts within the community even before they dominated Natick.[116]

Such problems were even worse in Natick's "sister" community of Hassanamisco, where, by 1730, Anglo-Americans outnumbered the natives. While the entrepreneurs who bought the Indian reserve fulfilled many of the terms of their contract, those who settled it under its new name of Grafton seemed unwilling to socialize with the natives. In June 1739, the General Court was told that settlers "Pretended they have Power to Remove the Indians out of the Place that was appointed for them and say they are no wais obligd to maintain Preaching nor schooling for the Indians." The settlers' arrogance was reported not by the Hassanamiscos, but by the original white proprietors, who had given substantial sums to the court as bonds and were still expected to meet their obligations. The court responded by requiring Grafton to build four pews for the Indians: two for men and two for women. In addition, there is no evidence that the proprietors or the town ever hired a schoolmaster for both Indians and whites, nor that the required school ever met. The Indians were clearly seen as social outcasts by whites in the town, for (unlike the Indians of Natick) none ever served as a Grafton town officer. The Nipmuc survivors in the town remained, willingly or not (but clearly contrary to the General Court's desires), a distinct community that continued to have a social and cultural life separate from that of the white Grafton inhabitants.[117]

Religious and social conflicts also marked the boundary between natives and colonists in Punkapoag. The Rev. Joseph Morse, who served the adjoining Dorchester Village congregation beginning in 1707, developed an unusual friendship with the Indians. His wife, Amity, taught the native children to read and write English, and when an epidemic in 1717 and 1718 devastated the Indians, he nursed them and (without compensation from the colony) gave them food, clothing, and materials for coffins for their dead. One writer noted that "the most pleasant part of Mors's life in Dorchester Village was his relations with the Indians. . . . His home became a favorite resort for them." Few Englishmen were willing to have "savages" enter their home, and Morse's friendship is all the more remarkable because Metacom's warriors had attacked and burned his home town, Medfield, when he was about three years old.[118]

But Morse's friendship with the Punkapoags contributed to his downfall, for at the same time that the Indians complained about white poachers Morse was also forced from his pulpit. A growing faction of the congregation attacked Morse on both theological and personal grounds. The minister was finally expelled by an ecclesiastical council in 1726 for "false Speaking . . . to ye Council" when he denied being drunk — sins remarkably like those whites believed the Indians frequently committed.[119] Morse may have been too friendly to the Indians, who were considered outcasts and low-life drunkards by many colonists. Indeed, some of Morse's parishioners who testified against him noted that they "would as soon trust a Punkpoug Indian as Mr. Mors."[120] Condemnation of Morse echoed (and was perhaps inspired by) that of the Indians. Tradition holds that after Morse agreed to leave the ministry, he "remained a member of the church, attending often enough to comply with the letter of the law, but . . . openly stuffing cotton into his ears to avoid having to listen to the sermon."[121]

The situation in Mashpee, as in Natick and Hassanamisco, points to the close ties between a community's religion and socioeconomic structure. Mashpee's maneuvers to control its church, like the group's efforts to keep the land, showed a high degree of conservatism, independence, and cleverness. In 1720, their beloved minister, Simon Popmonit, died at the age of eighty-six. The New England Company then urged the Indian enclave to accept Joseph Bourne, the great grandson of their first minister, Richard Bourne. The Mashpees resisted this, however, and told the officials that they would boycott the church (an act of civil disobedience, since provincial law required attendance) unless Bourne preached in their language. The company's leader, Samuel Sewall, noted how the Indians were "very fond of their own Nation, and their own Language." Indeed, many of the Indian congregants still understood only Wampanoag.[122]

Bourne responded to their challenge. He later reported that "some were at first Disturbed, not Understanding our English Language: But haveing Applied myself both to study & Speak In their Language, They understand me more & more easyly & Some of the Gretest opposers, are now become some of my most Candid Auditors."[123] In June 1726, a majority of the Indians agreed to accept Bourne, and he celebrated his ordination three years later with a sermon in the Wampanoag language. In addition to native control of their church, the ceremony also highlighted the ties between Indian groups in the region, for two of the three ministers ordaining Bourne were native pastors from the Vineyard.[124]

Unfortunately, Bourne's career ended in 1740 after he (in generosity or for medicinal reasons) gave a pint of rum to three Indians, an offense for which he was also fined and jailed for two months. His removal, however, offered the Mashpee community another chance for an Indian minister. When the Boston commissioners of the New England Company tried to get the Indians to accept a white minister from nearby Barnstable, they refused, saying they "did not like to hear him, and excused themselves by saying, that they had a minister whom they liked." This was Solomon Briant, who had headed a nearby Indian church since the mid-1720s and was now courted by Mashpee. The company controlled the funds to pay the minister's salary, however, and Briant "was not agreeable to the gentlemen of this county, or to the Commissioners in Boston" — the first no doubt hoped that an English minister would influence the Mashpees to sell their land and avoid conflicts with whites, and the latter sought the Anglicization of the natives. But the Indians, supported by Bourne, who remained in Mashpee until his death twenty-seven years later, won their case, and Briant maintained the primacy of the Wampanoag language in the community until his death in 1775. The man who the Mashpees rejected, ironically, wound up taking the pulpit in Pembroke, where he no doubt occasionally dealt with the Mattakeesits.[125]

Language was not the only surviving element of aboriginal culture that maintained boundaries between Indians and English in the churches, and in the larger society. Many precontact beliefs also persisted, just as echoes of pre-Christian folk beliefs survived among Puritan colonists. There are no records of Indian beliefs or practices in eighteenth-century eastern Massachusetts, but in 1807 an English visitor to Herring Pond and Mashpee found "six or seven masses of stone, standing in different parts of the woods, on which the Indians, though professing themselves Christians, still make offerings, and to which, for this reason, is given the name of Sacrifice Rocks." He noted two particular rocks crowned with oak and pine branches:

> These branches the Indians place there, from motives which they but obscurely explain, and for doing which their white neighbours therefore generally suppose that they have no reason to give. When questioned, they rarely go futher than to say, that they do so because they have been taught that it is right to do it, or because their fathers did so before them: if they add any thing to this, it is, that they expect blessings from the observance of the practice, and evils from the neglect. But, to whom is this worship offered? To a *manito;* and by *manito,* through the religious prejudice of the whites, is usually understood *a devil.*[126]

The Englishman also noted that the Mashpees were "very fearful of going about in the dark, in which they are constantly apprehensive of being presented with terrifying visions." Folklore from Mashpee and Gay Head concerning aboriginal ghosts, demons, and heroes, though often "colored" by African-American and European motifs, survived into the twentieth century, and were undoubtedly more pervasive and influential two hundred years earlier. The cultural barriers represented by the persistence of native languages, beliefs, and rituals (such as the shared pipe in the Nantucket church) made it difficult if not impossible for natives and colonists to worship together. Efforts by white ministers to erase such boundaries, as Peabody tried in Natick, created tensions and divisions within the Indian community.

)(

Persistent cultural differences were not, unfortunately, all that maintained a frontier between Indians and their white neighbors. Far more significant were escalating conflicts over resources. In the second quarter of the century, as the number of whites in and around native enclaves grew, the Indians who depended on wood, plants, grazing areas, and fish from their commons increasingly suffered from poaching. In part, this was a clash between two economic systems, for rural whites may have been more likely to poach or trespass on lands that seemed unowned or unused, that were used as commons by a people who kept no land records. Ironically, as these differences began to shrink toward midcentury, trespassing and poaching increased, perhaps because the province's general economic malaise in the 1730s led white farmers to seek additional resources on Indian lands. Economic relations between the two peoples were made even worse by the colonists' mistrust of and contempt for their strange neighbors. White racism not only barred Indians from the credit-debt system that underlay the rural New England economy, but also made Indian resources "fair game."

The smaller Indian reserves in Massachusetts, surrounded by growing colonial towns, seemed particularly vulnerable to poaching. Although the Punkapoags told the General Court in 1725 that their English neighbors "have been our kind Friends in many Instances," conflicting land uses soon soured relations between natives and newcomers.[127] Just two years later, the same Indians complained that "some of our English Neighbours are too ready to Incroach upon our timber and our wood, cutting it down to make coal with, and damnifying us greatly thereby."[128] A similar charge came from Teticut in 1733. Just nine years after the General Court created that reserve, the New England Company told the court that a "great Strip & Waste of Timber has been made by Trespassers on the Lands belonging to the Indians at Tetticut."[129] Wood, needed for cooking and heating, was an increasingly rare and expensive resource in eastern Massachusetts, especially given Boston's growing population, and the more lightly populated and less intensively developed Indian reserves presented a tempting target. Both the Punkapoags and Teticut (through New England Company officials) sought the assistance of the General Court against the Indians' white neighbors.

A number of poaching and trespassing cases arose from boundary disputes. While border conflicts between New England towns and even provinces were not uncommon, those between Indian and colonial communities were more vicious, in part because of the differences between the two peoples, and in part because the former's special status in provincial law required disputes to be mediated by the General Court. Here, too, Teticut suffered from its white neighbors, for in July 1741 a number of Teticuts complained to the General Court that, under color of an old unsettled lawsuit, three Englishmen had taken their fields and orchards and destroyed much of their timber.[130] The three tried to discredit the complaint by noting that only one Indian lived there at the time of the lawsuit and by claiming that the land at issue was part of the original grant to Bridgewater.[131] The General Court supported the Indians' side of the dispute and, one year later, appointed a committee to redraw the line between Bridgewater and Teticut. This committee, and the assembly as a whole, upheld the claims of the Teticuts against the settlers to the land on the south side of the Taunton River.[132]

Even worse were the problems faced by the Nantucket Indians. Their English neighbors not only forced them into debt servitude on whaling ships, but also wrought "great Injustice & Oppression" by forcing natives off their lands and taking their resources. In November 1718, the Indians charged that Nantucket whites not only cheated them of the full value of their labor, but "have pulled down the Indian Houses & built on their Land, that they plow across the Indians & plant in their Land, & take away their Horses & Cattle to prevent their Plowing."[133] The General Court took no action, accepting the explanation given by Nantucket's representative that this had happened only when the Indians built on English land. The island's natives found no relief, of course, and renewed their complaint in June 1723. This time the court ordered a hearing, but the issue was allowed to lapse for four years until the assembly again ordered an investigation — but again there is no evidence that the Indians gained relief.[134]

After the Nantucket Indians overthrew Benjamin Abel in 1740 for selling their land to whites, their new sachem brought the community's complaints, some generations old, to the General Court. Colonists had, they bitterly told the assembly, taken their horses, cows, and oxen without compensation. In addition, English landholders had raised grazing fees from three to four pounds and recently began demanding five pounds. The native (and old English) concept of a fair price was falling prey on the island to the growing stress on resources, due to the expanding English population and the period's rapid inflation. Worst of all, during the past eight years the colonists had let herds of sheep loose in the Indians' fields to "eat our corn most all up" but then refused to "pay us for hurt there creatures done In our land."[135] The trespass of English cattle in Indian fields was nothing new; in fact, it was one of the first sources of conflict between the two peoples, and even in the nineteenth century Vineyard Indians often found their fields violated by free-ranging cattle. The persistence of this problem testifies to the tenacity of native communal values that had no place for fences, and to the scarcity of wood that made fences difficult or impossible. Strife over cattle also points to the racism that inspired some colonists to commit vicious acts against Indians.

Indians on the east side of Martha's Vineyard, where most colonists on the island lived, also experienced growing pressure on their communal resources. In December 1737, "Edgartown" Indians (probably from Chappaquiddick) complained that a number of English proprietors had committed a "great wrong and injustice . . . in disturbing them in the improvement of their land."[136] The accused included Enoch Coffin, of one of the island's most prominent white families, Edgartown's blacksmith, justice of the peace, representative to the General Court, holder of various town offices, and owner of large areas of land and speculator in more through mortgages.[137] The "injustice" was probably fraud or trespass, as in many other instances on the island. On the other hand, the Indians could have been seeking a favorable resolution of a boundary conflict with local whites. Disputes between towns over boundaries were common in colonial New England, and Vineyard natives were fairly accomplished at using the provincial political system to bypass local officials. Assistance was not always readily obtained, however, for the Indians' complaint was put off to the next session and there is no subsequent indication that the court took action.

The skyrocketing value of wood and the shrinking distance between the two peoples also led some Indians, in addition to the sachems described above, to illicitly sell community resources to whites. Investigators into the Teticuts' complaints reported that the "great Strip and Waste" of timber was "by the Indians selling their Timber to the English for trifles."[138] Testimonies to this problem also came from the Indian communities. Natick was forced to ban the sale of timber to Englishmen in 1715.[139] In 1727, the Punkapoags not only sought help against white poachers but also asked that "we may be under a better Regulation, than we have been of Late, as to our corn, timber, orchards, meddowe, and upland that we have still in our hands," hinting at the involvement of Indians in the loss of community resources to whites.[140] By 1741, Christiantown felt compelled to ask the General Court for relief from "several ill disposed Persons" within the community who "cut down and sell off large Quantities of the Wood" growing on their common lands.[141] If this continued, they warned the court, in a few years they would have no wood for fires or for fencing. The need for the intervention of outside authorities hints that native social controls were beginning to lose their effectiveness.

Indian communal codes against the abuse of resources were weakened by the efforts of white neighbors to obtain wood from native reserves. Both Teticut and Christiantown could have dealt with the matter if the timber poaching was organized and carried out by members of their communities. But neighboring colonists helped subvert sachems' traditional privileges and responsibilities and no doubt encouraged other Indians to violate community rules and morals. Investigators into the Teticuts' problems looked no further than the Indians' culpability and simple market forces ("trifles"). The Christiantown Indians pointed, however, to the primary role played by Englishmen in arranging timber poaching and trespassing, reporting "a Design to cut and carry off some hundreds of Cords besides the vast Quantities that have already been carried away" — a "design" that would have required the assistance of white merchants and ship captains or carters.[142]

To deal with the wide range of problems reported by Indian enclaves, provincial authorities appointed Anglo-American men of good reputation, familiar with the dominant economy and legal system, and living nearby. These were secular officers with limited powers, quite unlike John Eliot or the Mayhews. In response to the "great Strip & Waste of Timber" at both Teticut and Christiantown, the General Court commissioned English timber overseers, two for Teticut and two for Christiantown, with the power to prosecute poachers and trespassers.[143] When trespass and timber cutting again became a problem, the legislature broadened the overseers' powers by allowing them to regulate the cutting of timber on the reserves.[144] The idea of appointing Indian overseers or trustees was not new: by 1720 Natick had an overseer who managed the community's monies from the Magunkaquag sale, and in 1727 the General Court made a similar arrangement for the money paid to the Hassanamiscos for their reserve.[145] The timber overseers for Teticut and Christiantown were appointed along similar lines.

A significant change in the pattern came with the appointment of a guardian for Punkapoag. In response to the "Incroach[ment] upon our timber and our wood, the Punkapoags told the court, "we are necessitated to pray for ye juxposition and assistance of some English person, Impowered by this great and gentl Court to take the care of us." They asked specifically for John Quincy, a lawyer well on his way to becoming one of the most powerful men in the province (and the grandfather of Abigail Adams). Quincy was to help them "be under a better Regulation" as well as to adjudicate "any small differences between any of us, and our English Neighbours."[146] This involved far greater and broader powers than overseers in other Indian villages, who were in charge of a single community resource or account, and closely matches the responsibility and authority of guardians under English law. Punkapoag's new guardian also filled the significant role of "culture broker" for the Indians; like John Eliot, Quincy mediated between the Indians and Anglo-American culture and law. A biographer noted that he served the Punkapoags for twenty years, "reaching his hand into his own pocket when public funds were short, and suffering his charges to camp on his farm, cut up his fences for firewood, and hang around his kitchen for small beer and cider."[147]

The special relationship between Indian groups and the General Court that Quincy represented cannot cloak the links between the trespassers and the local elite, who often met and worshipped in the same meetinghouse, shared family ties, and could even (like Enoch Coffin) be the same person. Thus some communities, most notably stubbornly conservative enclaves where native dialects, wigwams, and communal landholding endured, resisted the intervention of the authorities as well as trespasses by white neighbors. Gay Head (and later, Mashpee) skillfully manipulated the political system, including the occasional threat of violence, to improve their bargaining positions and exert a measure of control over the diplomatic exchange. Gay Head sharpened its skills in the struggle over the controversial Donegan deed, and was particularly effective when the fallout from that deed continued to plague the community.

In 1711, after Gay Head lost its long legal battle against New York governor Donegan's deed, the New England Company purchased the area as a boon for the Indian community. As so often in American history, however, the effort by reformers to do "the right thing" for Indians made matters worse, for the New England Company decided that the Indians should pay at least part of the costs.[148] Over Gay Head's protest, the Boston commissioners quickly leased six hundred acres of Gay Head Neck to

Ebenezer Allen for a decade.[149] In 1724, as Allen's lease was about to end, they arranged a new lease with the farmer, enlarging the area to one thousand acres at one hundred pounds per year. The Indians protested the new lease, telling Allen and the New England Company that "the Land was theirs and their Ancestors and that They never sold it," thus challenging both Donegan's original deed as well as the company's purchase.[150]

But the Gay Headers did not limit their opposition to petitions. In March 1726, Allen reported "the Violent Opposition made by the Indians to his taking possession of the 1000 acres." A group of men had met him at the boundary and threatened violence if he persisted in claiming the territory. Two months later, Allen told the company's Boston commissioners "that the Indians resolutely hinder not only his taking possession of the 1000 acres in his last Lease but also his keeping possession of the 600 acres in his former lease, that to his great damage the Indians impound his Cattle & pull down his fences alleging that the land is theirs." The commissioners lodged trespass charges against the Indians, creating the spectre of trials that (considering who ran the county courts) would have certainly resulted in guilty verdicts and large fines that could be paid only by selling the reserve.[151]

All sides preferred a negotiated settlement over further conflict, and in July 1727 the Gay Head Indians agreed to lease eight hundred acres to Allen for twenty-one years. They also agreed to a reduced rent due to the "Severall hundred pounds damage in his Stock of Sheep by means of the disturbance given by the Indians and for want of possession of the Land [earlier]."[152] Another eight hundred acres were set aside permanently for the Gay Headers, at a nominal rent (an ear of corn); according to the commissioners, however, this was barely sufficient for the number of native families there. The violent controversy, moreover, had left the Indians' land in poor shape, for they were reluctant to fertilize fields that might have been taken. While the fight damaged Gay Head, and the Indians did not stop Allen's lease, the community had scored a victory: they had fought for their land, forced their "betters" to negotiate, and won back a fifth of their territory.[153]

Clearly, at least some Indian enclaves realized that reliance upon English authority, in the guise of the New England Company, undermined their already weakened autonomy. When the General Court appointed guardians to guard Indian communities against trespassing, poaching, and fraud, their powers allowed (and encouraged) them to interfere with native ways and created an outside source of authority that easily generated factionalism within the enclave. Even worse, many overseers abused their positions. Samuel Sewall found irregularities in the Natick overseer's accounts, and often preferred "to furnish the Natives with Blankets, the better to guard against embezzlement."[154]

The Chappaquiddicks had particular difficulties with those who were supposed to help them. In August 1722, the Chappaquiddick sachem complained to the General Court through Edgartown's representative, Simon Butler, that his lawyer, Benjamin Haws, had defrauded him and his people.[155] Haws died in October, before he could answer the charges, but in response the assembly created a committee (including Butler) to oversee the Chappaquiddicks' rents and other monies.[156] But four years later the Indians returned to tell the court that Butler had turned out to be a scoundrel. English settlers were grazing excessive numbers of cattle on their common land, violating the 1715 agreement, and when the Indians tried to enforce their rights, Butler only encouraged the trespassers. The Governor's council looked into the situation and reported that the Indians had been "greatly injured" and that Butler, who held additional power as a justice of the peace, had violated provincial law by attempting to purchase (with other Englishmen) Chappaquiddick land without the court's permission.[157] Such problems grew worse after 1740, as more guardians were appointed to control the resources of Indian communities.

⟩⟨

The continued frontier between Indians and their white neighbors points to the persistence of aboriginal culture in eighteenth-century native enclaves. Indians in New England maintained different socioeconomic ways, languages, rituals, and legends. Even those in Natick and Hassanamisco, who tried to live more like their Christian English neighbors, retained some, though less obvious, social and cultural boundaries. While differences remained between inland and coastal Indian communities, during this period all enclaves developed new leadership patterns, rejecting the sachems whose traditional rights became oppressive under the influence of the colonial economy. Other problems common to all Indian groups in eastern Massachusetts, such as high mortality and low fertility rates, service in the military, and increasing migration and intermarriage, began to dissolve the borders separating the surviving native enclaves. Between 1720 and 1740, Indian communities orbited closer to New England's economy and culture, generating new pressures that began to shape a regional ethnic identity. The subsequent two decades would see that orbit decay, as the provincial government exerted more influence and the midcentury colonial wars devastated native groups.

CHAPTER 5

"Great Injuries & Oppressions"

Between 1740 and 1760, Indian enclaves in eastern Massachusetts were deluged by the demographic, economic, and political problems that had risen over the preceding two decades. While low fertility and high mortality rates continued to chip away at native communities, the destructive effects of renewed imperial warfare, including epidemics brought home by returning soldiers, left some enclaves with only widows, orphans, and old men. The survivors found that their demographic decay worsened the effects of the region's general economic woes, causing a growing number to become "impoverished and disheartened."[1] Families in groups that had embraced landholding in severalty were compelled to sell their land to whites in order to pay debts and buy "necessities," including medical care. Only the enclaves orbiting farthest from the colonial economy and culture escaped these shattering conditions.

The devastation of wars and epidemics was enlarged by the "great Injuries & Oppressions, which they have received from their English Neighbors, & particularly of their Guardians."[2] Aggressive whites poached timber and fish from Indian reserves, grazed cattle on native meadows, manipulated debts and deeds to obtain Indian land, or simply took advantage of border disputes to build homes on native reserves. Poaching and fraud were often aided and abetted, unfortunately, by the men appointed by the General Court to protect the Indians' lands and resources. As many native enclaves fell on hard times and some dissolved, an increasing number of Indians sought their fortunes elsewhere. Many became wanderers on the road, seeking a subsistence or work in white households. Some moved to Mashpee, Dudley, and other enclaves with more land and resources, creating new social and kinship ties between villages.

>(

While demographic decline and economic problems affected all Indians in the region, those in the orbits closest to New England society and culture suffered most. This trend is best seen in Natick. Initially, as discussed in the previous chapter, only a few Indians sold land to whites to fund economic improvements, but in the mid-1740s the number of land sales grew in response to the enclave's aging population, medical problems, rising indebtedness, and the province's terrible inflation. Natick's population declined slowly in the 1740s, from about 190 to 166, and in the 1750s shrank at a fantastic rate — to 37 in 1764.[3] While these losses might have opened more land to the survivors, labor rather than land was the key to competency in New England. Natick Indian families in the best of times were quite small, and towards midcentury many of their children (of all ages) disappeared in wars or died in epidemics. Their 1749 census not only noted a large number of widows, but also showed that nearly a quarter of the households consisted entirely of single adults.[4] Households that lacked sufficient labor reserves were particularly vulnerable to injury or sickness.

Cultural changes also played an important role in the Indians' economic problems. Natick had adopted Anglo-American landholding and agriculture, including gender work roles. As John Eliot had urged nearly a century before, men took up the plow and women took care of the increasingly English-style homes. The heads of New England farms depended on their sons to help them produce grain and cattle for local, regional, and international markets. When the men died in the colonial wars or left the community, the women left behind were unable to handle the new crops and technologies or to renew older traditions. Five Natick Indian households in 1749 contained only women, and they were unable to work the land, having successfully adopted colonial gender roles and lost their native agrarian skills. Ten years later, three widows asked to sell their combined holdings of forty-six acres because "being brought up in Household business [they] are incapable of improving said lands."[5] The acculturation that was to have been their salvation became, in the end, their destruction.

A growing number of Indian men and women, in Natick and other native enclaves, told the General Court that they were too old or incapacitated to work and owed money for medical and other debts, which they could meet only by selling bits of their land. The average age of Indians in the province rose as young men died in the colonial wars. The resulting demographic and economic problems are highlighted by the increasing number of requests by Natick Indians to sell land to whites, which jumped from twenty-two in the 1730s to fifty-seven in the 1740s (an increase of 150 percent), and then rose to sixty in the 1750s. Socioeconomic decline was also evident in the increasing number of sales to finance families leaving Natick for other towns in southern New England.[6]

As optimistic land sales (to aid economic growth or material comfort) declined sharply between 1740 and 1760, from 50 to only 9 percent, land sales to pay for medical assistance or food climbed rapidly, from 50 to nearly 73 percent. No doubt "bad" medical debts caused many of the legal fees, which drove another 12 percent of the land sale petitions in the 1740s. In 1743, deacon Joseph Ephraim petitioned the court for permission to sell twelve acres of land. "Growing old & little able to Labor, [he] designed to settle one of his sons (on whom he had much dependence) with him to assist him in his Old Age" but this son had recently become lame and could not work. Medical bills and the loss of his son's labor left Ephraim with debts "which your Petitionr can by no means pay; without either selling his Oxen (which would undo him as to his Husbandry Business) or selling some Lands, (of which he had yet a Considerable quantity)."[7] The Waban brothers, Moses and Joshua, were forced for the first time to sell family property in 1742 in order to build an English-style house for their aged and sick mother and to pay debts incurred by Moses' disabling illness.[8] By the 1740s, Natick Indians usually sold land to white settlers because of long periods of illness or to buy "necessities" because they were unable to labor.

At midcentury, medical problems posed a particular trap for the Indian communities that depended on land for capital. Like Natick, the Hassanamiscos increasingly suffered financially as well as physically. Some elderly members of the community, such as Peter and Sarah Muckamug, leased much of their land to white neighbors in order to live off the rents.[9] More were forced to sell land in order to quickly raise larger amounts of capital. In March 1741, John Abraham, son of Andrew, petitioned the General Court for permission to sell thirty acres. He suffered from the "King's Evill" (scrofula) and expected to die soon, but in the meantime he had over seventy pounds in medical debts and needed more to support himself.[10] Abraham's fatal illness may have been one more problem caused by the embrace of English ways. Scrofula, a form of tuberculosis affecting the lymph nodes, was often spread by unpasturized milk from infected cows.

Elderly women were particularly vulnerable. Sarah Burnee was placed by the Indian trustees in the care of a neighboring white, Hezekiah Ward, after she fell ill and was abandoned by her husband, William. By the time Sarah died in the summer of 1751, her medical bills totaled over thirteen pounds.[11] Abigail Printer petitioned in 1748 to sell two thirty-acre parcels of "pine plain," worth about £250, in order to support her mother, Sarah Printer.[12] Two years later, Sarah, who suffered from such terrible foot pains that she finally had the limb amputated, sold more land to pay fifty pounds in doctor bills.[13] Annuities, rent, and income from labor or farm produce were initially sufficient for everyday needs, but the costs of extraordinary illness and injuries, as in Natick, could be met only by selling land.

Hassanamisco land also found its way into white hands because of the enclave's embrace of English ways. Not only did the Indians adopt landholding in severalty, but the men of the community refused to leave their land to female heirs, so enthusiastically had they adopted Anglo-American gender paradigms. As a result, those without male heirs (a high percentage, considering their few children and the effects of colonial wars) left real estate to white male friends instead of wives, sisters, or daughters. Though Joshua Misco, in 1737, left his "cattle and swine and other Creatures," his personal estate, and most of his yearly interest earnings to his widow Deborah, and part of the annual payments to his mother Christian, he gave every one of his 260 acres and his "orcharding building and improvements" to his friend

Antipas Brigham, a member of the prominent Brigham family of Grafton, whom he also named as the will's executor.[14]

Similarly, in 1744, Moses Printer Jr. willed each of his three sisters, Sarah Lawrence, Mary Thomas of Natick, and Bethia Printer, a token four bushels of corn annually, but left all of his lands, clothing, horse, farm tools, and annual interest earnings to Ebenezer Goddard of Framingham. Ebenezer was the son of Edwin Goddard, one of the first Hassanamisco trustees, who took Moses into his home after the Indian's father and mother died in 1727. Like Misco, Printer named the largest beneficiary of his will to be the executor of the instrument.[15] The will may have been fraudulent though this is unlikely given the Indians' universe of competing colonial interests (guardians, governors, and others); more likely was the adoption by Hassanamisco men of Anglo-American gender roles and property holding.

While only a sixth of the original six-thousand-acre Punkapoag reserve remained, the Indians were still able to gain a livelihood from timber and game and by fishing along the seashore south of Boston, sometimes on the farm of their guardian, John Quincy, in Braintree. But, like the Hassanamiscos, many grew too old to labor and became increasingly dependent on annual interest from land sales and rents. In 1741, four Punkapoags told the General Court that "We stand in great need of the infirmities of old age being such with us that we are able to doe little or nothing toward obtaining a livelyhood."[16] Quincy disagreed, saying that the Indians were perfectly capable — but at the same time, he was forced to supply many with food and clothing, including "the old Indians and their wives haveing had this fall each of them a good Blanket."[17] Unfortunately, as the Massachusetts currency depreciated rapidly after 1735, the annual fixed rents and interest payments purchased less and less. As early as 1741, the Indians' debts rose to the point that the court allowed Quincy to begin spending the principal from their account.[18]

Punkapoag population and conditions continued to decline in the 1740s. Quincy's accounts show that the community decreased from just under thirty adults in 1735, evenly split between men and women, to about half that many men in 1747.[19] One year later he told the General Court that "the Number of Said Indians is diminished," and that "several of the Indians who Survive are Aged & Infirm."[20] The many petitions from whites asking to be reimbursed for nursing and burying Punkapoags — some far from their community — underscore the guardian's words.[21] By 1756, not enough remained in the Indian account to pay for past bills or new charges "for the Sickness and deaths of Indians, att their Houses, and others for medicines and attendance in Sickness." In addition, the "dayly" needs of elderly Indians "who are unable to help themselves att all" had to be met.[22] The court therefore authorized the guardians to sell three hundred acres, reducing the Punkapoag reserve by nearly half, to about two-thirds of a square mile.[23] Internal decline and external economic convulsions thus shattered the enclave.

The middle of the century likewise brought a sudden worsening in Teticut's fortunes. The area's relatively unchanged ecology allowed the community to maintain traditional ways — in 1754, for example, Job Ahauton, who had moved from Punkapoag in the 1730s, lived in a wigwam on his vast acreage — and shielded it from the colony's economic instability.[24] But the enclave's small population was not able to cope with the sudden onset of aging, illness, and injury that triggered a cascade of land sales to whites. Nearly a third of the eighteen sales (up from only two in the 1730s) were made to pay medical debts, and more than half paid debts and provided the funds for basic needs like food and clothing. John Simon, disabled and indebted for over one hundred pounds, harried by lawsuits, sold 35 acres in 1743.[25] James Thomas sold 25 acres in 1748 and 32 more in 1751 to support his aged parents and to meet other needs.[26] The Teticuts' deep debts and dire needs are indicated by the average of 53 acres in each sale between 1740 and 1759, more than twice the amount sold by Natick during the same period (21 acres). Little land was apparently left within the Teticut reserve after midcentury, for the number of land sales suddenly dropped off to six in the 1750s and three in the 1760s even as the Indians' problems seemed to worsen.[27]

Other Indian families in the area around Teticut, such as those in Assawompsett, were forced to sell their lands to meet medical and legal obligations. In 1743, Samuel Clark, called "an Indian of Middleborough," was authorized to sell his land, including a brook and ponds, to support his aged mother and his father's debts.[28] At about the same time, Jeremiah Anthony, also called a Middleborough Indian, told the General Court that he had been thrown into the Plymouth jail after losing a lawsuit, where he "was in danger of perishing" due to the severe winter. Another Englishman saved him and gained his release by loaning him money for the debt, but Anthony then needed to sell forty Assawompsett acres. He noted, however, that he had arranged to use the land as long as he lived.[29] Anthony drowned, unfortunately, twenty years later, without any children, but with substantial debts from his long sickness.[30] As the number of Indian families shrank, and the survivors sought each other's company, all of the natives in the area were referred to as "Middleborough Indians." In fact, after 1760, the Teticut name largely disappeared from the colonial documents. A number of native families remained at Assawompsett, which became better known as Betty's Neck and would ironically "outlive" Teticut.

Those Indian enclaves that created closer connections with the colonial economy in the early eighteenth century faced unforeseen, difficult consequences. Not only did they lack the material resources and experience that white farmers acquired from parents or neighbors, but their timing was particularly unfortunate. Just as the number of Indian land sales increased in the mid-1740s, the economy in rural Massachusetts slumped badly. In part this was due to King George's War, but population growth, resource exhaustion, and currency fluctuations also damaged the region. During the decade, real wealth (nominal wealth divided by the consumer price index) declined more than 4 percent, the first decline of the century. While the consumer price index rose 250 percent, the average price of land dropped 58 percent. Land, the Indians' primary source of capital, lost much of its relative value at this critical juncture. Established farmers benefited from increasing crop prices as the wars brought military contracts and Boston's population grew, and were able to buy more consumer goods, such as pictures, ceramics, and coffee pots, once considered luxury items but now manufactured in England and offered at lower prices.[31] While many Indian families at Natick and Hassanamisco joined in this consumer revolution, Indians were clearly harmed by their reliance on land sales for capital.

Indian groups on Cape Cod and the islands also suffered from epidemics, war, and economic problems, but most weathered these problems because of their larger populations and wider cultural boundaries. Elisha Tupper, the Sandwich minister and "inspector" of Indians at the Herring Pond, was scandalized at their isolation in 1751, for they "generally Dwell Ten or more miles from any Justice of the Peace for sd County, and many Disorders Contrary to law Prevale among them many of them not attending the worship of god in Publick on the saboth."[32] But that isolation cultivated a flourishing, far-flung community, for ten years later "more than an Hundred" were scattered around the three thousand-acre reserve "besides these Remote villages in Sandwich Plymouth and Rochester"—which probably referred to the twelve families living at "Monyment Ponds" (Kitteaumut) and the ten families at Sandwich (Mannamett) found by Ezra Stiles in 1760—making it larger than any other mainland Indian community except Mashpee.[33] This sizable population is all the more astonishing because it is about the same as reported in 1685 (120 for the Herring Pond reserve). Every other Indian enclave in the province declined between 1740 and 1760 because of epidemics and colonial wars. Herring Pond seems to have received immigrants from other groups — as Mashpee would later report — precisely because of the reserve's isolation. The newcomers, of course, represented (and would no doubt deepen) connections between groups.

Despite its apparent stability, Herring Pond was not exempt from the demographic decay and disasters that tore at Natick, Teticut, and other villages. In 1761, Tupper reported the community to be "Exceeding poor." He told Boston officials of the New England Company that ten of the Indians were seventy-five to ninety years old and unable to labor, though "most of them can travaill and Begg."[34] The annual assistance of fifty pounds provided by the company was not enough, and he had used his own money to purchase supplies for the Indians. Tupper's report indicates that the traditional communal ties that provided special status for the elderly had broken down under the pressures of the times. But the enclave's large population and isolation generally shielded it against the demographic and economic shocks that tore at other groups. Indians in the area maintained much of their aboriginal culture: like his father, Tupper still preached in Wampanoag, Stiles reported only wigwams in the area, and subsistence fishing remained a mainstay of the community.[35] An Englishman from Sandwich later remarked that the reserve was "convenient for fishing & planting & [had] plenty of Wood."[36] Like Mashpee, Herring Pond held the land in common, with families laying out fields that could be passed to heirs. These cultural boundaries shielded the Herring Pond community from the unstable provincial economy. Neither individuals nor the community needed to sell land during this troubled period.

Mashpee, only ten miles from Herring Pond and by 1740 the largest Indian community on the mainland (in area and population), showed similar stability during these turbulent times. In 1753, about 260 people (144 adults and 116 children) lived at the reserve, only twenty fewer than reported three decades earlier. Mashpee may have suffered a terrible epidemic, for the enclave told the New England Company commissioners that their minister, Solomon Briant, had recently lost all eleven of his children.[37] In addition, as a result of service in King George's War, the enclave had "lost many of our young men who have left many Widows and fatherless Children."[38] Yet their population remained stable and even grew despite those losses, Ezra

Stiles reporting 250 Indians on the reserve in 1762, and the resident English minister Gideon Hawley reporting 271 five years later.[39] Like Herring Pond, Mashpee welcomed many immigrants, some of whom came across the short strait from Martha's Vineyard (discussed later).

Mashpee's geographical isolation, like Herring Pond's, and its ability to maintain deep cultural boundaries against the colonists, seemed to play a major factor in the community's health. Most of the Indians lived behind hills shielding them from the northern and southern roads that connected English towns on the Cape. The Wampanoag language remained dominant at midcentury when the Indians refused the New England Company's offer of an English schoolmaster "because we cannot understand him, only a few can."[40] The enclave's proprietorship found an ideal compromise between native and English systems of landholding by reinforcing the community's social structure and control of the reserve while allowing families to set aside farm and pasture land and pass it to their children. The aboriginal material culture still dominated the reserve, for sixty of sixty-six homes in 1762 were wigwams.[41] No doubt as a result (or a cause), the Mashpees on the whole resisted the ties to Anglo-American culture sought by Natick and Hassanamisco. In 1753, the community told the General Court that their system "kept our young men at home to work so that we live pretty well" — though the petitioners also mentioned the loss of many of these young men in the recent war. Mashpee's ability to keep the colonial economy and culture at arm's length allowed the Indians, they noted, to better provide for "our Poor and aged."[42]

The Indian population on Martha's Vineyard shrank drastically from about eight hundred in 1720 to approximately three hundred in 1767.[43] The reasons for this decline remain a mystery, although no doubt like all native groups the Vineyard Indians suffered from disease and war and many emigrated when white islanders increased their pressure on Indian land and resources. Gay Head remained the "healthiest" of the island enclaves, with over two-thirds of all natives on the Vineyard in 1767. The reserve, like Mashpee, boasted excellent land, including some of the best grazing territory on the island.[44] Like Mashpee and Herring Pond, Gay Head was geographically isolated: an islet connected to the main island by a narrow neck. Its land holding system was like Mashpee's: both men and women were called "proprietors" and allowed to mark off land for family plots, though the groups held their land in common. Non-Indian spouses were denied full access to community resources, though their children were full-fledged proprietors.[45] Gay Head likewise jealously defended its resources against intrusions by whites, even resorting to violence in the late 1720s. Their success, like that of Mashpee and Herring Pond, came from the ability to maintain wide cultural boundaries against Anglo-American settlers.

The connections between Gay Head, other Indians on the Vineyard, and the native enclaves on Lower Cape Cod were based on more than culture and circumstances. Religious, political, and social relationships, burnished by frequent visits, welded the groups together into a regional community. As already noted, at the turn of the century Indian ministers traveled between groups on the island and the mainland. The tradition remained strong, as evidenced by Zachary Hossueit, the Indian Congregational minister who went at least once (in 1765, with his son) to Mashpee to preach.[46] Religion and politics, as always, were closely bound. Gay Head's 1749 complaint against the guardianship system closed with a plea to Elisha Tupper, the white minister at Sandwich who preached to the Herring Pond Indians in their language, "to defend us about this."[47] Either Tupper had developed a close relationship to Gay Headers who visited Herring Pond or he had visited Gay Head, but, in any case, Hossueit, who penned the complaint, clearly trusted his white colleague. There may also have been family connections across the strait, although only Amoses appeared in both Mashpee and Gay Head.

The recognition of a native network based on common interests and identity should not obscure the important differences that remained between enclaves. Early in the century some Vineyard Indians were skilled craftsmen, and at least one visitor to Gay Head, Samuel Sewall, was quite impressed by their adoption of English agriculture. By midcentury, Gay Head Indians depended on cattle raising, particularly sheep, and grazed about four hundred animals on their commons. Mashpee, on the other hand, relied largely on crops, fish from streams and ponds, and hunting. The two communities may also have been separated by theology, politics, and etiquette. When Hossueit preached at Mashpee, he "made an [unspecified] offense that Sabbath day in the teaching," for which he later apologized.[48] Gay Head was also unique among Indian enclaves for hosting two Christian denominations — a Baptist church and the Congregational church led by Hossueit — though this did not seem to cause tension within the enclave as it often did in colonial towns. Still, such differences were far less important than the similarities that brought these communities together in eighteenth-century Massachusetts.

Whether troubled or confident, Indian communities in Massachusetts were barely affected by the Great Awakening, which hit New England in 1740 and revealed the region's latent socioeconomic strife. Initially, many white ministers enthusiastically participated in the revival. But soon most ecclesiastical and political leaders felt besieged by the unleashed forces, as southern New England seethed with exhorters and enthusiasts who seemed determined to undermine the established religious and social hierarchy. The region's elite were particularly troubled by the chord that the Awakening struck among the lower orders, including the urban poor and African-American servants. The egalitarian and emotional aspects of the explosion even brought about the sudden conversion of natives in Connecticut and Rhode Island, who had previously scorned Christianity. The already-converted Massachusetts natives, however, hardly reacted.

As Indians from different villages in Massachusetts met, worshipped together, and exchanged stories about their white neighbors, they were certainly aware of the religious and political upheaval around them. But the Awakening had little appeal for these natives. In Natick, Oliver Peabody "approved of the Awakening," and his church grew as George Whitfield inflamed Boston, but only seven Indians joined during the revival.[49] The percentage of Indians in the Natick church did begin to rise during this period, going from 8 percent in the 1730s to 15 percent in the late 1740s.[50] But nothing from that town, nor among other Indian enclaves in the province, even hints at the emotional eruption that took place among natives in Connecticut and Rhode Island. Indians in eastern Massachusetts had, of course, already embraced Christianity, and native preachers such as Solomon Briant of Mashpee and Zachary Hossueit of Gay Head preached a gospel that contained many of the antinomian ideas spread by the more radical New Lights.[51] The reshaped social and cultural frontier between Indians and whites may also have helped bar the Awakening.

The social and religious turbulence of the period might have allowed or encouraged many whites near Indian reserves to cast an eager eye on their Indian neighbors' rich lands. Their transgressions indeed seemed to grow bolder in the 1740s and 1750s. On the other hand, aggressive colonists had troubled Indian enclaves for decades, even from the beginning of settlement. A more significant boost to the swelling tide of trespassing and poaching came from the social and demographic turbulence — including that buffeting native enclaves — of the renewed colonial wars.

While Indians had little interest in the Awakening, they were heavily involved in the wars that began in the mid-1740s with the collapse of the fragile peace between English and France. Initially, Britain declared war only on Spain in 1739, but this conflict, which became known as King George's War, drew in France in 1744 and then spread to the New World. Indian men in Massachusetts, who often served in the persistent frontier wars against the Abenakis in Maine, were enthusiastic participants in King George's War. Natick minister Stephen Badger noted that the native men were "very easily enticed" into military service.[52] Along with their cousins from Rhode Island and Connecticut, many served as indispensable scouts and fighters. One historian has noted that this service was not only an important source of income for the natives, but also, "in contrast to such alternatives as apprenticeship, whaling, and domestic service, it allowed young men to earn their manhood in traditional ways frowned upon by a surrounding white society."[53] It may also have seemed an important part of their socialization into the New England nation and provided essential capital when family farms declined and debts rose. The ultimate effects of that service, however, were terrible.

The demographic and economic health of Indian communities in Massachusetts, already in decline, went into a tailspin with the renewal of war in 1744. To begin with, of course, many men died or were crippled. While there are no statistics on casualties, one historian has estimated that about 8 percent of the men in Massachusetts died at the war, primarily from disease.[54] Indian soldiers, already more vulnerable to epidemics, certainly suffered a much higher mortality rate. A forty-man company from Yarmouth, for example, raised for the 1745 campaign against Louisburg (Cape Breton), included thirteen Indians. Only three native men returned; two were killed in battle and eight died of disease.[55] An historian found the names of twenty-seven Natick Indians who served in the colonial military between 1740 and 1758; Peabody noted in 1744 that ten Indians had left Natick to serve in the military and were feared dead, and five years later the community reported only thirty-four men left.[56] Only two Hassanamisco men, Peter Lawrence and William Thomas, survived the war: Moses Printer Jr., Andrew Abraham, and his brother-in-law, James Printer, died in the King's service at Annapolis Royal in Maine, and Joshua Misco, Amni Printer Jr., and Zechariah Tom died either in the war or at home.[57] Indeed, the Indian casualties of King George's War went far beyond those in the military.

War subjected whole Indian communities to the ravages of diseases bred among armies. Like so many other problems, this one was most visible in Natick, where about fifty Indians died during an epidemic between 1744 and 1746, probably brought back from military service by soldiers (as would happen again in 1759), and the number of native men fell to nearly half that of women.[58] A census taken by the community's leaders in 1749 reported 167 Indians in fifty-five households. There were 51 women, the same as in 1698, and just 3 more children than the 70 who appeared half a century before. The number of men, however, had dropped from 59 in 1698 to only 34. The census listed 11 widows (a fifth of all adult women) and the ratio of men to women went from 1.16 to 0.67. The percentage of children in the population rose from under 39 percent to over 81 percent.[59] Other communities that did not leave such complete records had similar problems. In 1753, Mashpee told the General Court that they "have also been Redy (and beyond our Strength) to go to the War for the Defense of our King and Country till we have lost many of our young men who have left many Widows and fatherless Children."[60] Three years later, the Mattakeesits also told the legislature that many in the community had lost their husbands, sons, and even their senses as a result of the colonial conflict.[61]

War also threatened the livelihood of Indian families and their communities not only because it bred many widows and orphans, but because it produced many veterans who could barely gain their livelihoods. After William Thomas of Natick recovered from gout and joined the army, his wife died of consumption during his absence of six years, leaving their young child with a wet nurse for the nine remaining months of its life. When Thomas returned, he fell sick for nine months, and by 1750 found himself "Greatly indebted and reduced in circumstances."[62] Incapacitated by sickness contracted in the military, in 1749 Benjamin Tray asked to sell thirty acres of land in order to pay medical debts and to support his mother and grandmother.[63] Stephen David, a Teticut Indian, faced debts that his family incurred for food and clothing while he served in the Cape Breton expedition of 1745. He also owed creditors for money borrowed when he "inconsiderately" enlisted for another term of service, changed his mind, deserted, and was caught and fined.[64] Another Teticut, John Simon, was wounded and unable to work after the war. The General Court gave the Middleborough overseers of the poor forty shillings per year to support Simon, who became the Indian community's minister.[65] Matthew George, of Punkapoag, served in Maine, where he reinjured his back. He was discharged and sought medical help near Teticut before returning home.[66]

The war also brought a new group of Indians to the Bay Colony. Eastern Abenakis, in southern and middle Maine, had long resisted European colonization, sometimes allying with the French and other times trying to reach an accommodation with the English. By the onset of King George's War, internal tensions within the Abenaki confederation mirrored the colonial conflict, and a number of Pigwackets, the southernmost of the five Eastern Abenaki groups, decided to fight for Massachusetts. In the winter of 1744, reports reached Boston that Pigwackets were scouting for the militia along the Saco River, and that many wished to resettle further south.[67] Provincial authorities began looking for a resettlement site, and two years later finally found a spot in Rochester, south of Assawompsett Pond, in an area rich in fishing grounds and where the owners of the land asked to be paid only for the wood that the Indians burned. Two Rochester whites were appointed to be the Pigwackets' guardians, and to buy a fishing boat, axes, and hoes for the Indians.[68] One year later the court paid £170 for the care, support, and apparent relocation of the Pigwackets.[69] The precise number and composition of the refugees, unfortunately, was never recorded. Over the next three years this enclave cost the province treasury over one thousand pounds and then disappeared from view, as its members mingled with the Freetown, Dartmouth, or Middleborough Indian communities.[70]

In 1754, six years after a truce ended King George's War, England and France resumed their conflict in what became known as the Seven Years or French and Indian War. That war and its aftermath brought the English colonies deeper into the imperial system. Massachusetts formed the northeastern border between the English and French colonies, and inevitably gained both the benefits and the problems of "frontline" status. The province served, however, more as a supplier of soldiers than of food or war goods. About 30 percent of the men in the province served in the war; while the number of casualties remains a mystery, one historian has estimated that about 10 percent of the army died on the battlefield or "in a disease racked garrison."[71] Another noted that soldiers were twice as likely to die of disease as civilians in Boston and faced more than four times the risk as their neighbors who remained in rural Massachusetts. "At its worst, life during the late campaigns was routinely riskier than it had been during the worst epidemics in New England's history."[72]

The Natick Indians, already hit hard by the previous conflict, were decimated by the Seven Years War. In 1754, there were twenty-five families "plus several individuals"; ten years later only thirty-seven Indians remained.

Badger noted that many of the men "were engaged in the [military] service; not a small number died while in it; others returned home, and brought contagious sickness with them; it spread very fast, and carried off some whole families. This was in 1759. In the space of about three months, more than twenty of them died, all of the same disease, which was a putrid fever; it carried them off in a few days."[73] The terrible tragedy wrought by the war is reflected in the dry statistics of the *Vital Records.* Mortality rates for Natick Indian males peaked after 1740, stayed high until the start of the war in 1755, and then immediately plummeted to their lowest levels. No male deaths are reported after the end of the war, suggesting that most of the adult men vanished in the war. Women and children at home were the victims of the 1759 epidemic: the deaths of women shot up from six in the previous half decade to eighteen, and the deaths of unnamed individuals, almost certainly children, went from one to nine.

As in the aftermath of the previous war, many of the Indian men who survived were unable to earn a living because of their injuries or debilitating sickness. Their infirmities further weakened Indian communities by opening the gates to colonists. In June 1756, Joseph Poignet, wounded and discharged from the army, sold some of his land to a white settler because the injury created medical debts and prevented him from supporting his family.[74] Joshua Ephraim served only two years in the army, but caught a fever that paralyzed an arm and later forced its amputation; he then had to sell land to colonists to pay medical debts.[75] In 1757, Thomas Awassamog sold twenty acres to whites in order to pay medical debts and to support himself as "under his infirmities contracted by means of the hardships he has undergone in his Majesty's Service for many years past, & which have rendered him unable to labour."[76] Four years later he told the General Court that he had served in the army for more than three decades, where he "endured such great hardships as have brought upon the Gout, and more lately the Palsy and two apoplectic Fits." Awassamog faced additional debts and "great distress" because the white majority in Natick did not think they were responsible to help poverty-stricken Indians.[77]

Land sale requests do not, of course, reveal the full impact of the war on Indian enclaves. For example, only one individual from Potawaumacut, on Cape Cod between Eastham and Harwich, asked to sell land during or after the war: Leah Ned, a widow "advanced in years," who, no doubt as a result of the wars, had "nor Relations Left that is able to provide for me."[78] But Ned was not the only Potawaumacut widow: two years after the end of the Seven Years War a visitor noted fourteen — one more than the number of married women. While some of the husbands may have drowned on whaling voyages, since Indians on the Cape were heavily involved in that industry, many must have died in the military. Thus there were many more native widows and orphans of the war than those represented by petitions to sell land.[79]

)(

The hammer blows of the colonial wars were magnified by the Indians' bellicose, encroaching white neighbors. As in the second quarter of the century, trespassing and poaching on the Indian reserves was part and parcel of the racism, numbers, and poverty of their white neighbors. In addition, the "classic" means for defrauding Indians through the judicious application of liquor and the law, also resurfaced as a major problem for native families and enclaves. When colonists and Indians shared the same town, as in Natick and Hassanamisco, whites pushed the natives into a marginal position, dominated town offices, and established their own schools and churches or moved these town institutions away from where natives lived. Conflict with whites convulsed every Indian community in Massachusetts after 1740.

The critical gaze of Stephen Badger, Natick's minister in the second half of the century, penetrated into the racist attitudes that fueled the settlers' aggressive behavior. The Indians, he noted, "are generally considered by white people, and placed, as if by common consent, in an inferior and degraded situation, and treated accordingly." Many of the whites living in or near native enclaves "have been under temptations to encourage their Indian neighbours in idleness, intemperance, and needless expenses, and thereby to involve them in debt for the sake of preparing the way for the sale and purchase of their lands," usually at "a very low rate, in order to have their debts discharged." As a result, many of the Indians became "impoverished and disheartened." Those in Natick

> became more indolent and remiss in their attention to the improvement of their lands, to which they had before been encouraged, and in some degree lost their credit; their civil and military privileges were gradually lessened, and finally and exclusively transferred to the English inhabitants, who were become more numerous, and some of whom, it is to be apprehended, took every advantage of them that they could, under colour of legal authority, and without incurring its censure, to dishearten and depress them.[80]

Of course, not all whites "took every advantage" of the Indians, for the legal, economic, political, and even cultural conflicts were not only between natives and colonists. The aggressive behavior of many settlers, in fact, created battles among whites — occasionally revealing the class divisions indicated by Badger's words. The minister's opinions were colored, in fact, by his conflicts after 1775 with many white families in Natick over the location of the meetinghouse and his salary.[81] Settlers were also able to gain Indian allies or manipulate debtors, gaining useful leverage and generating conflicts within native communities.

The only place and time in which Indians and whites came together in nearly equivalent numbers and power was Natick in the late 1730s and early 1740s. Unfortunately, the settlers were increasing as the natives rapidly declined in both numbers and power, helping aggressive whites "finally and exclusively" take the Indians' "civil and military privileges." As colonists began moving into Natick in the late 1720s, they soon dominated town offices such as clerk and treasurer that demanded literacy and monetary skills, while the natives continued to monopolize the board of selectmen and to command other posts of authority such as constable and tithingman. The end to the Indians' political participation in Natick came from the white's demographic dominance in the mid-1740s. By January 1746, the natives had faded to 30 percent of Natick's population, following the epidemic of 1744–46 and the addition in 1744 of about thirteen families in Hog End — a large section of Needham that protruded into Natick's northeastern quarter.[82] Their numbers and the newcomers' ambition proved the Indian's undoing.

English families on the northern side of town, following the incorporation of Hog End, tried to isolate themselves from the Indians (and other whites) in the south. In December 1744, they asked the General Court to be set off as a separate town. The court rejected the request, but one year later transformed the native plantation into a parish — a religious community instead of a political entity. Not one Indian ever again achieved office in Natick. The newcomers to the town also strove to move the meetinghouse north, away from where most of the Indians lived. Their efforts not only violated an agreement with the General Court, but alienated other Natick whites who lived on the southern side of the town, closer to the meetinghouse. Since the Indians officially owned the Natick meetinghouse, and the court would not allow the building to be moved without the natives' approval, both sides were forced either to gain the support of the natives or to argue that their position was best for the Indian community. The battle over the meetinghouse continued into the early 1800s — allowing the Indians, despite their loss of civil "privileges," to retain a small measure of political power in the town.[83]

A much more widespread and disruptive threat came from whites who sought Indian land. The more aggressive colonists not only easily avoided the "censure" of "legal authority," but were quite capable of using its "colour." Alcohol proved a particularly useful tool. The Mashpees complained in 1755 that their English neighbors "Doth bate [us] with Strong Licker" to get them to sell their land: "It is a old saying that when the Drunk Is In the Wit is out."[84] One cold winter night Job Ahauton, the Punkapoag expatriate, was plied with liquor by Stephen David "so as to intoxicate him, and then drawing him in to execute a Deed for Conveying away his Lands in Teticut for a trifling Consideration." Job contested the validity of the deal before the General Court; while he accepted (or was forced to accept) the document, he had no memory of actually signing the deed and condemned those who got him drunk.[85] David defended himself and the deed in turn by attacking Job's character, "trusting that your Excellency and Honrs are so wise and just that you will not condemn one poor honest temperate Indian upon the bare naked word of another Indian who owns himself to be a Drunk."[86] Like Ahauton, many Indians found liquor greasing their descent into a nightmare of lawsuits.

Court actions filed by whites claiming Indian debts (whether from alcohol or medicine) made matters worse, for the Anglo-American legal system was still a mystery to Indians. Most never even bothered to contest lawsuits, resulting in the addition of fines and court costs and forcing the sale of more land. Even settlers who were apparently helpful gained from this system. Isaac Waban was bailed out twice by Isaac Coolidge of Sudbury, whose assistance Natick Indians often sought to help get a better price when selling their land. When Waban's debts to Coolidge proved too great, the Indian fled Massachusetts and Coolidge got his lands.[87] The unfortunate Stephen David was unable to sell enough land to redeem medical and legal debts, and in 1760 absconded to Albany.[88] Waban and David were not alone, for many Indian men fled the province in an effort to avoid crushing debts or the legal battlefield.[89] These fugitives only steepened the demographic decline of their families and communities, and of course their efforts were in vain. Courts and justices of the peace ordered their land sold in their absence or their remaining relatives were forced to meet debts by selling their own land.

Indians could be besieged by the law collectively as well as individually. In September 1743, Teticut was compelled to sell eighty acres in order to pay

£150 in debts from "defending their Rights in the law from the invasions of their English neighbours," and six months later the courtroom battle was still raging.⁹⁰ Even the General Court was forced to acknowledge the "great Loss & Injury" suffered by Indians as a result of "designing & ill-minded men."⁹¹ Of course, the court (as in so many other cases) failed to take effective action to halt the "Injury."

Those who could not meet their debts or were unable to flee the province were committed to involuntary servitude. Many Nantucket Indian men found themselves aboard whaling vessels as a result of a trifling or fraudulent debt. But men were not the only ones to fall afoul of the debt system. Alice Sachemus, a widow with an infant, found herself in the Plymouth jail at the behest of a white debtor, John Otis, of Barnstable — perhaps because of her late husband's debt. Sachemus was bound over to Otis for three years of domestic service. Otis also promised "yt the Infant Child of ye sd Alice shall be no Charge to ye Town where it is kept" — so mother and child were apparently kept apart. Sachemus's situation worsened: two years later Otis sold her indenture to Consider Howland of Plymouth, and Howland in turn sold her to Jabis Allen of Killingsley — not only outside the province, far from her home and child, but also several months after her involuntary service was supposed to expire.⁹²

Calls by provincial officials for reforms were usually ineffective. In December 1760, Governor Francis Bernard asked the legislature to pass new laws to prevent the scourge of Indians forced into servitude by their debts to whites — debts often created or manipulated by colonists (such as whaleboat captains) who wanted native labor. First, Indians should be barred from contracting large and unnecessary debts "which they can pay only by selling themselves." Second, parents should not be allowed to sell their children [!] nor make them responsible for their debts. Third, Indians who broke laws should be whipped or placed in stocks but never fined, for inevitably the offenders were forced to sell themselves into servitude. Finally, Indians should be excused altogether from legal charges "which in little Squabbles that ought to have been made up without Expence have sometimes brought ruin, and in consequence Slavery upon a whole Family." These proposals, which would have required drastic changes in the dominant legal and economic system, found little support.⁹³

While involuntary servitude continued to plague Indians, a more wide-spread and disruptive problem was the efforts by whites to gain title to native land. The Mashpees complained that the capitalist system manipulated by settlers undermined the enclave's communal landholding system. Some individuals were, contrary to the village's desires and provincial policy, trying to sell pieces of the reserve to whites. If the sales went ahead, others in the group faced the choice of also selling land (and thereby destroying the community's land base) or of losing out altogether, for "he that Can sell the Most will Be the best [wealthiest] fellow."[94]

The Teticuts, seemingly suspended halfway between Natick's and Mashpee's landholding systems, had particular problems. In 1748, John Thomas of Teticut fought (without success) the request by his brother James to sell land from the reserve.[95] Stephen David tried to sell about a hundred acres upon returning from King George's War, even though the community had complained fifteen years earlier that, as an outsider, he had no right to sell community land.[96] A few years later, two Teticuts complained to the General Court about separate incidents in which another Indian and a white man connived to steal their land. John Thomas had sold ten acres of Katherine Sachemus' land to a Bridgewater man, and David got Job Ahauton drunk and obtained a deed to his land at the home of Elkanah Leonard, a lawyer and leading Bridgewater citizen.[97] Both Thomas and David blamed unnamed whites for the accusations: Thomas supposed that "some person of a Different Complection Stood near to Encourage" Sachemus's lies, and David told the court that if liquor did not inspire Ahauton's complaint, then "he was made a Tool of by Some designing Person."[98] The Teticut minister, John Simon, complained that by 1753 his people were "often imposed upon by the English, and the Lands sold much under their Value, the Indians thereby led into an Idle & dissolute way of Living, & so reduced to Poverty, and many times the Lands sold by those who have no good Title to them, with many other Evils arising from this Liberty."[99] The General Court finally responded to Simon's cry by requiring Thomas and David to set aside small parcels of their holdings as a permanent Teticut reserve — like Mashpee and Gay Head — never to be sold or leased. But there is no subsequent mention in any documents of such restrictions.[100]

No doubt only some of the settlers' efforts to obtain Indian lands reached the attention of the General Court and were preserved for our enlightenment. The only documented Hassanamisco conflict took place in 1739, when the original white proprietors told the General Court that the new town's inhabitants "pretended they have Power to Remove the Indians out of the Place that was appointed for them."[101] Yet oral history points to other conflicts with prominent Grafton settlers. In 1920, a member of a Hassanamisco family, Sarah Cisco, told anthropologist Frank Speck that her clan still remembered two prominent white families from the mid-eighteenth century, the Brighams and Goddards, encroaching upon the Indians' lands. Edward Goddard was a Hassanamisco overseer from 1727 until 1743, and the Brighams were also important in the region. "These neighbors were alleged to have used means to intimidate the Indian folks to an extent that caused 'the Indians to talk in low voices in the native tongue when discussing matters pertaining to the land dispute.' "[102]

But in most cases, colonists generally found it easier and faster to avoid the law and to simply take Indian resources. Most native enclaves divided only a small percentage of their lands into small farming plots. All continued to depend heavily on their still-large commons for fish, wood, game, and building materials. By comparison, their English neighbors had divided most if not all of their common lands by the early eighteenth century and faced a shortage of precisely the resources still plentiful on Indian reserves. Thus poaching posed a growing though hardly new threat at midcentury.

Poaching was a problem even in Natick, where the Indians had created a proprietorship and divided a large percentage of their land in part to gain legal protection from the dominant landholding system. The natives retained until 1763 "hundreds of acres" of common land for grazing, fish, and wood, some barred to white residents of the town. Many of the English, however, were not about to allow the Indians special privileges, particularly when colonists were now in the majority. In February 1744, Ebenezer Felch, a white resident of Natick, complained that "a great part of the wood and Timber is cut off by the English in other Towns. . . . I have seen a great many trees fell and barked and some barked standing all [through?] their wood and timber; so that it seems if care is not speedily taken [the Indians] wont have wood to burn, nor fencing stuff to fence with." While Felch blamed the problem on the greed of outsiders and the Indians' wasteful habits ("for they burn much wood"), he and other English Natick residents also had little regard for the natives' common resources.[103]

Four years later the Indians charged that "Felch and others, English Inhabitants of sd Parish (without our consent, and against our wills) have of late so far Trespassed upon our said priviledges, as to take Possession of our best fishing-ground." The Natick natives told the General Court that "our families have been in a great measure supplyed" by the "Fish of Various sorts, especially Ale-wives in plenty" obtained from the ponds. They had traditionally set their nets at the narrow opening to Cochituate Pond. Now, however, Felch and others "have Entered into articles of agreement, in writing, Provided a Seine &c; which we very much dislike." The settlers had joined to build a fish trap at the place long used by the Indians. The natives asked the court to guarantee their "old and valluable liberty of fishing."[104] Perhaps the English were not aware of the "priviledges" long held by Natick Indians. The colonists more likely, however, refused to recognize a preexisting exclusive right to what seemed (to them) unowned or "improperly" exploited resources. One should also not rule out, of course, simple greed and racism.

Isolation and traditional ways did not bar the loss of fish to whites. In 1762, one year after Herring Pond's guardian complained about the Indians' isolation and poverty, they approached provincial authorities for the first time to ask for assistance against neighboring colonists taking their fish. They complained that inhabitants of Sandwich and other nearby towns "make great Profits of the Alewives which pass up in the River called the Herring River which River is fed by ponds lying chiefly in sd Plymouth, and our lands ly adjoining chiefly along by sd Ponds and River, and we are not allowed the Privilege of taking sd Fish for market nor any part of the profit of the yearly produce of the Fish so taken."[105] The Indians wanted a share in those profits to offset the depletion of their primary food source and the impoverishment of their community. The coastal community's geographic isolation made it impossible to prevent whites from dipping into the stream that reached far from their borders. But isolation and aboriginal ways did not stop the Indians from learning about the "profit of the yearly produce" of the fish taken to market and wanting a share. The General Court did not answer the Indians' plea.

The Mashpees felt even more besieged by neighboring whites, who were not only taking fish from their ponds and streams, but also invading their lands and poaching their wood. In April 1752, no longer able to ignore "the great hurt and damage done by English men invading their marsh and Land and culling their wood and fencing stuff," the Indian enclave appointed a committee to "look into means of getting [the] English out."[106] They soon decided to take their case to provincial authorities, and in June petitioned the General Court (in the native language) for relief. The Mashpees began by reminding the court that the same sachems who had given most of the Cape to the English had also created Mashpee, and had put limitations on the deed that had been upheld by New Plymouth.

We shall not give it away, nor shall it be sold, nor shall it be lent, but we shall always use it as long as we live, we together with all our children, and our children's children, and our descendants, and together with all their descendants. They shall always use it as long as Christian Indians live. We shall use it forever and ever. Unless we all peacefully agree to give it away or to sell it. But as of now not one of all of us Indians has yet agreed to give away, or sell, or lend this Indian land, or marsh, or wood.

They were increasingly bothered, however, by their white neighbors. "Against our will these Englishmen take away from us what was our land. They parcel it out to each other, and the marsh along with it, against our will. And as for our streams, they do not allow us peacefully to be when we peaceably go fishing. They beat us greatly, and they have houses on our land against our will."[107]

The problem worsened, and one year later they again told the court that "Englishmen so much want our Land they begin to [come] here upon our land [take] out our fencing stuff catch most all the fish came up our rivers we find we must starve quickly unless you help us."[108] And in 1757, the Mashpees pleaded for assistance against squatters and poachers. The settlers' encroachments on the Indian reserve had increased, and the Indians wanted clear boundaries that could be enforced. "We Desire the line to be Run between us & the English [,] that they join to us, and trespath on us, on Every Quarter, some in one way & some in another." Even worse, their best river for alewives, key to their subsistence, had been "ruined" by whites. "The English have Improved it about 17 years for nothing only paying for the Ketching." Before their white neighbors intruded, the Indians normally caught 200 to 350 barrels of fish a year. Now, however, the English were hauling about 2,000 barrels of fish every year away from Mashpee. Those using the Indians' fishing grounds had nothing but contempt for the natives: they had been "tricked" out of the best fishing spots along the river, and one was recently thrown into the water when he tried to set nets among the English. While Herring Pond Indians asked only for a share of the profits when it confronted a similar problem five years later, the Mashpees wanted provincial authorities to completely bar Englishmen from catching fish along the river for market. But the General Court failed to take any action to enforce boundaries or to stop the fishing disputes.[109]

Potawaumacut, further east along Cape Cod, also found white neighbors encroaching on a key resource. The community was closely tied to the colonial economy through whaling, probably because its reserve lacked the good planting and meadow land and the plentiful ponds and streams possessed by Mashpee. By the 1730s, many men from the enclave were whalers, either on the community's or on English-owned vessels. In fact, one of the Potawaumacuts, Samuel Cooke, captained a shore whaling boat with an all-white crew![110] In March 1758, the enclave complained to the General Court that Harwich and Eastham had "encroached on their property, and that the Town of Eastham have Sold to Samuel Smith Esqr and Mr. Sylvanus Snow a certain Neck of Beach and Thatch Ground on one side of Billingsgate most commodiously situated for the Whaling business, and which has from time immemorial been improved by them for that purpose."[111] Snow had begun charging the Indians for the privilege of whaling at Billingsgate, where they had traditionally launched whaleboats and landed the huge sea mammals. The controversy may also have involved a conflict between two groups of whites, in which one party "used" Cooke's aboriginal rights to get around an adverse court ruling.[112] Eastham voted to give the Indians the right to whale at Billingsgate point and to cut thatch there for their whalehouses, but the General Court for unknown reasons rejected the arrangement.[113] That was the end of the matter for the provincial authorities, but the Potawaumacuts ended up more dependent on colonial whaling masters, if they were lucky, or provincial charity, if they were not.

The Indians on Nantucket, who had spearheaded the whaling industry in Massachusetts, also felt pressed by their white neighbors. In March 1743, after the General Court gave short shrift to their charges about cattle trespasses and confiscation of their animals, they again complained about the behavior of their white neighbors. The natives felt that English judges were giving short shrift to their efforts to recover loans made to colonists — a sign that some Indians were using the county legal system, though they were unhappy with its administration. In addition they charged that, as before, settlers were taking their lands and leaving them insufficient area to farm. The court (again) ordered an investigation by two Nantucket justices, who reported that, although the natives had leased out "a great Many acors of Pla[n]ting Land to the English," they still held over a thousand acres, more than enough for the thirty surviving families. The English did not, they assured the court, hinder or molest the Indians.[114]

But the court had already cast its verdict by appointing John Coffin and Abishai Folger, who had financial and family ties to those about whom the Indians complained, to investigate the charges against English justice. So of course when the two confronted the Nantucket sachem about the Indians' charges, John Quaap had (supposedly) answered "that they never Put in any such Complaint." No doubt he saw the futility or danger of pursuing the issue since the court insisted on appointing local elites to investigate the Indians' concerns. The sachem and his family still suffered for his leadership, for five years later Paul Quaab, a brother or close relative, was seized by a constable and fined by justice Josiah Coffin (a relative of John Coffin) supposedly for refusing to go whaling in payment of a debt.[115]

Indians on Nantucket continued to feel hindered and molested by their English neighbors, and to seek relief from provincial authorities. Their problems with bound labor had never ebbed, and in 1746 they tried to frame the problem in religious terms, charging the colonists with compelling whalemen and other bound laborers to violate the sabbath. English whaling captains forced them to row and kill whales and "let us no time to Read our [Bibles] on Sabbath days." Even when Indians were not forced to work, their circumstances were shaped by their masters so that they would "Rather go to see there friends on the Sabbath days then to come to meeting." In addition, they charged that whaling captains and merchants refused to give a full accounting of earnings and debts, and that they were probably being defrauded of their labor. One wonders whether the Indians were attempting to spark sympathy, given the old Puritan perception that the Quakers (who dominated Nantucket) spurned "proper" religious regulation. The Indians' guardians, including Abishai Folger and two Coffins, later told the General Court that, as always, they were unable to find a single instance of fraud.[116]

And, of course, older conflicts over land rights and resources, which revolved around the former sachems' authority to sell community land and resources, had never been resolved. By March 1747, the Indians were again charging the English with "hindering them from planting upon their own Land & feeding their Creatures there."[117] In 1748, Paul Quaab, probably the sachem's brother, was fined for trying to stop a white man from taking wood from the Indian reserve. When questioned, the selectmen of Sherburne, the largest English village, denied the natives' complaints but noted that "we have Purchased of their Avowed Sachems and other owners for which we have good Deeds for." By comparison, they said, none of the petitioners "were allowed any other Land by the Sachems but a planting Right" for which they paid yearly tribute. The English therefore felt that they held ultimate control of the land, and that the Indians had no complaint if English cattle ate their corn. The Indians, on the other hand, insisted that "all we want is our Land . . . to make use of as we have all our dayes past." The intrusion of an alien culture had caused the traditional right of a sachem to manage community resources — a power that had increased when Europeans first arrived — to clash with a community's traditional right to use its land. Once again, after (supposedly) investigating the charges, the Indian guardians reported no truth to the Indians' complaints and the assembly dropped the issue.[118]

The Indians, however, continued seeking succor from the General Court and in July 1751 again called attention to conflicts over resources on the island. Their labor was for naught, for "We plow our ground and they take it from us and sow oats on it, some of our plowed Land they turn over again, and when some of us mow our grass English take the same from us." The natives still claimed half of the island, while the English pressed their owner-ship to "a greater proportion," probably over three-quarters, by brandishing an old deed. Unlike Gay Headers, Nantucket Indians were unwilling to resort to direct action against English trespass — or felt too weak to stand against the consequences. The natives sought legal remedies, but found the local courts dominated by the very men (or their relatives) causing their problems, and therefore asked for their disputes with whites to be tried in another county. As in the 1743 petition describing the inability to gain justice in the island's courts, the Indians told the assembly that when challenged, Englishmen boasted that "we can have no Remedy" — a boast that they found "true in Respect to any tryl by any of ye Courts on that place."[119]

Over the next three years a committee reviewed the situation, but in the meantime ordered the Indian guardians "to take effectual care that the Indians be supported & protected in the enjoyment of their wonted Priviledges & Improvements" — so apparently the Indians' many petitions were bearing fruit. The Indian guardians again scoffed at their charges' complaints, telling the court that the colonists recognized the traditional sachem's rights to land and resources, and did not interfere with the Indians who had been given horse-holding rights by sachems — thereby implying that they *did* confiscate horses from those who they felt lacked such rights. Sherburne proprietors denied that they had taken the Indians' land, but admitted that the island lacked "Disinterested" judges of Indian-white disputes.[120] In 1754, the Indians again claimed that they were still "the Rightfull Owners of a Considerable Part of the valuable Lands" on Nantucket, but that the English had taken their land, leaving them only enough for each family to have a house and small garden. When they tried to graze their animals on the commons, Englishmen confiscated the livestock. "We Cant Keep a Cow horse nor Sheep unless we will submit to hire the Preveledge of the English."[121]

The sudden flurry of efforts by the Nantucket Indians to regain or reclaim their lands and resources and to obtain relief from forced labor indicates that they were trying to lessen their dependence on the whaling industry by expanding agricultural production. This would explain why the English proprietors treated the Indians' claims as something new, as well as why whites tried to dismiss those claims — in order to keep both the land and their laborers. The issue remained stalled in the General Court until a committee was appointed in August 1757 to hold hearings on Nantucket. The events, held in the English meetinghouse at Sherburne, drew "a large concourse" of English and Indian spectators and lasted three or four days, after which the judge ruled in favor of the English.[122] While the Indians were doubtless dissatisfied with this judgment, they also realized that, after fifteen years of effort, they would receive no relief from provincial authorities. The real end of the controversy came, tragically, five years later with the death of over two-thirds of the Indians on the island from an epidemic.

)(

The Indians' most common tactic to ward off their aggressive neighbors was to appeal to the governor and General Court for assistance: to cry, as did the Mashpees in 1753, "Oh! you kind gentlemen in Boston, in Massachusetts Bay, now we beseech you: defend us, and they would not trouble us any more on our land."[123] Other options were useless: overt resistance would be crushed and county courts were unresponsive. The Indians' connections to provincial authorities offered at least occasional relief. Unfortunately, the general solution picked by the General Court in 1746, to appoint guardians for all Indian communities, seemed to create even more problems.

Indians were familiar, of course, with prominent men such as John Eliot and Daniel Gookin acting as agents for the colonial government, and, between 1725 and 1745, trustees with limited powers were appointed to oversee wood in Teticut and Natick and community funds in Hassanamisco and Punkapoag. But, towards midcentury, as the number of Indian complaints about whites trespassing and poaching increased, provincial authorities began to consider exercising more authority over native communities and resources. Also on the rise were complaints by colonists about Indian poverty and alcoholism. In 1741, for example, Punkapoag guardian John Quincy told the court that he preferred to pay for supplies instead of giving interest payments, for if the Indians were given money "at once they would go no further than the nearest place where they could get drink for it, and not leave till twas all spent." He found to his disgust that "they are often intoxicated and it is as nothing to see them lying about the House drunk."[124] Trustees also complained about their lack of authority to "improve" the Indians. The Hassanamisco overseers in 1743 called the legislature's attention to the Indians' "Incapacity [and] also of the Indisposition to Act or contrive for their own benefit," and urged the assembly "to bring both their persons Lands & Moneys under Some New & better Regulation."[125] These respected men clearly considered Indian guardians with broad powers, like those appointed for orphans and other legal "incompetents," absolutely necessary.

Three years later, the General Court passed the act for "Better Regulating the Indians," authorizing the appointment of three guardians for each native enclave in the colony. These guardians were given the power not only to act as justices and to manage the community's account, but also to take land that the Indians were not using and lease it to white farmers or cattlemen. Guardians were to submit annual reports to the court — few of which are extant, if they were ever submitted. Three men were elected by a joint meeting of the Governor's Council and assembly for each of eight Indian communities (or cluster of small enclaves): Natick; Plymouth, Pembroke, and Middleborough; Stoughton (Punkapoag); Yarmouth, Harwich and Eastham (Potawaumacut); Grafton and Dudley; Mashpee, Barnstable, Sandwich, and Falmouth; Martha's Vineyard; and Nantucket. These are similar to the "spheres" of Indian communities discussed in chapter 3. A few years later, guardians were appointed to oversee the affairs of Freetown, the Indian reserve in the southeast created by the General Court at the turn of the century.[126] As a result, Dudley, Mashpee, and other Indian enclaves in the Commonwealth suddenly found their land and fortunes controlled by outsiders.[127]

The General Court appointed Indian guardians under the English common-law principle that orphans or mental incompetents with property should have a "father" appointed by the courts to manage the estate and supervise his or her future. Indian groups under the sovereignty of colonial governments were similarly considered incompetent to handle the intricacies of English law.[128] Their guardians, while filling the active roles held earlier by John Eliot and other missionaries, were not ecclesiastical figures; instead, most worked as merchants, lawyers, or farmers while holding political authority in their county and province: militia officers, justices of the peace, selectmen, and General Court representatives. For example, John Quincy, Punkapoag's guardian from 1727–48, was a lawyer and for many years delegate from the town of Quincy to the General Court and that body's speaker. Few were eager for the post, particularly since they received no salary, though expenses were supposed to be paid by the community whom they "assisted" — a situation that inevitably created conflicts with the Indians who had not asked for the officers. Newly appointed guardians found a thankless task with few (legal) rewards, caught between the strange ways of the Indians and the obvious needs (or greed) of white neighbors, relatives, and friends.

No doubt guardians seemed, to those who led the province, a way of "Regulating" Indians and controlling illegal actions against native groups. The General Court held broad authority as a judicial and legislative body, but lacked extensive power since New England lacked the tradition and bureaucracy of an active central government. Thus it had little real power to interfere with the will or actions of an entire community, particularly on behalf of an unpopular minority such as Indians. Its power also rested in large part on the town and county elite, who were often friends of those responsible, or were even themselves responsible, for the Indians' problems. In 1741, the Governor's Council considered drawing up a bill since "notwithstanding the Laws already in force, the Indians residing in this Government are greatly imposed on by some of his Majesty's English Subjects."[129] Nothing resulted, and seven years later the council again called for a bill because "the Indians inhabiting within this Province, have been often imposed upon by designing & ill-minded men in the disposing of their Lands, either by Wills or Conveyances to one another, or otherwise to the great Loss & Injury of themselves & Families."[130] The government referred the issue to the recently appointed officers, proclaiming that no land sale would be approved unless "recommended by the respective Guardian of the sd Indians."[131]

Guardians proved a double-edged sword for Indian groups. While the General Court failed to take direct action against the Indians' loss of lands and resources, the guardians that they appointed *could* offer Indian groups an important measure of protection. Natives were still generally unfamiliar and uncomfortable with Anglo-American law — in fact, many were still unable to understand the English language — particularly since the law was, by the middle of the eighteenth century, increasing in complexity. They also lacked the social connections that allowed uneducated colonists to influence the political and legal system. The guardians' assistance can be glimpsed in the often-bitter battles that erupted between some and the Indians' white neighbors in the 1740s, 1750s, and 1760s. Unfortunately, many were like the villains in gothic novels, committing fraud, theft, and squandering community resources, and in the process hastening the decline and dissolution of native enclaves. In fact, during the second half of the eighteenth century nearly every Indian community that held common property appealed to the General Court for relief from their guardians.

Guardians could fail their charges without malicious intent. Bad loans and the economic upheavals of the 1730s and 1740s jeopardized the money held by the province for Indian groups that sold or leased land, such as the Hassanamiscos and Punkapoags. Trustees loaned these funds to Englishmen, and then doled out the yearly interest payments to the Indians. In 1741, four Punkapoag men complained to the court that they were not receiving as much annual interest money as in the past, and that some of the goods provided by Quincy in lieu of cash "is not half so good."[132] The trustee admitted that the Indians had received lower payments during the past few years. This was a result, he told the court, of the poor financial condition of "the generality" of borrowers; in fact, many had failed to pay their interest for the past two to five years. The only way to obtain additional interest income was to sue in "almost every Court" in the province.[133] By 1756, at least one of these bonds was held by a bankrupt estate and could not be recovered.[134]

Inflation also destroyed the value of the funds in the account, particularly given the low fixed interest rate charged by guardians. When Quincy asked to resign in February 1748, he noted that he held £636. 15s. 6d. in bonds (old tenor); inflation made this money worth only about half of its 1740 value.[135] Thus provincial financial conditions, rather than fraud, was responsible for Hassanamiscos (as they told the legislature in 1744) having "been kept out of our Interest Money almost Two years last past by which means we have been great Soufferours."[136] The General Court proved even more incompetent than their agents, for in 1745 they decided to exchange the old Hassanamisco loans for new bonds at an ounce of silver for 28s. 8d. — an act perhaps designed to help prop up the plunging provincial currency but which resulted in the rapid depreciation of the Indians' funds.[137] Negligence was also a threat, as a committee investigating charges against the Punkapoag guardians in 1754 found their accounts kept "in a lax & bad Manner, either in Chaulks or Memory."[138]

One of the guardians' primary duties was to manage the resources of "their" Indians: to prevent poaching and trespassing, lease surplus planting and grazing land, and sell wood and fish to whites. But the Indian communities that retained such resources also held much of their land as commons — a system quite different from Anglo-American ways. What was surplus to the English was necessary to the Indians. Conflicts were inevitable. In September 1753, the Mashpees complained to the legislature about those who "take away our lands and marsh and hire it out to English men they say they are our Guardians and have orders from you to do so."[139] The loss of supposedly surplus land was driving young men away to work on whaling ships. Three months later, they cried that the guardians had

> *allmost ruined [us] by having* our lands and Medows taken from us, that is great part of them: for we have not so much as we want to use, and we that are aged and cannot labour used to let our land and so gitt corn, we used to take Cattle to the [meadow] and so gitt Cattle, but we are not allowed medow now to Do that [,] English Men use our land and it will soon be Worn out, they Cut off our Wood, and some set their Houses upon our land, we are allowed to use some small peices of land but these will soon be worn out.[140]

The Mashpees obtained no relief, and four years later renewed their complaints. Guardians had leased eight of their best fields plus "ye grater Part of our medow" for a term of eleven years, and the Indians were afraid that when they regained the land it would be worn out from the intensive planting and grazing practiced by English farmers. They were also barred from taking bark and wood from the commons. The guardians did not understand, or were not interested in understanding, native reliance on undivided resources.[141]

Gay Head was similarly plagued by its guardians. From the beginning of the century, the conservative native enclave had fought tenaciously against the leasing of their lands to Englishmen, from Lord Donegan to neighboring farmers, and in 1746 forged an agreement that detailed the grazing rights on Gay Head Neck for both communities.[142] But the newly appointed guardians quickly destroyed that agreement, leasing in October 1747 much of Gay Head's pasture to English cattlemen for six years. The community immediately protested to the General Court, telling the assembly that the guardians had rented out their best woodland, were denying them critical firewood, and had made the leases without reserving sufficient pasture for the Indians' cattle.[143] The guardians scorned the Indians' "groundless and Vexatious" charges, and (as usual) the court dropped the issue.[144] But two years later Gay Head renewed its complaints, telling the court that they were becoming "poorer and poorer" from their lack of pasture, and that next year they would not even have enough land to plant. Many of them were "suffering from want," but their requests to the guardians for assistance were always spurned.[145] Again they received no relief, nor were there any changes in response to their third complaint four years later.[146]

English guardians also refused to recognize the evolving patterns of Indian inheritance. The Chabanakongkomuns told the General Court that in 1756 their guardians had taken "the grass and fruit of our land" — probably not fraud but the sale and leasing of "surplus" to other whites — "particularly of Jonathan Pagan's plantation." Pegan had given use of his land and control of his affairs to a relative, Joseph Pegan, while Jonathan left to join the colonial militia, but the guardians refused to recognize Joseph's claim and leased the land to whites.[147] Three decades later, the Mashpees complained that "if any [of] our near kindred dies they [guardians] takes their int[e]rest and hires it out and the Nearest relation Cannot have it."[148] The General Court's representatives believed that "Better Regulating" the Indians included guiding native landholding into line with the provincial legal system, presenting the Indians with a choice: either to divide their commons in severalty, with deeds that could be defended in court (and easily sold to whites), or to see its pieces leased and produce sold to whites.

Of course, the official reason to lease Indian land was to create a community fund, like those owned by Punkapoag and Hassanamisco, that could be applied by the guardians for the "betterment" of the enclave and sick or elderly individuals. But this system created new problems for Indian groups. In 1744, the Hassanamiscos asked the court to appoint trustees who lived closer to Grafton so they could collect their annual allotments without "such Great expence of Time and Travel."[149] Since guardians were allowed to pay their expenses with community funds, Indians who disliked the guardians and their actions were infuriated at the idea of paying for what they opposed. In 1757, the Mashpees charged that, contrary to the court's intent in "Better Regulating" them, "our Poor and aged are not so well Provided for as formerly for our Guardians cannot spend their Time for nothing and live a great way from us" — a complaint also made by Gay Head. Mashpee's guardians not only charged the community for their unwanted attention, but insisted on meeting the Indians at a distant tavern (probably in Sandwich) where fighting frequently broke out "and some of us [are] abused by English men."[150]

The Indian funds also offered unique opportunities for fraudulent profit, particularly given the General Court's lax oversight and the guardians' independence from their charges. In September 1749, the Gay Head Indians charged that their loathed guardians were taking the lease payments that totaled about £470 per year and giving each of them only twenty-nine shillings each.[151] Four years later, when the guardians moved to renew the leases, the Gay Headers again protested that they had received little money from the previous arrangements.[152] Six months later, the court finally noticed the years of fraud and the shocked assembly demanded receipts for the "very extraordinary" expenses: particularly the huge sum (£133) charged by the guardians for their time.[153] In the end, the court refused to reimburse 90 percent of the charges, implicitly rebuking men who staked their lives on their honorable reputations, and appointed others to the post.[154] A few years later the Chabanakongkomuns, now usually called the Dudley Indians, for the English town that surrounded their 640-acre reserve, reported a more elaborate fraud. Their guardians had asked the legislature to approve some debts "said to be owed by us," and had submitted a petition supporting the request that "is said to be signed by at least some of us, but both were done without our knowledge or permission."[155] There is no other record of this petition, which either shows that the Indians were mistaken or, more likely, reminds us that we have only a partial record of this period.

While embezzlement was a problem, Indian enclaves found that English abuse of their resources continued to be the greater threat. Guardians were, of course, supposed to prevent this problem, but (at least in the eyes of some native groups) their powers made matters worse. When Gay Headers first complained that they were being "deceived regarding the money" from leases, they also lamented that, since the court appointed the officers, the settlers had been able "to treat us as they pleased." The guardians were, the Indians charged, "particularly" part of the "great Injuries & Oppressions which they have received from their English Neighbours." For example, the guardians had leased some of their meadows for far below their real value.[156] In 1758, the Dudley Indians complained not only that their guardians had submitted false charges, but also that they had failed to prevent other whites from poaching wood and timber. Perhaps the guardians' error was neglect rather than fraud, for they were also responsible for the Hassanamiscos in Grafton — but neglect can be deliberate, particularly when racism is a factor. Indeed, the Nipmuc guardians did not neglect the opportunity to profit, for the Dudleys also charged them with grazing their cattle in the Indians' fields and pastures without permission or compensation.[157]

Five years later, the Dudley guardians persuaded the General Court to allow William Dudley's heirs to purchase two-thirds of the remaining reserve for two hundred pounds. The Indians, they told the court, no longer farmed the tract, and so had broken the stipulation on the lease obtained three decades before from Dudley. The truth, however, was that the Indians had owned the land since the 1680s (see chapter 2), and that in 1724, when Dudley managed to shrink their holdings to a square mile (in a somewhat mysterious and probably fraudulent manner), he inserted the phrase "to plant and improve" into the deed. The money was needed more than the land, the guardians told the court, to meet growing medical bills and other "necessaries." The court agreed to the proposal, and in exchange the Dudley heirs were to pay fifty pounds into the Indians' account (controlled by the guardians) and nine pounds each year as long as the Indians "improved" their remaining land.[158]

Trespassing, poaching, and fraud often met on Indian reserves, for the guardians appointed by the General Court to care for the Indians' interests could be among the worst violators of native rights. The Vineyard Indian guardians appointed to replace those who had "deceived" the Gay Headers carried out their own abuses on the other side of the island, on Chappaquiddick. In 1715, natives and colonists on the islet had arranged a treaty that specified how many goats, cows, and sheep could be grazed by both groups, and confirmed that the reserve could never be sold or leased to whites. In March 1761, the Indians accused the English of making "clandestine purchases of the Sachem and his Descendants till they have got near half the Island."[159] General Court investigators found that two of the Vineyard guardians led "a Number of the English" in "open contempt" of the compact, making illegal and fraudulent purchases of Indian land through "clandestine purchases of the Sachem and his Descendants," obtaining "near half the Island" and creating "great difficulties" for the natives. Colonists had also poached the Indians' wood and violated the treaty's grazing limits. When Indians tried to challenge these wrongs, they were forced into long whaling voyages. No other Chappaquiddick complaints about the guardians had reached the court, which speaks loudly about the meaning of silence in the records and the histories based on those records. The investigators asked — and the General Court agreed — that special agents be appointed to prevent poaching and trespassing, and that disputes between whites and Indians be tried on Cape Cod (Barnstable County) instead of the island (Dukes County).[160] The fraudulent purchases were not returned, however, because the settlers' loud protests soon led the court to recognize their holdings if they paid the estimated value of the land.[161]

The court's special agent proved just as useful. Jonathan Newman reported that the Indians had welcomed him and voted to help "my Endeavours to put a stop to the Disorders & Trespasses committed upon that Island." The method that he "hit upon" to stop wood poaching, however, probably generated more astonishment than relief: he "directed the Indians, whenever they find any wood lying upon any Part of the

Shoar of sd Island, in [an] Order to be carry'd, off, immediately to take it away & convert it to their own Use."[162] Two years later, in January 1766, the Chappaquiddicks were forced to again complain to the General Court about continued trespassing and poaching. Whites continued to invade their territory to take wood and brush and, by not securing their pastured cattle during the summer, took advantage of an easy source of nourishment for the foraging quadrupeds: the sprouting corn planted by the Indians.[163] Once again the island's English inhabitants managed to delay changes, and two years later the Indians told the court that not only did the colonists' cattle continue to destroy their cornfields, but

> our Petition Latly offends the people of Edgartown / as if they Took the Delay of this Matter as the fittest oppertunity to Destroy us / Seem to Double their deligence to our Disadvantages / and Imploying one Certain Indian as we Suppose to Cut our wood In Great Quantitys and Convey the Same to the water from whence they / the English / take it / and unless there is some speedy stop put unto our wood will Be gone upon which we must Leave the Island to our Destroyers.[164]

A committee again visited, found their complaints all too accurate, and recommended barring cattle from the island between April 10 and October 30 each year, and fines for English poachers and straying cattle.[165]

When local interests again stalled action, the Indians returned to the General Court (for the fourth time) in May 1773. They again reminded the court that English inhabitants were flouting the 1715 contract and continued to poach their wood and to make illegal land purchases. Since none of the settlers had been removed, "others have thereby been Encorraged to move on & if they can Purchase a right of any one Indian they immediately Erect a House and Inclose a Tract of Land & get their wood off our Common Land & have even of Late dispossed some of us of our old improvements."[166] Again the court's committee found rampant fraud, abuse, and violations of provincial law against Indian land sales, all possible only with the acquiescence of the local elite. The court silently acknowledged the role played by the powerful when it adopted the committee's recommendation to make "equitable adjustments" in order to avoid hardships and "great Injustice" to the English even though the colonists had made their illegal purchases with "eyes open."[167] The committee found that the boundaries described in most of the deeds transferring Indian lands to whites enclosed more land than the documents were supposed to convey, that some of the deeds indicated that the Indians had been given nothing for their land, and that in most cases "if not in every one" the consideration paid was not nearly the value of the land. While the assembly finally did set limits on grazing for whites and passed strict fines for violators and wood poachers, the Chappaquiddicks' problems were not over.[168] Following the Revolution, the state legislature again recognized the boundary between the native community and white settlers on the islet, but the latter never built the fence demanded by the assembly and the Indians continued to find their grass and corn devastated by livestock.[169]

The Punkapoags, however, suffered the worst abuse of power. In 1748, their guardian, John Quincy, retired from that office and was replaced by Samuel Miller and John Shepard. The two quickly made life intolerable for the Indians. Five years later, seven Punkapoags, probably a majority of adults in the shrinking community, complained that Miller and Shepard "have in their Accounts charged many things wrongfully." Even worse, they lamented, "Since they were set over us our woodlands have been plundered by many people so that our Cedar Swamps & Timber Trees have been destroy[ed], and our firewood cut off of our Land, to that degree that our Lands are now Thousands of pounds of less value than they were ten years ago — and we have had no recompence for the same." In addition, Shepard, who was a justice of the peace, had for no apparent reason thrown three of the complainants into prison where they were "kept a great while in the most distressed condition." The Punkapoags also told the court that they "doubt not but you our Fathers are disposed to shew us more kindnes than would show to the Eastward Indians," showing that Indians in southern New England were sensitive about the Abenakis, whom they often went to fight.[170]

Investigators confirmed all of the Indians' charges: the accounts were "kept in a lax & bad Manner, either in Chaulks or Memory," and the guardians had allowed whites to clear-cut ten heavily wooded acres, take ten cords of wood in another location, and cut at least two hundred valuable trees from the reserve's cedar swamp as well as two tons of ship timber. As a result, "there is but a small Number of Timber now standing on the whole of said Indians Lands, and the Wood greatly diminished." Shepard in particular had profited by the Indians' "great wrong and damage," pocketing the cutting fees and taking for himself "three or four large Trees." Shepard was also condemned for his "Barbarity" and "illegal Proceedings as a Justice of the Peace." Investigators were particularly upset that, during the month in which Samuel Mohoo and his wife were illegally jailed, several of their small children "were left in a lonely Wigwam, where they must unavoidably have perished."[171] The investigating committee recommended compensating the Punkapoags one hundred pounds for the damage; this money, of course, would be placed in the account administered by guardians — an irony that escaped the adjudicators.

The committee's recommendation suddenly made Miller and Shepard aware of their danger. The two protested their innocence, called the witnesses "perfidious Men" and "hardened monsters," blamed others for the apparent fraud, and boasted additional evidence that would clear their reputations.[172] Additional hearings confirmed that the guardians had allowed "very great Strip & Waste of Wood & Timber" on the Indians' land, and also uncovered their intimidation of witnesses. "Several of the Witnesses were very unwilling to declare the whole of what they knew in the Matter, and could not be induced to speak freely . . . those Witnesses were on the Part of Major Shepard." Another witness told them Shepard had offered to forgive a large debt if he testified for the guardian. The General Court ruled Shepard the primary agent of fraud, fined him eighty pounds, and barred him from all government posts. Miller, who had given a "humbling" confession of his "Indolence and want of Care," was forgiven.[173]

The court immediately appointed new guardians, who reported in August 1756 that the Punkapoags were in "great Danger . . . of their English Neighbours encroaching & trespassing upon their Lands." No records remained from previous boundary surveys, so "a great deal of dist[ress] and Contention" existed "between the sd Indians & the Inhabitants whose land bounds on sd Indians land." The guardians therefore requested, and received authorization for, a new survey of the reserve's boundaries.[174] When the new survey was completed, it showed that only 711 acres remained in Punkapoag. The court then authorized the guardians to sell three hundred acres in order to meet the Indians' outstanding debts and support their future needs, reducing the reserve to about two-thirds of a square mile.[175]

Not all guardians were frauds and cheats. Some, perhaps even most, defended their charges against aggressive white settlers. In fact, at least one of the controversies that reached the General Court was apparently generated as part of a campaign to discredit and remove an ethical guardian. A complaint by four Punkapoag men in 1741 against John Quincy was (according to Quincy) hatched four years before by an Englishman living in adjoining Stoughton who had borrowed money from the Indian account, failed to pay interest, and was successfully sued by Quincy. That man and others "who have stirred" up the controversy "aimed at having not only the managemt of the Indians and their affairs in their hands, but also the

Remaindr of their Land on which is a good growth of wood & Timber which your Respondt has been Instrumental of preserving hitherto in a great measure and on which their Eyes have been for Several years."[176] Only Amos Ahauton defended the petition against Quincy, and lacked evidence to back his complaints. The General Court found that the charges "appeared groundless and abusive, prompted it is likely by some malevolent and disaffected Person (whose resentments were perhaps excited by a suit at law against him for non payment of some of the indians money)."[177]

And not all whites sought every opportunity to injure Indians; in fact, some served as allies against abusive guardians. For example, the seven Punkapoags who pressed charges against Miller and Shepard told the General Court that they were directed to make their appeal by several white neighbors who "see that we are wronged."[178] Those advising the Indians were either morally disgusted at the guardians' abuses or had been unable to join in the "feast" laid out by Shepard. The accused guardians claimed in reply that the complaint was "the artifice & contrivance of some of the vicinity who are continually filling the ears of those Indian Inhabitants with groundless surmises of Injury done [them]"[179] But the court followed the advice of its investigators and confirmed their guilt.

Conflicts involving guardians also reflected schisms within Indian communities. The challenge to Quincy, for example, spotlighted an otherwise invisible split within that native enclave, as one group that claimed to be the true Punkapoag proprietors demanded his replacement by Samuel Miller of nearby Milton.[180] Seven years later, after Quincy retired and was replaced by Miller, Shepard, and another (who soon quit), eight Indians, including Quincy's primary antagonist, Amos Ahauton, told the legislature that the new trustees were "to our great Satisfaction & Advantage." They had heard rumors that people claiming to be Punkapoag proprietors had asked for Quincy's return, but those individuals "are not propr[ietor]s; & Consequently have no Right to petition as such." Restoring Quincy "would be greatly to our Damage on many accounts, particularly by reason of his Distance [in Braintree] from us, yr Petitionrs being advanced in Years & unable to Travell."[181] Of course, over the following five years Miller and Shepard "damaged" Punkapoag "on many accounts."

To the south, the Plymouth County Indian guardians worsened existing tensions within a native community. The dispute among the Mattakeesits over traditional rights and community responsibility, which had begun in the 1730s with timber sales by "Queen Sachem" Patience Keurp, again erupted in 1754 after the guardians leased all but three acres of the reserve to white farmers for five years. On 13 June 1755, ten Mattakeesits asked the General Court to annul the contracts, for some of them had been tricked into asking for longer leases "equal to selling it forever, which we cannot consent to, being to turn ourselves and our Children forever from off the land."[182] But Patience Thomas, one of the signatories, also announced (on the same day) that as the Mattakeesit "sachemiss" she was claiming the entire reserve for herself and her grandson Caleb Brand. Thomas also noted that, as sachem, she was obligated to use the small income from the leases to support other Indians. The two were perfectly willing to have the guardians lease part of the reserve to white farmers, as long as they received the annual payments and retained sufficient acreage for their personal needs. Other Indians in the area, they told the court, "had no rights" to the land.[183]

When word of the Thomas-Brand petition reached the community, twelve "poor Matteekeeset Indians" petitioned the court to dismiss Thomas's request and to annul all of the leases.[184] A few months earlier an Englishman in Pembroke had told the court that

> Patience Abigail & Caleb are minded to turn off all the rest, Continually Contending & quarreling with them, & by the help of others who got sd Petitioners in their Debt are laying Schemes to out them, who really have a right therein some by blood & others by birth & long uninterupted living where their ancestors lived, & to perpetuate the Scheme, [at?] times to take Leases to puzzle them & pay nothing & then to sell the land [in order] to out the rest poor old Creatures, & so to get the rent to be paid to sd petitioners to pay their debts.[185]

Despite these protests, the court backed Thomas's petition, probably at the behest of the guardians.[186] In August 1756, over 170 acres supposedly "belonging to Patience Thomas, Abigail Quason, and Caleb Brand" were sold, and one year later Patience Thomas and a few other "proprietors of lands at Mattakeeset" persuaded the court to build her a "suitable house."[187]

The Mattakeesit controversy featured, in addition to the obvious conflict of interests within the Indian community, a land grab, hypocrisy, and tragedy. The land grab and hypocrisy came with the Plymouth County Indian guardians, who had touched off the battle when they rented out nearly all of the Indian enclave's land to Pembroke whites and then (with the support of the lessors) backed Patience Thomas's effort to "turn off all the rest" by renegotiating longer leases that benefited her and harmed other Mattakeesits. Their motivations became suspect when they stressed their support for the sachem's "traditional" authority, but had refused to back the Teticuts' equally "traditional" opposition to Stephen David's land sales. While no one accused the guardians of defrauding the Indians or profiting from the sales, it was clear that they made whichever decision best facilitated the transfer of land from Indians to Englishmen, increased the Indians' funds (which they controlled), and strengthened their authority over the native community. The tragedy in the Mattakeesit controversy was that, once again, the "faceless" colonial economy had cultured and then exploded the gap between a sachem's traditional responsibilities and privileges.

The Mattakeesit controversy points to a subtle but destructive aspect of the guardianship system created by the General Court: guardians could easily subvert the authority of native leaders and undermine community cohesion. Ironically, at the beginning of the century, the leaders of middle and outer Cape Cod Indian villages had asked the General Court for regulations to help them maintain "order and discipline." But the guardians appointed by the court for "Better Regulating" native groups refused, as the Nantucket Indians complained in January 1747, to allow Indians to appoint their own judges, so that "we cannot punish one another for our unlawful deeds."[188] Similar troubles emerged among the Mashpees five years later when, as a result of the guardians' independent authority, "our wicked neighbours have advised young men & others not to submit to our Rules & orders because we had no power to make them."[189] By 1757, Mashpee's guardians sought to exert their control over the community, the Indians charged, by barring them "from the Priviledges of our Commons," selling the wood to whites, and then giving "all its Profits" to "some Particular Indians."[190] Although in most cases the guardians' interference was too subtle to draw complaints, every Indian enclave must have been affected, for guardians controlled common resources and held supreme political and legal power. Only the General Court could overrule their actions, and when that rare event happened it was inevitably too late.

Alone of all Indians, the Mashpees refused to accept subordination and fought the guardianship system from its inception. For nearly a century, with only one brief victory, the Cape Cod enclave sought every opportunity to reclaim its autonomy. In December 1753, when complaining that the guardians, though "Good Honest men," had beggared them, the Indians demanded either the abolishment of the office or the right to yearly elect their guardians. They had thought their sacrifice in King George's War meant that they "had Deserved so well of our Country as to have Injoyed our lands as English men do theirs."[191] Instead, one year later the General Court renewed the guardianship system, and the Mashpees' problems seemed to increase.[192] In 1757, they presented a long list of complaints against the guardians, described above, and angrily told the assembly that "We Desire no more Guardians to manage as they doe. They do us more hurt than good, we chuse to be as we were before they were set up."[193] To amplify their voice the Mashpees enlisted the support of English missionary Gideon Hawley, who had helped John Sergeant in Stockbridge and preached among the Iroquois. By asking Hawley to join Solomon Briant in their church's pulpit, they gained his strong voice in provincial politics without losing control of their critical institution.

When the General Court again ignored their pleas, the Mashpees took the astonishingly radical measure (for Indians) of sending a representative to London to petition the King for relief. The action demonstrated the Indians' political sophistication, for they were following the example of other dissidents (such as Quakers) and of the provincial legislature. Reuben Cognehew's odyssey is the stuff of legends: he boarded a ship in Rhode Island, was kidnapped by the captain to be sold as a slave in the West Indies but escaped when the ship wrecked on Hispanola, was rescued by a British man-of-war and impressed into the Navy until an admiral freed him in Jamaica, and then finally arrived in London where he was given a favorable reception by the King's Royal Council. The council, no doubt, welcomed the opportunity to increase the Crown's authority in Massachusetts. The petition that Cognehew presented to the council complained that "the English Inhabitants of the said Province of Massachusetts Bay have of late years unjustly encroached upon the said Lands, and have hindered and obstructed the Indians in the exercise of that just right they have to fish in the River Mashpee within the said limits." Their efforts to gain help from the General Court "have been constantly frustrated by the Art and Deceit of such Agents [guardians] as they have been obliged to employ in this affair." The Royal Council in August 1760 ordered the Bay Colony's governor to lay the petition before the General Court and to demand justice for all of the Indians in Massachusetts.[194]

The assembly began a long series of discussions with the Mashpees, though it managed to avoid the broad demand of the council's order. In 1763, Cognehew, who had returned to Mashpee, traveled to Boston with Hawley, Briant, and another Indian, Joseph Richards, to approve the act restoring self-government to Mashpee.[195] Thereafter the Indians managed their resources and chose their constables, clerk, and other officers, though instead of selectmen the Indians elected five overseers (two of whom had to be whites) who held more power. Mashpee also won the legislature's ban on Anglo-American settlement in the district, while keeping the right to bring in new "colored" proprietors by a majority vote.[196] Three years later the Barnstable delegate who also acted as the Mashpees' agent to the General Court, Isaac Hinckly, persuaded the assembly to renew the act, noting that the Mashpees were "Easy & Quiet under such officers as they have Chosen from Time to Time."[197] Indeed, between 1763 and the reimposition of guardianship in 1788, the Mashpees did not press any complaints in the court.

After 1760, the number of complaints from Indian enclaves about their guardians' fraud, abuse, or mismanagement declined remarkably. The only notable incident involved the Hassanamiscos' account (as one might expect) and was reported by other guardians. Stephen Maynard, who became a Nipmuc guardian in 1776, borrowed $1,327 and, after becoming insolvent around 1790, fled the province and died around 1803. The embezzled funds were never recovered, leaving (in 1807) only $925 in the Hassanamisco account.[198] Perhaps the system had undergone a "shakedown" period that had cleaned out the obvious incompetents and frauds. Or perhaps the Indians had successfully gotten rid of the worst men during the 1750s and afterwards simply tolerated the incompetents that remained. As already noted, the guardians' legal and financial skills and political connections *could* be useful to Indian enclaves. But one might conclude that the natives still at the mercy of guardians had little left to steal or mismanage.

)(

The cynic's view is supported by the tragic dissolution of inland Indian communities in the 1750s. Most notable was Natick's decline, as disabled men, widows, and orphans came to dominate the community. Deacon Joseph Ephraim asked in 1755 to sell his land because he was "greatly advanc'd in Years and unable to Labour," and needed the money to pay debts and to support himself.[199] At the same time, Daniel Thomas also petitioned to sell his land, for he was quite ill, his wife had died the year before, and his two small children were with nurses who would continue to need payment.[200] In April 1758, Sarah Tray told the court that she had been widowed for seventeen years, was sixty years old, blind in one eye, and (obviously) unable to work.[201] One year later, Sarah Rumneymarsh, also widowed, related "her great Want and infirmities being now Eighty years of Age, and without any means of Support."[202] Whites acted as guardians for the Indian orphans, paying their expenses by selling the children's land. Samuel Morse, white guardian for the late Sarah Waban's daughter, sold some of her estate in April and November 1754, and again in June 1756, and in 1765 also sold land belonging to the orphaned Hezekiah Comecho.[203] Natick was a dwindling, poverty-stricken community: in 1760 the remaining Indians asked the General Court to extend the lease of a grain mill in the town, which was "of absolute necessity to us, and our Familys, as [the miller] grinds Toll-free for us, and otherways extends his Charity to the poor among us."[204]

The regional networks that had previously brought Indians to Natick now facilitated their emigration. That movement hastened the economic as well as the demographic decline of the native community, for those who left soon sold their remaining land in Natick to pay for needs elsewhere. In 1750, when Samuel Bowman's heirs asked the General Court to sell his remaining fifty acres in Natick, Samuel's widow remained in Worcester with Samuel Jr., and one of his daughters and son-in-law lived in Sturbridge (southwest of Grafton and west of Dudley). All were dependent on charity, and noted that they were "strangers" to Natick.[205] Mary Toss, sister of Natick proprietor Samuel Ompetowin, inherited her brother's rights and lands in 1722, and married Jeffrey Henry in 1739. By 1746, the couple had moved to Providence, Rhode Island, where Mary had lived as a child, and sold more than seventy acres in Natick to pay debts and buy more land in the city.[206] Nine years later the Henrys sold their remaining rights in Natick in order to support themselves as they had "grown old & unable to support themselves by Labour."[207]

Not all roads led away from Natick. Cesear Ferrit, possibly of Punkapoag ancestry, purchased land there in 1751. Raised in an English family in Milton and "Taught Husbandry-business," he moved to Boston, but, driven by high unemployment and the cost of living in the city, he had "a desire to dwell at Natick among his own Nation the aboriginal natives."[208] In 1720, Sarah and Thomas Lawrence married and moved from Boston to Natick: Sarah, a Pennacook born in Natick but living in Cambridge and Boston for over ten years, had met Thomas, a Cape Cod Indian mariner, through the native network in the city.[209] In 1731, Nathaniel Hill of Brookline (an African-American) married Patience Quassont in Newton; seventeen years and three children later they moved to Natick, where they obtained land through Isaac Monequassin (probably Patience's father).[210]

Unfortunately, the Indian enclave's problems were regional and systemic — as indicated in the example of the four Hassanamisco women who signed the 1760 mill petition — and newcomers to Natick were caught up in its decline. Ferrit, like so many of "his own Nation," rode a disheartening cycle of expanding operations in an effort to meet debts (including his first purchase of land in the town) and then fell short and was forced to sell part or all of the recent land purchases to pay debts and medical costs.[211] The Hills were forced only two years after moving to the town to sell fifteen acres to pay debts, build a house, and buy food, and then in 1758 parted with another thirty acres to pay medical debts and support themselves in "their advanced age."[212] When Patience died about a year later the family returned to Brookline, and after Nathaniel's death in 1772, their children in Brookline and Cambridge sold the Monequassin lands.[213] Thus even newcomers to Natick were drowned in the community's dissolution.

Between 1755 and 1765, an astonishing number of Indians left Natick, driven out by socioeconomic problems and their neighbors' contempt. About 160 Indians lived in Natick in 1754; ten years later only 37 remained.[214] Over a hundred people (102), after accounting for births and deaths, vanished from the town — nearly 63 percent, and an annual average of ten persons or about two families. Others had left Natick before, such as Benjamin Wiser and Samuel Bowman, but the tempo and nature of this movement had radically changed. Those leaving at this time moved in search of sustenance, not improvement. The 1763 census found "37 Indians only; but in this return, probably the wandering Indians were not included"[215] — the first such description of Natick natives since the Treaty of Utrecht had ended the town's frontier status fifty years before. English observers since then depicted a stable community that had forsaken seasonal migrations for a permanent settlement. With the sudden drop in reported population had appeared the characterization "wandering Indians."

Looking back from 1797, Stephen Badger, who had arrived in Natick in 1752, wrote that many of his native congregants were "strangely disposed and addicted to wander from place to place, and to make excursions into various parts of the country, and sometimes at no small distance from their proper homes." The minister noted that

> Some of them, after an absence of near twenty years, have returned to their native home. The most trifling and uninteresting cause have been assigned, by some of them, for their travelling thirty, forty, fifty miles, and more; and this sometimes in the most unfavourable seasons of the year, and in very bad weather. They have not infrequently taken infant and other children with them in their journies. . . . This wandering and irregular practice, especially when applicable to the females, not only exposes their virtue and their morals, but is a great injury to their own

health, and to that of their children that accompany them, and lays a foundation for consumptive sickness, which has generally (exclusive of accidental causes) been the means of their deaths.[216]

The Natick Indians were not alone. Many Punkapoags left their reserve to "wander" the region, looking elsewhere for relatives, better opportunities, or perhaps ancestral fishing grounds and fields. In 1741, Zachariah Quock died in the home of Isaac Royal, one of Stoughton's leading merchants.[217] Seven years later, Sarah Mamentag fell ill and traveled towards Natick — probably seeking medical care, perhaps from Peter Brand — but never arrived, ending her days in the house of a white man in Dedham.[218] Elizabeth Pumham journeyed as far as Boston, where she died in the home of Sepio Lock, a free African American, during a smallpox epidemic.[219]

A number of factors drove Indians onto the road: social, political, and economic pressure from white settlers, poverty and loss of hope, employment or near slavery in the whaling trade, new connections made between formerly distant native enclaves during visits, by marriage, or in the army during the many military campaigns, or other opportunities that suddenly opened in other towns. Some made a successful transition, some struggled in their new homes, while others, like many of their poor white contemporaries, never again found a place to call home. Forced by debts to sell critical land, suffering from disease, facing an ever-increasing white majority, having recently lost political control, and subjected to the gall of racism, it is no wonder many Indians felt forced out of their towns. Most probably moved to other towns where relatives already lived, particularly Boston, which in 1764 had at least as many Indians as Natick.[220] Others, however, continued looking for work or a place to stay, a sad shadow of their ancestors, who migrated seasonally from food source to food source. Unfortunately, changes in the region's ecology prevented subsistence in the old ways. Family bands now asked for food from Anglo-Americans who lived where fields or fishing spots had existed. Badger noted that many boldly entered "into the houses of which they seem to think they have some kind of right to enter, as their forefathers were the original proprietors and possessors of the land."[221]

But Indians were not the only people on the road. Many towns in Massachusetts began to suffer the effects of the region's chronic economic problems. An increasing number of poor families were forced to leave their homes in search of land or work elsewhere. Other towns, however, lacked land, work, and the means (or desire) to support these wanderers. Families and communities were willing to take care of their own, but the flood of homeless proved too much. Warning-out, a legal remedy for villages to halt aid to the needy, began to work like a merry-go-round, moving people from one town to another. Many native families from disintegrating or shrinking enclaves joined whites on provincial roads, some of which, ironically, followed aboriginal paths. Another irony: since Indians were legally the responsibility of their guardians or (ultimately) of the province, towns were probably more willing to host indigent natives than whites. Creditors could obtain reimbursement from the guardians of the individual's community, or from the General Court if the needy's home could not be determined.[222]

At midcentury, wandering Indians were frequent visitors in towns from Westfield to Plymouth. Those who appear in the record represent a small percentage of the total, and are there only because a town or family had to support, nurse, and too often bury them. In the winter of 1742, an Indian woman was passing through Brookline, just west of Boston, when she "was taken with fits in such a degree that the select men were obliged to take care of her; and provide nursing and attendence for her until she was able to Leave the Town. She apparently belonged to no other town in the province."[223] The three Indian women who in 1758 were "Providentially Cast into the Town of Maulden," ten miles north of Boston, were not so lucky. All three fell sick, were unable to care for themselves for three months, and sometimes required the services of three or four people. Two of the women died, and the Malden selectmen asked the court to pay for two shifts to bury them in, the coffins, the sexton "for Diging the Graves & Toling the Bells," and "the Negros that Carry'd them To the Grave."[224]

The towns just south of Boston were particularly likely to see these unfortunate travelers. Daniel Allen, who served for many years in the Massachusetts army in Maine, became sick and was discharged in September 1741. Before he left, his friends, apparently from Mashpee or elsewhere on Cape Cod, told him that he would be welcomed in their community. Unfortunately, he got only as far as Braintree: the town's selectmen placed him with a white family where he died ten weeks later.[225] In November 1747, Sarah Quill, "no inhabitant of any town in the province," was traveling through Dorchester when she became ill and came to Mary Plimton's house to die.[226] Before falling victim to severe arthritis in 1751 while passing through Roxbury, Hannah Comsett had, for three decades, "been strolling about from town to town getting her living where she coud but never lived During that time the space of one year at any Town at any time."[227] Mercy Amerquit, born somewhere on Cape Cod, came to the house of

John Robinson in Dorchester with her two-month-old child in October 1751. He expected that she would leave soon and in the meantime agreed to employ her as a domestic servant — but in January 1752 she fell ill and soon died.[228]

)(

The years of demographic decline, economic upheaval, epidemics, fraud, trespassing, and poaching threatened all Indian enclaves in eastern Massachusetts by midcentury. The once-prosperous Natick Indian community and the smaller enclaves of Hassanamisco, Punkapoag, and Teticut were rapidly dissolving; as a result, the General Court received a growing number of tragic stories about homeless Indian travelers. Of course, not all wandered the roads: many were welcomed in Mashpee, Gay Head, and other Indian villages, while others moved to the expanding cities of Boston and Worcester and "vanished" among their growing African-American populations. Those who remained on the Indian reserves began to build houses, learned English, and married African Americans; in this sense perhaps the guardians achieved their goal of "Better Regulating the Indians." But, as we shall see, new habits and newcomers were assimilated into the Indian way of life and helped to forge a regional ethnic community.

CHAPTER 6

"Indians and their mixt posterity"

Between the end of the Seven Years War and the conclusion of the American Revolution, many Indian groups in eastern Massachusetts disintegrated. Members of enclaves that had sold land to white settlers found themselves a shrinking, marginalized minority, pursued by poverty, illness, and homelessness. Some moved to neighborhoods within the growing cities. Others left to join the few native villages that retained substantial communal resources. These enclaves increasingly served as sanctuaries where natives could often ignore or transcend the handicaps imposed by Anglo-American culture.

In the wake of the colonial wars, an increasing percentage of Indians within and without the refuges were the "mixt posterity" of intermarriages, as many widows and young women found African American husbands.[1] The growing rate of intermarriage and the developing network of native enclaves, urban neighborhoods, and isolated families reshaped old social and community boundaries. A constellation of values emerged in the form of a startlingly modern ethnic identity that transcended race and place. The Indians' increasing participation in the regional and international economy, while limited by racism and patterned on community values, also offered opportunities to spin new relationships between different groups and races.

)(

The Indian population of eastern Massachusetts, which had shrunk dramatically during King Philip's War, diminished further by 1760 as inland enclaves seemed to teeter on the brink of extinction. In 1762, Ezra Stiles compared his tally of natives, 1,573, with the 4,168 found by Rawson and Danforth in 1698 — only a third of those in the province at the beginning of the century.[2] Stiles's dismal snapshot pointed to the terrible demographic conditions in Indian enclaves, for many men died in the colonial wars or brought back epidemics, and some groups would seemingly vanish by the end of the Revolution.

Yet these figures, along with the doom announced by many whites and bemoaned in the recorded words of many Indians, do not tell the whole story. While natives disappeared from view in white-dominated towns like Natick and Middleborough, they did not disappear into a twilight zone but settled in other enclaves, in backwoods places, or in city neighborhoods away from the view of Anglo-American observers. Hints of their presence appeared in the 1764 census, which showed a widely scattered Indian population in Plymouth and Barnstable counties; one can reasonably assume that many escaped the notice of the white enumerators. A more obvious gap in the records came with the Indians' increasingly common marriage to African Americans. A growing number of people born into and belonging to Indian communities were viewed by whites as "negroes."

The apparent evaporation of an Indian group was particularly dramatic in Natick, the first "praying town." In 1700, Natick had about as many inhabitants as Mashpee or Gay Head and as few, if any, whites. But intertwined demographic and economic problems during the 1740s led to a rapid decline in the Natick Indians' population, and by 1764 few were left in Natick. About six times as many adult whites as total Indians lived in the town, and the number of natives (37) was nearly matched by the town's population of blacks (34).³ Fourteen years later Natick contained only 21 Indians: 11 women, 4 men, and 6 children under fourteen years of age. The aging of the Indian community, first indicated by landsale petitions in the 1750s for "necessities," had grown worse: the women's median age of forty-three meant that most were past childbearing age, and only three were between the ages of three and twenty-seven — so the next generation would shrink even further.⁴

Few resources would be left for that next generation, for most of the remaining natives, crippled by old age and injuries, were forced to sell their land for food and medicine. Esther Speen, a widow afflicted with a debilitating ulcer and supporting a six year-old child, needed to pay debts and buy food, clothing, and medicine.⁵ Widows Sarah and Deborah Comecho faced heavy debts and suffered from crippling arthritis.⁶ Elizabeth Tray told the General Court in 1773 that she had no children or any relations living near her; she had supported herself until she broke her arm, and now, unable to labor, needed to sell land to buy necessities.⁷ Around 1760, Eunice Spywood's husband "absconded and left her in very distressing circumstances, and has never returned." Several years later she and her children fell ill; while Eunice survived, her children all died, and she found herself unable to meet their medical and funeral costs.⁸ Then in July 1769, Eunice took in Sarah Wamsquam, the wandering Pennacook widow who had been born in Natick and raised in a white household in Cambridge; alone and in poor health, Spywood could barely support Sarah, who "tho utterly helpless is very voracious." When she asked the General Court for help, the Natick guardian added a note that "the Indians are not able to support her — nor themselves."⁹

The Natick Indians' suffering and debt was not entirely the results of war, disease, and injury. For some, problems also sprang from efforts to improve their lives in the colonial manner, as glimpsed in the changing fortunes of John Ephraim, son of deacon Joseph. For two decades, John expanded his farming operations and improved his household's comfort — the only Natick Indian to sell land between 1740 and 1760 for positive reasons — but then in 1761 was forced to sell forty acres, not only to pay debts from his "considerable purchase of Land, building a House and Barn, setting up a Team," but also to relieve the "great discouragement" of "the Support of an aged Father and the Education and Expence upon his Children."[10] Two years later, in debt for "necessaries," Ephraim parted with another fifty acres, including the small house and barn that he had built in better times — though he still held the larger house and barn on a thirty-acre tract.[11] His affairs may have steadied for a while, but in 1772 he told the General Court that he could no longer work. Sixty-three years old, Ephraim suffered from gout and other illnesses, had recently broken his wrist, and, due to sickness and death in his family, owed forty pounds to numerous creditors. He asked to sell the remaining land that lay far from his homestead in order to pay debts and to support his family in the future.[12]

The Revolutionary War was Natick's final blow. Decades later, the few surviving Natick Indians would tell the General Court that "almost all that were able did go into the Service of the United States and either died in the service or soon after their return home. We your petitioners are their widows, there not being one male left now that was then of age to go to war." Those who survived the war found themselves "forced to go from place to place to git our living." The changes had begun with the Seven Years' War, they told the court; before that conflict, they had a missionary, money for the meetinghouse, and assistance from England: "But now, how are things altered as to us! Our husbands are dead! Our minister the revd Stephen Badger is dead also! The meeting house which we had undoubtedly some right unto, stands as a monument, shocking to behold with all the glass broken, the sashes dashed to pieces, clapboards off, & the inside of the house, equally frightfull."[13] As at the beginning of the century, the Natick meetinghouse served as a metaphor for the condition of the Indian enclave.

The Hassanamiscos also faced hard times. Many traveled through the region seeking a living in English households, settling in backwoods areas, or staying in other Indian enclaves, particularly Natick. Innkeepers and merchants who advanced food and clothing to needy natives frequently claimed payment from the Hassanamiscos' account[14] As in Natick, part of the problem came from changes in the community's material culture as well as the enclave's aging and demographic imbalance. By 1761, widow Sarah Lawrence was "advanced in years & often infirm," in debt for food and clothing, and her house was "very Craizy and Leaky that I can neither keep warm there in Cold weather nor dry in Wett." To repair her home and pay her debts, she sold more than thirty acres — including an adjoining lot belonging to her sister, Mary Tom, who lived in Natick.[15] Nine years later, Deborah and Patience David told the court that "they are wholly destitute of an House to shelter themselves from the inclemency of the Weather," and asked to sell enough land to build a small home.[16] A house instead of a wigwam had become a basic need, but the elderly Hassanamiscos were unable to build such structures and needed the capital to buy materials and hire laborers. And as in Natick, most of the remaining Hassanamiscos were older women; in 1770, the town's selectmen told the General Court that the Indians "are greatly reduced that there is but one male Indian left."[17]

The Revolution also affected the Hassanamiscos, though not as drastically as it affected Natick. All three Hassanamisco guardians entered the Continental Army in 1776, and replacements failed to meet their obligations.[18] In the wake of the Revolution, all but one Hassanamisco family (the Ciscos) sold their land and abandoned Grafton, moving elsewhere in the county, many to the growing city of Worcester where they worked as laborers or domestics.[19] Even as members of the community began moving apart, however, they and their descendants spun a network that gave the scattered people a sense of community as Hassanamisco Nipmucs, and brought families together for festivals and religious celebrations.[20]

The Chabanakongkomuns, in Dudley, shared the demographic decline and some of the economic problems of their cousins in Natick and Hassanamisco. According to the enclave's guardians in 1763, the Indians "are now mostly Females," and more of their land needed to be sold in order to meet growing medical bills and other "necessaries."[21] In May 1767, Ezra Stiles found "now Ten families or less. Diminished three Quarters in Memory. Mr. Gleason of Dudley says there are but Two Men, & inclusive of these but nine Souls Indians now living."[22] The guardians' accounts reflect these small numbers, for one year after Stiles's visit six households obtained assistance, half headed by apparently unmarried women.[23] Like the other two inland communities, the Indians in Dudley held a diminishing amount of land. Stiles wrote that of "a Mile square in the Center of Dudley reserved for Indians . . . about 25 Acres are lately sold by Permission of the General Assembly."[24] In fact, in 1763 William Dudley's heirs had purchased not 25 but 440 acres, or two-thirds of the Indians' "Mile Square."[25] Only thirty-five years later, all but 26 acres were sold to cover debts and to "give the Town Liberty to act and dispose of [the Indians'] Interests as they do with their other Poor."[26]

The Indians who remained in the shrinking reserve mixed farm labor and subsistence hunting, fishing, and gathering, an economy quite different from that of their relatives in Natick and Grafton. The Chabanakongkomuns could maintain these older ways because their isolated village lay far from colonial roads, in the middle of a forested valley guarded by two high hills, with substantial resources, including a cedar swamp and a large lake. The continuation of their subsistence economy was later condemned by state investigators, who reported with undisguised disgust that Indians on the reserve "had reached a lower deep than any other in the State. A few get an honest living by cultivating their land, and by going out to work. The rest subsist upon the bounty of the State, and by prostitution. They have no schools and no preaching, are ignorant, improvident, and degraded to the lowest degree."[27] Another observer reported that the reserve had "became a resort for the idle and dissolute of the county about, to the great detriment of morals and annoyance of the sober and orderly portion of the community."[28] But state welfare ("bounty") was hardly sufficient to maintain a family, and prostitution (assuming that Indians were involved in the trade) could only support a few. The earliest colonists had, of course, called native men "idle and dissolute" for resting in the village while the women worked. The similarly scornful language of the contemporary observers points to how the residents of the reserve (of all races) continued to support themselves through small-scale intensive agriculture, hunting, gathering, and occasional labor for neighboring whites.

Kinship, social, and political connections joined the Nipmucs, Massachusetts, and Pennacooks who settled in Natick after King Philip's War. By the turn of the century, those who stayed in Natick and those who re-settled Hassanamisco and Chabanakongkomun developed new boundaries around their communities, as highlighted by the Natick proprietorship in 1719. But the kinship ties between the three enclaves were enlarged when conditions worsened at midcentury, as individuals or their relatives moved around the region, stretching village relationships while expanding family and community networks. After Thomas Awassamog of Natick married Deborah Abraham of Hassanamisco, the two traveled throughout the area as Deborah bore children in Natick, Medfield, and Needham.[29] Their offspring became threads in the nearly invisible, inchoate, regional network that joined enclaves and isolated families. While such far-flung kinship connections were not unique, they were singular in creating the foundation for an Indian ethnic identity, as described below.

Even as the Awassamog children scattered, they maintained links to their father's village. Thomas Jr. married a Dudley woman, Hannah Quitticus, in 1758, and within a decade joined that enclave, drawing on the Dudley account for clothing, food, and redemption of debts in Natick. Years later, the Dudley Indian account paid for his funeral, even though he died in

Natick.[30] One of Thomas's sisters, Submit, born in Natick in 1735, ended up four decades later in the Holliston home of Ebenezer Hill, about ten miles south of Natick, "in a very low and languishing State of Health."[31] Seven years later she married Solomon Wamsquam, another Natick Indian, in Hopkinton, about five miles northeast of Holliston and halfway between Natick and Grafton.[32] The Awassamog descendants, along with many others from Dudley, Grafton, and Worcester, occasionally visited Natick to renew ties with their families and other remnants of that Indian community. Stephen Badger marveled at how "some of them, after an absence of near twenty years, have returned to their native home."[33]

But connections to Natick weakened and dissolved as the offspring of marriages developed closer bonds and better opportunities elsewhere. Elizabeth Brooks was born in Natick but left as a young woman to live elsewhere for years before buying thirty acres in the town of Dudley near the Chabanakongkomun enclave. She married Senah, an African American (or mixed-blood) from Natick, and they raised several "Industrious and frugal" children "with good morals." Brooks had various relatives in Natick, including Senah's mother. In 1783, her sister Eunice Spywood died, leaving her eleven acres in Natick "with a poor house and no firewood" and substantial debts. Unfortunately, while Elizabeth was away seeing to family and the estate, her home in Dudley burned down. Sixty years old, without possessions and facing debts, she preferred, though "depressed and destitute," to return to Dudley and sold her inherited land to finance her life there. While family ties kept Elizabeth Brooks as part of the Natick Indian community on one level, her home was elsewhere. Family and community-as-identity became detached from the land that had been home to the enclave.[34]

The family connections among the Chabanakongkomun, Hassanamisco, and Natick Indians and the movement of individuals throughout the region point to the Indians' evolving network. This network facilitated movement between the three enclaves, as highlighted by the Awassamog children who were scattered yet linked to their ancestral village, by the Wisers and Bowmans from Natick who moved out to Worcester and Dudley in the 1730s, and by the four Hassanamisco women living in Natick in 1760. Dudley funds not only paid for the Natick medical and funeral expenses of Thomas Awassamog, but also reimbursed travel expenses for two Pegan women, Anna and Mary, to visit Natick in December 1768.[35] At about the same time, Elizabeth Brooks moved from Natick to Dudley. Individuals who moved from one enclave to another, like Senah, retained kinship and economic links to former homes as they developed new connections in their new villages.

Few of the immigrants moved to Punkapoag, and the second praying town continued to shrink in population and size. The reasons for the decline remain a mystery; possible explanations are the reserve's small size, proximity to English settlements, long-standing social and political conflicts with those who settled Natick, and distance from Indian villages in the southeast. Some of the Punkapoags left the enclave to follow their kinship connections to Pembroke or Middleborough. In 1764, there were nineteen Indians in Stoughton, the colonial town that included the Punkapoag reserve.[36] Four years later, five Punkapoags told the General Court that they were "the greater part of the remaining part of Said Tribe, now almost extinct." The Punkapoag reserve had shrunk, like the one in Dudley, from 1,000 acres in 1740 to 411 acres in 1757, and would disappear entirely between 1760 and 1780. The five who claimed to be most of the tribe also noted "that their Lands are full in proportion diminishing with their numbers, but the poor natives cannot give a solid reason therefore." As in Dudley, Punkapoag land was sold to pay debts arising from basic needs, and the Indians (unlike those in Natick or Hassanamisco) relied on fishing and gathering economies and avoided extensive English-style agriculture. Even in 1768, the five supposed Punkapoag survivors noted their "dispirs'd scattered manner of living."[37]

Unfortunately, Punkapoag shared Natick's medical and economic misfortunes, as the reserve's inhabitants grew increasingly helpless and more elderly after 1760. When Samuel Mohoo died during the winter of 1763, he left eleven orphans, seven of whom were too young to provide for themselves. The Punkapoag account was exhausted by the heavy strain of past years, and without those funds the children were "in a suffering and almost starving condition and without Suitable Clothing in this Cold Season of the year." In response, the General Court permitted the Punkapoag guardians to bind out Indian orphans until the age of twenty-one, just as town officials were empowered to handle indigent orphans in their communities.[38] Two years later, the court enlarged this directive to include "the Mulattoes, Children of the Punkapoag Indians."[39] Thus *Indians* and *poverty* had become synonymous in the towns around Boston. Such measures provided only a small safety valve for the enclave's unfortunates, and as bills for food, supplies, and medical and funeral expenses continued to mount, the General Court allowed the Punkapoag's guardian to sell their land again and again in 1769, 1773, and 1776.[40]

The Punkapoags also suffered from their white neighbors' aggression. In 1768, members of a Stoughton town meeting voted to build a road through the Indian reserve and had the road surveyed, both without obtaining the approval of either the natives or the General Court. While the Punkapoag guardian squashed the project, he was unable (due to the costs of a lawsuit) to keep white settlers from trespassing on the small reserve.[41] The Indians also complained that they were "unable to prevent the Incroachments of Avaricious men — who would fain take from us that very little part which we are allow'd to possess of our former abundance." The assembly had arranged to have sixteen acres in Stoughton, including a meadow and an orchard, worked by a white farmer; in exchange the Punkapoags were to be allowed part of the produce. But the natives "are not suffer'd to occupy even that so small part," for the farmer threatened to kill them "if we attempt to take an apple from the orchard which yields many barrels of cyder in a year, nor will he suffer us to gather cranberrys from off our own meadow for our support."[42] The "Great Court" did nothing, however, and a century later their great grandchildren were still trying to regain that land.[43]

Those who left the shrinking, poverty-stricken Punkapoag reserve to live among their relatives in southeastern Massachusetts found similar conditions in their new homes. The 1764 census shows a small number of Indian families in the eastern part of the region, scattered throughout instead of living together in neighborhoods — for most of the towns in Plymouth County reported similar numbers of Indians. Apparently Teticut, Assawompsett, and Mattakeesit were no longer centers of native population, perhaps because of the many land sales since 1740. Even the enclave in Rochester, all or mostly resettled by Pigwackets, contained only ten males and twenty-seven females — though some of the twenty-two "negroes" in the town may have married into this native community.[44] Farther east, the large Indian population reported by the town of Plymouth maintained two distinct enclaves: Kitteaumut (along Manumit Pond), where Ezra Stiles found "perhaps a doz. Wigwams" housing about thirty individuals in 1763, and the legally protected reserve of Herring Pond, on the line between Plymouth and Barnstable counties.[45]

But the census depiction of a tiny, diffused native population in the county is somewhat misleading. As Indians in the area sold land, the original territories of Teticut, Assawompsett, and Mattakeesit were swallowed by the prolific colonial villages. Thus the native families that remained in Teticut in 1764 could have been counted as residents of six different towns. Three years before the census, Ezra Stiles spoke with "Simon, an Ind. preacher" —

probably John Simons, who lived in Teticut and later moved southeast to Rochester — who told him that twelve to fifteen Indian families remained in Assawompsett. Stiles also noted twelve native families in "Pembroke & Situate" (Mattakeesit).[46] While increasing white settlement must have left a few native farmsteads somewhat isolated, Indians preferred (like most people) to live near friends and relatives.

The census figures are also flawed because many Indian or "mixed" families escaped enumeration. Some lived remote from English settlements, in places disliked by or unknown to the colonists. The frequent intermarriage of Indians and African Americans also makes censuses recorded by whites suspect. One wonders whether (or how) the census taker counted Indians like the Wampanoag Ruth Moses. In 1746, she married Kofi, a freed African American, and over the next twenty years they moved back and forth to the Vineyard, often living among Indians. They finally settled in Dartmouth in 1766, after Kofi purchased a farm where they raised several children, one of whom, Paul Cuffe, led the first back-to-Africa movement.[47] Neither Pequot nor the poor white relatives of the famous William Apess, who led the Mashpee revolt in the early nineteenth century, can be traced. In fact, Apess's birth (like those of many Indians, blacks, and poor whites) was not documented, and he does not appear in any federal census.[48]

Regardless of where most Indians lived in Plymouth County, the inland reserves continued to shrink as desperate natives sold land to pay white creditors for medicine, nursing, food, and liquor. Elderly Stephen David fled to Albany to escape numerous creditors, who sold his thirty acres in 1760.[49] By January 1762, the guardian for Indians in the county annually distributed blankets to natives who seemed "proper object[s] of Charity."[50] Six months later, Esther Anthony, one of those who received charity, sought to sell all of her Teticut lands to satisfy creditors. Her husband had drowned during the winter and she had no children or other source of income for her few remaining years.[51] Similar problems forced other Middleborough Indians to sell lands in the 1760s and early 1770s.[52]

By 1790, the only Indians reported in Middleborough were eight families living at Betty's Neck (Assawompsett), with reputations of being "poor and improvident . . . very intemperate, the corn and rye raised on their land being usually sold for liquor."[53] Few if any natives lived on the north or west sides of the town, once part of the Teticut reserve. Thirty-five years later, state investigators counted only four to six Indians who held land in the town, though that number occasionally rose to about twenty from the "temporary residence of other Indians among them" — as individuals and families traveled along the natives' regional "highway."[54] Mattakeesit was even smaller, only one or two Indian families remaining in East Bridgewater.[55]

Indians in the western half of southeastern Massachusetts, once the core of the Wampanoag confederation and now Bristol County, were also scattered. The county contained only one Indian reserve, Freetown, created by the General Court in 1701 with a grant of 190 acres to Wampanoags who had fought for the province. The village vanished from provincial records for a half century, although the appointment of a guardian in 1746 showed that the enclave had not disappeared. In 1763, the General Court was told that "contentions are risen among their Descendants concerning the Lands" in the reserve, and dispatched a committee to settle the issue.[56] While the committee allotted land to seventy-two adults, few lived year-round on the reserve; the visitors found only seven houses (probably wood huts, not wigwams) and nine cultivated acres.[57] Either a community had never developed in Freetown, and most families retained their primary social ties and residences elsewhere, or most of the Indians lived in scattered wigwams and maintained a traditional living by hunting, fishing, and finding occasional work elsewhere.

Some Freetown families probably spent all or much of the year in neighboring Dartmouth, the Quaker-established town that lay along Buzzard's Bay and was noted for the rich estuaries within its vast territory and its burgeoning maritime trade. The town's abundant resources, acreage, and employment supported a number of native communities, only some of which are documented. In 1698, there were a number of Indian villages and congregations within Dartmouth, from Sakonnet (Saconet) in the west to Achushnet in the east, and over the following half century natives remained in scattered groups, as the population pressures that pushed Indians elsewhere into large enclaves either did not exist in this region or pushed in the opposite direction. A large number lived within the white community. Ezra Stiles noted in 1760 that a man counted seventy-five natives in Dartmouth "mostly living with English" — probably domestics and sailors renting rooms.[58] Even his census was misleading, however, for a century later, several elderly residents of the area, including those of Indian descent, told of "great numbers" of Indians around 1760 living in clusters of wigwams along the Westport River, between Westport and Dartmouth, growing corn and maintaining their burial grounds.[59]

The two very different pictures of Dartmouth Indian residence and socioeconomic patterns are both accurate, representing the worlds of "urban" and "rural" native groups. Dartmouth is an excellent microcosm of the New England Indian universe in the second half of the century. Unmarried young people increasingly left villages like Dartmouth for Boston, New Bedford, and other port towns that offered adventure, income, spouses, and opportunities to escape a marginalized status and reduce the pressure on a community's shrinking resources. Those who remained on the reserves were the elderly, children, and the successful few who held sufficient capital, land, livestock, and children.

But the seemingly vast differences between the urban and rural worlds are misleading, for many if not most Indians moved between the two fairly readily and even often, as employment fluctuated and social and family obligations pushed and pulled. Individuals who left their village for a port town socialized with other Indians, and when they found a spouse and perhaps sufficient capital for a farm, returned or found a new rural home. A state investigator visiting New Bedford found a large number of Indians from a variety of tribes, few of whom "consider themselves permanently located there, but generally, are looking forward to the time, more or less remote, when they shall return to the places of their nativity, finally to mingle their dust with that of their fathers."[60] New social and family networks emerged as natives from Freetown moved between that reserve, the developing ports around Dartmouth, and more isolated villages along the Westport River. Unfortunately, as the inhabitants of the smaller villages were forced to sell more land and the surrounding white population grew, as in Natick and Grafton, little or nothing was left for the exiles.

The few Indian villages on Cape Cod outside Mashpee also dissolved after 1760. Like Indians in the villages along the Westport River, those in Yarmouth, Falmouth, and other English towns were largely invisible throughout the first half of the century. Yarmouth set aside "Indiantown" in 1713 and its inhabitants promptly disappeared behind a veil of silence, although local folklore tells that the community was devastated by the midcentury colonial wars. In the 1760s, the enclave reemerged in several censuses that showed only six to eight families, all living in wigwams.[61] The small group maintained family ties with Herring Pond through the daughter of an Indiantown founder, and social and religious connections to nearby Potawaumacut.[62]

Potawaumacut, the largest Indian enclave on the Cape outside Mashpee, was badly hurt by the participation of its men in the Seven Years War as well as the whaling trade. When Ezra Stiles visited Potawaumacut in 1762 he found more widows than married couples.[63] During this period, the Potawaumacuts experienced some of the same challenges to resources and rights as Indiantown, but more successfully defended their land and privileges. Not only did they regain unlimited access to a privately owned beach for landing whales, but the enclave's leader reclaimed his right to cut wood on a former reserve purchased by whites.[64] Efforts to maintain their community, however, would be frustrated by the same demographic problems that hurt many native groups in the late eighteenth century.

Far less is known about the small native enclaves that remained within other English towns on Cape Cod. Inspectors dispatched to the Cape in 1767 by the New England Company reported nine wigwams at Scanton (near Mashpee), at least twenty Indians living in Falmouth, eight families in Pocasset (Sandwich), and a number in Wareham who "live mostly in English families." This scattering of Indian groups is reflected in the 1764 census, which shows a few natives in nearly every town on Cape Cod.[65] The sizable community in Falmouth is particularly notable, for despite their absence from provincial documents, Indians held a large amount of land in the town and high prestige in the region. Their minister until 1742, Solomon Briant, stood at the nexus of a large family and religious network reaching from Dartmouth in the west to Mashpee in the east. Briant's move to Mashpee, and his successor Josiah Cognehew's kinship to Mashpee's emissary to London in 1760 highlight the deep connections between the Indians in Falmouth (and elsewhere on the lower Cape) and Mashpee.[66] The disappearance of these smaller groups by the Revolution marked their absorption into the larger enclaves.

An unknown number of Cape Cod Indians wandered homeless, like so many other natives in the wake of the Seven Years War. In October 1756, Samuel How of Dorchester found Hannah Quason, an aged Indian probably from Harwich, "Lying in the Road," near his gate. "Rather than have her Perish in the Way," How "took her into his House, as humanity & Compassion Obliged him to do," where she died twenty days later.[67] Eight years later, Hannah Cowitt, from either Mashpee or Martha's Vineyard, came to Duxbury, where she fell ill and was nursed back to health at the town's expense.[68] These individuals shared the provincial roads with Indians from other places. In 1757, Mary Moses became sick in Roxbury while traveling through the area and was taken to the barn of physician John Davis, where she stayed for several years — and apparently recovered.[69] Even towns in western Massachusetts found themselves supporting traveling indigent Indians.

A typical wanderer was Sarah Wamsquam, the Pennacook mentioned earlier who had grown up in Cambridge before moving to Natick about 1720. She inherited just three acres when her husband died of tuberculosis in 1755, and so was forced to travel from town to town, though three of her children survived in Natick, looking for work or (as a Natick guardian later wrote) "begged from door to Door," never staying long in any one town. In January 1767, Wamsquam noted that she had no home in the province, and sold her little land to avoid "Perish[ing] in the Streets in this severe Season."[70] By the close of the decade, nearly seventy years old and unable to "Travel one mile in a day," Sarah returned to Natick to seek assistance at Stephen Badger's house. Ironically, she arrived while the minister was away asking the General Court for money to support Indian paupers.[71]

As the number of landless Indians increased, towns sought ways to support aged and indigent natives. Indian communal resources could be tapped to pay expenses. During the 1760s the Hassanamisco guardians often reimbursed innkeepers who put up traveling Indians whose homes were still nominally in Grafton. Often neighboring towns, such as Needham and Sherborn, near Natick, or Westborough, next to Grafton, submitted bills to the respective Indian guardians. When the land or money was gone, however, towns looked to the General Court for a stable source of financial assistance. In 1767, Natick guardians asked the legislature to support indigent Indians in the town, and two years later Stephen Badgers asked the assembly to guarantee future funding.[72] While the court created a committee to consider "the state of the poor Indians of the province," and authorized individual requests for assistance, it created no systemic relief.[73] Towns with Indian communities opposed any move by the court to require them to provide natives with poor relief, in part because Indians were exempt from local taxes, and in part because, as a Natick guardian noted, such arrangements would attract "so many other Indians to come [to Natick] as shall hear of it — and Towns that shall have an Indian in them shall be likely to send him when he shall want relief."[74]

Many of the wandering Indians, like poor whites in the region, found homes in the growing port towns, particularly Boston. Unfortunately, the urban poor are rarely documented, and the African Americans and Indians who formed the lowest socioeconomic class are particularly invisible. The 1764 census shows only twenty-one male and sixteen female Indians in Boston (ironically matching Natick's numbers) and only a few in neighboring towns. But anecdotal evidence hints at a much greater native presence, such as the Indians who went to gain a trade and later returned to Natick. An Indian community of sailors, domestics, and travelers emerged in the Boston area, many disappearing into the back streets and alleys of the city — including Crispus Attucks, a sailor and one of the Boston Massacre's martyrs, who may have been a Natick Indian.[75] No doubt a large number found employment on ships, and many failed to return. Those who did return extended and enriched Indian kinship networks when they brought with them new mates from other native groups or even non-Indians.

Three native communities gained in population and power in the second half of the century as they drew immigrants from dissolving Indian communities throughout the region. Herring Pond, Mashpee, and Gay Head became centers of the evolving New England Indian network, in large part because of their large, resource-rich, legally protected reserves. All three managed to maintain pieces of their traditions far longer than the smaller enclaves, although the pressures that brought other natives into the fold also pushed the groups into closer ties to the dominant economic and material culture.

Indians on the three thousand acres in the Herring Pond reserve lived in small family groups, as in Dartmouth, scattered among the rolling hills and many ponds at the entrance to Cape Cod. Their settlement pattern may have been shaped by the light sandy soil, which could not be intensively farmed, or because the scarcity of English settlers and the many ponds in the area allowed the natives to maintain a more aboriginal economy.[76] Over time the community incorporated nearby smaller enclaves. Elisha Tupper, who ministered to Indians in the area, noted "more than an Hundred" at Herring Pond, while the 1764 census reported a total of 121 Indians in Plymouth and Sandwich, which included Pocasset, Kitteaumut, and an emerging group called the "Black Ground Indians."[77] Herring Pond clearly became the community's core by 1767, when the New England Company built a new meetinghouse there for Tupper. Twelve years later a white minister wrote that the group at Herring Pond had grown (to 108) "partly in a natural way their Births having much exceeded the Deaths; & partly by their coming from other Places & settling there." The village's particular attraction, he noted, was its "large Tract of Land convenient for fishing & planting & plenty of Wood.[78]

Mashpee grew even more rapidly, becoming the largest Indian enclave in Massachusetts. In 1762, Ezra Stiles noted 250 people in seventy-five households. At that time Mashpee families were quite small; Stiles found "not four to a Fam. at a medium," and recorded that only nine children had been born during the previous year.[79] Not mentioned by Stiles but no doubt the major cause of the low birthrate was the large number of Mashpee men recently killed in the colonial wars. Many in the village were immigrants, and a large number were not natives, for the census three years later reported 230 "Indians" and 31 "Negroes."[80] Of course, these racial categories may say more about the observer than the community, for just two years after the census Gideon Hawley reported 271 Indians "and mulattos" — but no "Negroes."[81] The community's growth rate increased over the next decade, for in June 1776, a year after Solomon Briant's death, Hawley reported eighty-one households with 327 people, including 14 "negroes."[82] The minister acknowledged Mashpee's natural increase, but noted that the growth was "cheifly By the coming of Indians from other places for of late years we have families from a distance and some men from New London & Narragansett who have incorporated with the Mashpee tribe."[83]

The enclave's unique self-government, plentiful resources, and role as a native cultural center attracted refugees from other Indian villages, further increasing Mashpee's importance and power. In 1765, Mashpee became the only Indian community in Massachusetts to govern itself and to manage its resources without the interference of white guardians. Visitors often remarked on the reserve's bountiful forests, streams, ponds, clamming beaches, and meadows. And by the 1760s, Indians from southeastern Massachusetts, Cape Cod, and Martha's Vineyard gathered in Mashpee to "celebrate the holy communion together."[84] At the time, Hawley recorded immigrants from Falmouth and the Vineyard, and years later told a fellow minister that the reserve "has been an asylum for Indians and their mixt posterity," and had received immigrants from "Narraganset as well as Middlebury [Middleborough], Natick, N. Bedford [Dartmouth], etc."[85]

Those who came to Mashpee may also have been drawn in part by the community's ability to preserve certain elements of traditional culture. The reserve's resources, of course, allowed families to maintain a subsistence economy; even in 1802 a white observer complained that "their stores are generally very small, as an Indian depends for his daily bread upon his daily success."[86] The Wampanoag dialect, perhaps somewhat reshaped by the influence of the Natick Bible and other Massachusett writings, remained dominant in Mashpee. Visitors to the Indians' annual regional gathering in 1767 noted that the services were conducted entirely in the native language.[87] More intriguingly, while whites noticed only the prayers, preaching, and sacraments, the celebration retained echoes of aboriginal holidays, beginning with its timing in mid-September, the traditional date for harvest festivals. Of course, the traditions now celebrated or remembered by natives were revised versions of aboriginal habits — transformed in the 150-year crucible of religious, economic, and ecological evolution.

The revised "aboriginal" culture continued to evolve in the decades following the Seven Years War. The change can be glimpsed in the types of Mashpee homes reported by white observers. In 1762, 60 out of 66 homes were wigwams (90 percent); just five years later there were 52 wigwams out of 73 homes (71 percent); nine years after that, in 1776, only 26 wigwams (out of 68 homes, or 38 percent) existed in Mashpee.[88] The switch from wigwams to "shingled houses" symbolized a broader transformation of the community's material culture, for even the remaining wigwams contained English-made or designed goods. In 1761, Ezra Stiles sketched two wigwams at Niantic, Connecticut — perhaps a day's journey from Mashpee — whose design and materials showed, according to anthropologist William Sturtevant, "remarkably detailed similarities across space and time."[89] But within those traditional homes were cupboards (or shelves), tables, and chairs.

The newcomers who helped Mashpee grow were at least partially responsible for this cultural change, for many came from places like Natick. They had been drawn to Mashpee by its resources and autonomy, but, like late twentieth-century American urbanites moving to rural villages, brought new tastes and desires that unconsciously transformed their new home. Briant's death in 1775 heralded another force for change, for when Gideon Hawley gained the pulpit, he tried to "Anglicize" his congregation, promoting the use of English and discouraging less orthodox worship (perhaps the pipe ceremony noted in the Nantucket church?) and "unChristian" social activities. But the connection between religion, culture, and politics was obvious, and the number of Indians in Hawley's audience shrank rapidly. Thus Mashpee's culture and the community's identity, like that of native groups everywhere on the continent, did not "die" or "degenerate" (as many white observers thought) but shifted or evolved along with the group's members and their fortunes.

Whether living in a wigwam or a house, everyone in Mashpee was influenced by the dominant Anglo-American culture and economy. Immigration was one major cause, but more significant was the increasing pressure by neighboring whites on the enclave's resources, including the degradation of rivers by milldams. Levi Mie of Mashpee told the legislature in 1791 that white men "says that it is the Indians that spoils the river . . . [but it is] the wite people & ther mills Before there was so many wite people on our land & so many mill on our stream there was fish pleanty to supply the hole town and great many for market & now we cant suply our own famely's."⁹⁰ Such pressure forced many to seek a living outside the reserve.

As in other coastal Indian communities, men sought employment in whaling and women as domestics in white households. Some took fish, wood, and other Mashpee resources to sell elsewhere. Unfortunately, these connections brought death as well as income to the community, for whaling killed many, and the women and men who came back to visit or live often returned with liquor and disease. Yellow fever hit Mashpee hard in December 1776, when Hawley told a friend that "a terrible sickness has raged among my poor people. . . . I have buried 8 with it in a few weeks and have several at the point of death and I fear it will carry off numbers before ending."⁹¹ Many Mashpee men died far from home in the colonial wars, and when the Revolution broke out large numbers left to serve and to perish in that conflict. Their service points to the tangled web of Indian culture in New England, for aboriginal warrior traditions and legends, political allegiances, and republic ideology were all motivations — along with economics, as the loyalist Hawley noted when he wrote "what can they do but [en]list into the army!"⁹² The thirty-five Mashpee widows in 1788 attest to the community's sacrifice for the new nation.⁹³

Some Mashpees traveled regularly to Nantucket and Martha's Vineyard to sell loads of wood and crafts, where they were welcomed by white customers and stayed with relatives. No doubt they noticed the large number of natives from the mainland who found new homes among the still-strong Indian enclaves on both islands, groups that retained good pasture, farm, and wood lands, and from which men could easily find work in the booming whaling trade.⁹⁴ Most of the newcomers to the Vineyard went to Gay Head, which contained some of the best land on the entire island. The population of Chappaquiddick and Christiantown stayed level, but the numbers in Gay Head increased from 112 people in 1747 to 165 in 1765, 203 in 1786, and perhaps 276 in 1790, stabilizing at about 270 during the first half of the nineteenth century.⁹⁵ Some were drawn by Gay Head's resources and communal strength, others by marriage and family ties. Zurviah of Natick, for example, married Samuel Ompany of Gay Head and sold her land to finance a new house on the Vineyard.⁹⁶ Indians who came to Gay Head were given full rights in the community, with access to land and other resources.

Indians who came to Nantucket found many natives living in Miacomet, just outside the colonial port of Sherburne. Tragically, the ability of Miacomet's inhabitants to work among the English primed the Indians of that Island for a devastating epidemic. In August 1763, an Indian woman washing the clothes of sick sailors in a white household became extremely ill. Her relatives brought her home, but she experienced "much pain, a high fever & then soon appear[ed] yellow," dying in about three days. The disease, possibly yellow fever, spread throughout the village, then to other Indians on the island. By the time the epidemic suddenly ended in February 1764, 222 of the Indians had died (62 percent), leaving 136 Nantucket Indians and shattering the native community.[97] The disease spread beyond the island through the Indians' trade and family networks, for that winter Sam Pognit of Mashpee and "the squaw from Nantucket" both brought "yellow fever" to Mashpee — though luckily only five adults died.[98]

Crevecoeur visited Nantucket shortly after the epidemic ended, and found the surviving Indians clustered together "in decent houses along the shores of Miacomet pond." He noted their recent high mortality, and remarked that the Indians "appear to be a race doomed to recede and disappear before the superior genius of the Europeans."[99] Indeed, their vast silence in the provincial records, following the avalanche of protests in the 1740s and 1750s, is striking. Yet the Indian population was still relatively high compared to other native enclaves in the province, and continued to play an important role in the island's fishing trade. The smaller number of Indian men could not, however, meet the insatiable demand for whalemen, so captains and merchants "imported" an increasing number of African Americans and Cape Verdeans. Many of the newcomers married Indians and their descendants, creating a new village near Miacomet dubbed New Guinea, where blacks, Indians, and "mixed-bloods" lived.[100] In 1792, a Nantucket historian noted that the Indians were "reduced to four males and sixteen families," and fifteen years later an English visitor found that "of the unmixed race, two or three females compose the entire list."[101] The so-called "last Nantucket Indian," Abram Quary, died on 25 November 1854.[102]

)(

Natives and native enclaves in eighteenth-century southern New England found their sense of identity shifting as a growing number of the native women married African men. Intermarriage became more frequent as Indian men died in the colonial wars or on whaling ships, or fled the province to escape debts. African men and their male descendants took their place, largely because labor demands in New England brought nearly twice as many enslaved or bound men as women to the region, creating a demographic imbalance that complemented that of the Indians. White prejudice, and the Indians' and blacks' shared low socioeconomic status, also helped drive individuals from the two groups together. The rising tide of intermarriage forced the larger Indian communities in eastern Massachusetts to reexamine their political, cultural, and economic boundaries. Small enclaves, on the other hand, despite the problems that could arise from the newcomers, were simply grateful to be able to survive. Regardless of the size of their village or the state of their kinship network, all Indians developed a new sense of themselves as an ethnic group, shaped from the *inside* by the rising tide of intermarriage and from the *outside* by the rising tide of white prejudice.

Enslaved and free Africans and their descendants in New England increased from less than a thousand in New England in 1700 to about eleven thousand at midcentury. At the beginning of the century about 70 percent had been born in Africa or the West Indies, but by 1750 only about 35 percent were foreign born, and the importation of slaves plunged after midcentury. Most blacks were men brought to work, whether enslaved or bound servants, as semiskilled assistants to urban artisans or as domestic help for upper-class households, particularly those of ministers. At midcentury 2,700 adult African Americans, including nearly twice as many black men as women (1.75) lived scattered around Massachusetts. About half resided in Boston and the neighboring towns, and formed nearly 10 percent of the port's population. Other clusters developed in the port towns of Salem, Ipswich, Newbury, and Dartmouth.[103] Between 1760 and 1800, as the population of blacks in Boston grew, adapted, and helped develop a unique African American folk culture, they forged new religious and social institutions.

Some African Americans found mates among native groups. Blacks met Indians in cities, while serving in ministerial households, or during errands, finding to their surprise and pleasure a people lacking the prejudice of whites. Many marriages developed when Indian women peddling crafts or working as domestics met African-American men in the bustling streets of Boston or in the fields of rural New England. Mashpee minister Gideon Hawley remarked that "many of our women have found negroe husbands, as they were stroling in the country and bro't them home."[104]

African men in New England gained a number of advantages by marrying Indian women, who were in many cases their only possible mates, given the lack of black women, frequent isolation in otherwise all-white households and rural communities, and white prejudices. Even if an Indian wife could not purchase their freedom, their children would be born free.[105]

Slave or free, black men who married Indian women gained access to, though not legal control over, native land and other resources. Last, but not least, an African man could gain a community with an Indian wife, for native groups generally welcomed (or adopted) newcomers without prejudice. Marrying into an Indian community provided social, economic, and psychological gains in a hostile Anglo-American world.

Indian communities, on the other hand, found mixed marriages to be a mixed blessing. With the death and disappearance of many Indian men, African American men filled the obvious need of Indian women for mates. At the end of the Seven Years' War there were 1.3 females for every male among Indians in Massachusetts, and among adults the imbalance was about two to one.[106] Small rural inland villages, such as Natick and Punkapoag, were saved from extinction as Indian women married blacks. In addition, new knowledge and abilities (and genes) came with African American spouses, helping native groups adapt to the changing colonial world. But new conflicts erupted within Indian groups as African men gained a reputation as better husbands than native men. Around 1770, William Brown's Narragansett grandmother bought her African American husband "in order to change her mode of living. It was customary for the woman to do all the drudgery and hard work in-doors and out. The Indian men thought it a disgrace for them to work; they thought they did their part by hunting and procuring game. The Indian women observing the colored men working for their wives, and living after the manner of white people, in comfortable homes, felt anxious to change their position in life." As a result, Brown believed, Indian men had a "very bitter feeling" against blacks.[107]

Time and identity may have colored the author's account: Brown wrote in the early 1880s, when industrial capitalism had become a paradigm instead of a radical challenge, and he saw himself as an African American able to succeed in America. In addition, his description of the occupations held by Indian men bear only a partial resemblance to the reality of the mid- and late eighteenth century; while many Indian men continued to hunt and fish, most worked as farmers, laborers, or mariners. But Brown's account contains an essential truth: Indian men were growing concerned at the tendency of Indian women to marry African American men. The white guardian of Chappaquiddick and Christiantown noted that "there were many disputes among them oweing to their Females Marying Negroes whom they did not wish to have any right to their lands," and that Christiantown men filed lawsuits in the early 1800s to stop African American men from marrying into their community.[108] By the mid-nineteenth century, the Gay Head Indians were "jealous of the influence of [black] foreigners, having had much trouble with some of those who have intermarried with their women and settled amongst them."[109]

African American men and Indian women were pulled into marriage by their complementary demographic imbalance, and then pushed into a shared social and economic underclass by Anglo-American prejudice. The colonists' distaste, contempt, and lingering fear of Indians joined with their gelling belief that blacks were inherently inferior. The prejudice that pushed "colored" people together was made manifest in 1706 when the General Court debated a bill "for the Better Preventing of a Spurious and Mixt Issue," criminalizing sexual relations or marriage between a European and an Indian, a black, or a mulatto.[110] Samuel Sewall, afraid that such a law would be "an Oppression provoking to God, and that will promote Murders and other Abominations," used all of his immense influence to remove Indians from the act.[111] He succeeded, but custom continued to frown on native-white matches, and the ban on intermarriage was extended to Indians in 1786, six years after the Massachusetts Superior Court outlawed slavery in the state, and would not be removed until the middle of the nineteenth century.[112]

Anglo-American prejudice was also expressed in the inability or un-willingness of white observers to distinguish between Indians and African Americans. While Natick minister Stephen Badger was sensitive to how whites mistreated that town's Indians, he also noted it was "almost impossible to come to any determination" of the native population, for they "are intermarried with *blacks,* and some with whites; and the various shades between these, and those that are descended from them."[113] The white men who gathered statistics or demographic data either saw "negro" faces among the children of intermarriages, or lumped Indians and African Americans together as "people of color" and assigned both to the same low social and political niche. Indeed, the federal census, beginning in 1790, identified households only as "white," "slave," or "all other free persons."

The statistics assembled by whites on "people of color" (Indians, blacks, and mulattoes) after the Seven Years War, as intermarriage became common, are at best questionable and at worst racist distortions. The evolving ideology of race among Anglo-Americans distorted even the most careful observations. Gideon Hawley, Mashpee's Anglo-American minister, made a detailed census of the community in 1776 and identified only fourteen men (4 percent of the 327 nonwhites) as "negroes. He seemed satisfied with the situation, noting only that the large number of women widowed in the Seven Years War "hath been the means of introducing among my people the African blood."[114] But during the social and political upheaval of the Revolution, Hawley became horrified at the willingness of Mashpee Indians to marry African Americans. Twelve years after his first census, the minister reported that nearly 70 percent of the 400 Mashpees were "greatly and variously mixed," and that only 25 men and 110 women were "pure bloods."[115] While many of the newcomers who swelled Mashpee's population were African Americans, the swift change from 4 percent "negro" to 70 percent "mixed" was, in large part, within Hawley's mind.

Hawley was, like other Anglo-Americans, increasingly obsessed by race. And skin color was a large part of race, for Hawley now referred to all Mashpees as "blacks," and in 1791 told the Massachusetts governor, John Hancock, that "the children who are lately born are mostly mongrels." Racial "science" was in its infancy, of course, and the minister's hostility to African Americans and their "mongrels" was tempered by his fascinating view of blood lines, for while Hawley fought against the newcomers' influence in Mashpee, he also believed that mulatto men made "better husbands." "Their women are more prolific, and children healthier," he noted, "since their intermarriage with English, Germans, & Negroes."[116] The "Germans" included four Hessian deserters from Burgoyne's army who had married native women, "whereby we have a motley medley of characters more heterogenous, if possible, and some of them not less turbulent, than the elements."[117]

Hawley and Badger both confessed that Indians married whites, but few Anglo-Americans were willing to acknowledge such unions. Marriages between whites and Indians, while not illegal, violated Anglo-American boundaries. Ministers generally refused to bless or even acknowledge marriages between whites and Indians, yet enough scattered hints exist to show that such households were hidden rather than nonexistent. A state investigator later noted that almost every marriage in the Yarmouth Indian community since 1700 had been between whites and Indians; an astonishing observation, but unfortunately left unelaborated.[118] Caesar Ferrit, who moved from Boston to Natick in 1751 "to live among his own Nation the aboriginal natives," also boasted, according to a local historian, "that the blood of four nations run in his veins; for one of his Grandfathers was a Dutchman, the other a Frenchman; and one of his grandmothers an Indian, and the other an African."[119] Over several generations, intermarriages might blur the once-firm lines between ethnic groups. Ferrit married a white New

England woman and his children might have passed as whites. Questions of romance aside, most white men who married Indians were already scorned by the dominant culture and gained many of the same socioeconomic benefits as African American spouses. But while Indian-white unions were more frequent than town records indicate, they were relatively rare due to Anglo-American prejudice, as highlighted by the Massachusetts law to prevent "a Spurious and Mixt Issue."

Boundaries between Indians and African Americans, on the other hand, were so porous that by the end of the Revolution white observers were unable (and perhaps unwilling) to draw the line between Indians and blacks. Both groups struggled to create communities within the dominant Anglo-American world. Like the Indians, Africans from different regions and cultures forged, under the pressure of isolation and servitude among a foreign and hostile people, a new ethnic group: African Americans.

As both groups developed their own ethnic identities, clear boundaries between the two evolved even as individuals crossed those borders to marry and have children. Ethnic groups define themselves by particular bits of shared culture, such as food, language, or clothing. Yet ethnicity is as much social as cultural, for such "markers" change over time even as the group's boundaries persist. Though not all aspects of culture serve as boundary markers, individuals claiming membership in a particular ethnic group implicitly agree to measure themselves by their community's standards. While those standards vary over time and even between localities, a group's existence depends on its maintenance of social boundaries.

During the eighteenth century, Indians in southern New England developed social and cultural markers for their ethnic community, including communal resources, a distinct folklore, inclusive meetings, kinship ties to other Indians, individual behavior (such as how one made a living), social conduct (membership in the group's church), and perhaps most important, though difficult for the historian to document, the desire to make a legitimate claim to be Indian.[120] The primary purpose of such markers is to define a community's boundaries to outsiders, and only indirectly to govern relationships within the community. "Thus the persistence of ethnic groups in contact implies not only criteria and signals for identification, but also a structuring of interaction which allows the persistence of cultural differences."[121]

Exclusion also shaped Indian ethnic boundaries, for white perceptions of "Indianness" helped fashion their cultural markers, and white prejudice against Indians reinforced those boundaries. The workings of exclusion in ethnic identity can be glimpsed in the few known instances of Indian-white intermarriage. Their descendants did not look like Indians or blacks and so, we think, could have easily abandoned their community in order to "improve" their material and social conditions. But the family background of individuals was common knowledge in a small village such as Yarmouth and the surrounding towns, particularly when the town's ancestors had done something as scandalous as enter into common-law marriages with "savages." No "respectable" person would want his or her children to marry the offspring of such unions — though enough poor whites were interested to keep the pattern going in that town. Leaving the community in order to pass as white was also difficult, for family background formed a large part of an individual's reputation. Ethnic boundaries were reinforced by the prejudice of outsiders as well as the needs of insiders.

The insider- and outsider-imposed borders that separated Indians and whites also formed boundaries separating Indians and African Americans, even as many individuals crossed between these two groups. Anthropologist Frederick Barth notes that the "social processes of exclusion and incorporation" within ethnic groups mean that "discrete categories are maintained despite changing participation and membership" and "contact and interdependence."[122] Unlike whites, Indians traditionally welcomed mixed marriages as a way to bring new skills and power into the community. But those thus adopted were likewise expected to adopt their new community, to meet certain standards of conduct and to raise their children as members of the group. As the rate and influence of intermarriage increased, Indian enclaves were forced to redefine themselves. Smaller groups that lacked numbers and retained few communal resources, such as Natick and Hassanamisco, depended on African American spouses for survival. Their ethnic boundaries were therefore fairly weak and permeable, consisting primarily of "ascription and identification" and invisible to almost all but members and outsiders wishing to join the group. The seemingly weak boundaries were strengthened, ironically, by the Anglo-American guardians who controlled the Indian groups' funds.

The Indian groups first reshaped by intermarriage were the smaller inland enclaves of Natick and Hassanamisco, which developed close connections to the dominant economy, were hammered by poverty, disease, and war, and by the 1730s were swamped by Anglo-American settlers. In the 1720s, as the colonial population expanded into the middle of New England, Sarah Muckamugg left her home in Hassanamisco for Providence, Rhode Island, where she met, married, and had several children with Aaron

Whipple, a "Negro servant" (or slave).[123] In 1731, Patience Quassont of Natick married African American Nathaniel Hill of Brookline in that town, and seventeen years later Elizabeth Awassamog married Stepney Senah in Medway; both couples moved back to Natick.[124] When the Natick Indians asked the General Court in 1760 to maintain Samuel Stratton's milling monopoly in the town, four of the eighteen signatories were identified as "Negro": Nathaniel Hill, Cato Francis, James Feegoo, and Jean Fare.[125]

The records that trace the offspring of these marriages illustrate the difficulty of relying on local and provincial documents for ethnic identification. Joseph Aaron, the son of Aaron Whipple and Sarah Muckamugg, returned to Hassanamisco and (after a prolonged battle with the Indian guardians) successfully claimed membership in the community and the rights to his mother's property — including her stake in the Hassanamisco Indian account managed by the province.[126] The Senahs's son, Joseph, was listed at birth in the Natick records as "negro," but years later he moved to Dudley and married Elizabeth Brooks, a Natick Indian, thereby demonstrating his "Indianness."[127] The daughters of Nathaniel and Patience Hill followed a different path. After Patience died in 1769, her widower and children returned to Brookline, where he died five years later. In 1774, Elizabeth Hill, still in Brookline, and Hannah Hill, who had moved to Cambridge, sold their family's remaining lands in Natick to pay their father's and their own medical debts — and then vanished from state and local Indian records, having seemingly severed their connections to their mother's ethnic community.[128] But the social networks that brought Indians and their descendants together in cities and towns outside native enclaves seldom appeared in records made by white officials.

By 1740, both Natick and Hassanamisco had divided most of their communal property and found their villages inundated by white settlers. These conditions eased the entrance of African American men into the Indian communities as the native men disappeared in the midcentury colonial wars. Blacks who married Natick Indian women must have been seen by other Indians as equal members of their community, for they were being buried in the Indian cemetery whereas others "deposit their dead in the burying ground of the white people."[129] The groups' landholding in severalty also allowed newcomers an unequaled opportunity to improve their socioeconomic condition through marriage. Hill and his wife, for example, sold large pieces of her land in his attempt to build a profitable farm in Natick. The Indians' remaining common rights were also useful to African American spouses, as shown by their effort to retain the milling privileges provided by Stratton's monopoly.[130]

The mixed blessings of intermarriage for the Indian communities were particularly clear among the Hassanamiscos. The enclave survived in large part because the Indian women married African American men. While this confused white observers, the contradictions in their accounts point to the importance of intermarriage. In 1762, Ezra Stiles saw "the Burying place & Graves of 60 or more Indians" in Grafton, and "Now not a Male Ind. in the Town, & perh. 5 Squaws who marry Negroes"; yet just one year later he noted four Indian families in the enclave, including four men, five women, six boys and seven girls.[131] About three generations later a state investigator found twenty Hassanamisco families with seventy-six individuals and reported that

> little trace of Indian descent is apparent in the members of this tribe. It is most marked in the few who have mixed chiefly with the whites, yet some of these have no perceptible indications of it, and have become identified with the white race. The remainder of the tribe have the distinguishing marks of African descent and mixed African and white, of various grades, from the light quadroon and mulatto, to the apparently nearly pure negro, and, in every successive generation the slight remaining characteristics of the race become less apparent.[132]

Sixty years later, anthropologist Frank Speck noted the survival of the scattered, "mixed" Hassanamisco community. "Group solidarity has vanished at the far end of acculturation," he wrote, "but one must admit that the group, though interfused and obscured, is one consciously apart in name and identity."[133]

Unfortunately, without strong community controls over resources, the ambitions of African American spouses could wreak substantial damage to an Indian enclave. William Burnee, a free African American given the appropriate "Fortune," married Hassanamisco Sarah Robbins, giving Burnee access to her land and her annual interest from the Hassanamisco account. In 1744, his wife bore him a daughter, also named Sarah, but then fell ill; he abandoned her to the care of a white man in whose home she died in 1751.[134] Fortune's infant daughter gave him the legal avenue to control the Robbins's farm and annual interest receipts. But the land was sold to pay Sarah Robbins's medical debts (though the interest payments continued), so in November 1752 Burnee married another Hassanamisco, Abigail Printer.[135] After Abigail died in 1776, Fortune continued to use and profit from the combined land and annual interest income.[136] While Fortune was barred from selling his wives' lands without the General Court's permission, he held their property in all but title.

Burnee's mercenary actions (as well as Nathaniel Hill's more moral efforts) seem to show that the shrunken, impoverished native communities made no distinctions between Indians and African Americans. Yet a narrow border of ethnic identity did separate the two groups. Natick's graveyard is an excellent example of how these boundaries existed even in death, and how marriage acted as a bridge over that boundary. But even some of those who married into the Indian enclaves might not be accepted as full members of the community. The Hassanamiscos' white guardians, for example, considered Burnee a "foreigner" and therefore not eligible for Hassanamisco funds. Of course, a gap probably existed between Indian and white perception of the native community's identity and boundaries. Yet when Burnee married again, sometime before 1793, it was (according to a guardian) to "an old negro wench," not an Indian. And, no doubt, the Hassanamiscos as well as their guardians were angered when he willed the Robbins and Printer properties to a white lawyer, including a third of the remaining Indians' shrinking funds. Burnee had not become a Hassanamisco Indian.[137]

Ethnic identity is a dynamic relationship between individuals, family, and community. Individuals choose a particular identity, usually following one of their parents, but must follow the "social processes of exclusion and incorporation" (cultural boundaries) demanded by their chosen community.[138] Boundaries change over time and often vary between factions within a community, but individuals must still meet certain expectations to gain recognition as members. The complex relationship of these factors appear in the paths taken by the Lawrence sisters of Hassanamisco and their offspring. In 1763, Esther Lawrence married Sharp Freeborn, a free African American, and went with him to his home in Paxton, northwest of Worcester.[139] Five years later the family severed their connections to Hassanamisco by selling Esther's remaining land in Grafton. She renewed those ties in 1790 even though she stayed in Paxton.[140] Esther's sister, Patience, also married an African American, Cesear Gimbee, but the two stayed in Grafton on her property, raising four children within the Hassanamisco community.[141] When Patience and then Cesear died while their sons, Cesear and Moses, were still minors, the boys' cousin, Elnathan Freeborn, son of Esther and Sharp, became their guardian.[142]

Elnathan and the two Gimbee boys were equally entitled under Massachusetts law to Hassanamisco funds, for both had an Indian mother and an African-American father — in fact, their mothers were sisters. Yet neither Elnathan nor any other Freeborn descendant ever claimed an Indian identity or tried to obtain money from the Hassanamisco account. Sharp Freeborn's descendants instead saw themselves as African Americans, even when they cared for their Indian cousins. The ethnic boundaries that separated the Indian Gimbees from the African American Freeborns had a number of potential sources. The Hassanamiscos' boundary markers excluded the Freeborns because the family chose another place to live: Sharp Freeborn sold his Indian wife's land in Grafton, Esther remained in Paxton after his death, and their children and grandchildren never joined the enclave. And, of course, another major element in the New England Indian ethnic identity, as demonstrated by Elnathan's actions, was individual choice.

The Cuffee family of Dartmouth is another illuminating example of the relationship between individual choice and community boundaries in shaping ethnic identity. In 1746, Kofi Slocum, a freed African slave who had been in New England for two decades, married Ruth Moses, a Wampanoag Indian. The family lived in various places in coastal southeastern Massachusetts, even residing at the Gay Head Indian community during the 1760s. In 1766, Kofi bought 116 acres in Dartmouth, perhaps near Ruth's family, before dying six years later. Kofi's sons took their father's African name as the family name, but vacillated between being "Indian" and "African." Since Indian land was exempt from taxes under Massachusetts law, Paul and John Cuffee asked the Bristol County court to declare them Indians, but their effort failed. Another of Kofi's sons, Jonathan, later moved to Martha's Vineyard and soon was signing petitions as one of the Gay Head Indians. Paul married a Pequot woman, but by the turn of the century had clearly embraced his father's heritage; he became a rich merchant, involved himself in many African American institutions in the region, and spearheaded the first back-to-Africa movement. Paul chose his father's identity and Jonathan chose his mother's, and both were accepted by their chosen communities.[143]

The few Indian enclaves in Massachusetts that held a fairly high degree of social and economic autonomy, such as Mashpee, could also create more rigid ethnic boundaries. But unlike the increasingly rigid Anglo-American racial barriers, Mashpee's boundaries were porous enough to allow in and assimilate newcomers of any skin color. Some Mashpee men did fear that

"Negroes & English . . . will get away our Lands & all our Privileges," but intermarriage increased rapidly after 1760 as the enclave welcomed new blood in the wake of their great losses in the Seven Years' War and the American Revolution.[144] African American and white newcomers offered new skills and connections outside Mashpee. Immigrant Indians, including Narragansetts, Mohegans, and Montauks from Long Island, helped to extend the Indians' regional network and ensure the persistence and creative adaptation of native customs.[145] The Indian enclave's proprietorship and hard-won autonomy allowed it to build both high boundaries and clearly defined gates within those walls. Immigrants were allowed in the gates by marrying members of the community. Newcomers inside the walls, however, could not be Mashpee proprietors. Only their "mixed" offspring, raised within and socialized by the community, were recognized by other Mashpees as fully "Indian" and entitled to claim communal resources. Nearly identical ethnic boundaries emerged at about the same time in the Indian enclaves on Martha's Vineyard.[146]

Gender was embedded in the ethnic boundaries created by Indian villages with communal landholding, for only those born into the community could directly claim its resources — and as Indian women increasingly married African American men, they controlled that gate. Mashpee highlighted the gulf between Indian and English gender roles. When the village created its proprietorship in the 1720s, not only did it incorporate traditional landholding practices, but allowed women to be proprietors and therefore vote on community concerns and claim land in a manner contrary to English law. With the death of many Indian men in the midcentury colonial wars and the increasing number of "foreign" husbands, women must have become the majority of proprietors in Mashpee — a fascinating echo of how people in the region managed their land before colonization. While the landholding patterns in other villages such as Gay Head and Chappaquiddick are poorly documented, the power held by Mashpee women could not have been unique.

Anglo-American observers, as one might expect, did not see the ability of Indians to manage the influx of newcomers. Gideon Hawley complained that the Mashpees' fishing was "being ruined" by the "Negroes mulatoes and poor whites who have crowded upon this territory," and told a friend that the immigrants were "depriving the legal or natural proprietors of this plantation of their birth right."[147] He warned Governor John Hancock that the Indians would, for a little rum, trade their lands to "poor whites, who will come and settle around them and intermix with them; but whose posterity in the issue will be, but little above savages."[148] Hawley was proved wrong, for intermarriage did not weaken the Indian community. In fact, some non-Indian immigrants strove to be more "native" than those born in Mashpee. A visitor in 1808 found that although "almost every one of the Indians had a wooden house," an English sailor who had married a Mashpee woman and was one of the wealthier members of the community insisted on living in a wigwam.[149]

The ability of the Mashpee community to socialize the large number of newcomers was manifest in the gradual evolution of the enclave's culture. As noted above, the community maintained many traditions even as families adopted bits of New England's material culture. Wigwams remained a prominent part of the Mashpee landscape at the end of the eighteenth century, yet many of these aboriginal homes contained brick fireplaces and furniture "generally of the same description with that of poorer whites."[150] Mashpee farmers stubbornly refused to manure their soil despite the advice of white reformers.[151] After Indian crafts became a reliable source of income, the rising output of traditional baskets and mats took on new patterns and colors in response to changes in materials and market demands. Surviving Mashpee stories show that "ancient shamanistic powers such as transformation, magical flight, control of spirits, herbal cures, and herbal witchcraft lived uninterrupted beneath the surface of acculturated forms."[152] The Mashpee boundary was a porous one, but the natives' demographic and social dominance safeguarded the group's land, customs, and integrity.

When Gideon Hawley tried to anglicize the Mashpees during the Revolution, their anger exposed the Indian core in the Christian congregation. Until Solomon Briant's death in 1774, at the age of eighty (followed one day later by his wife), he preached only in Wampanoag, keeping the language dominant in the enclave.[153] But when Hawley gained the pulpit, he proclaimed the intention to preach only in English, and strove to replace native leaders with "men of the first character."[154] The new minister's efforts to reform the community alienated his congregation. Two years after Briant's death, Hawley reported that "alas the spirit of religion is low among us," and a decade later all but a few Mashpees formally announced their estrangement from the orthodox minister by ordaining John Freeman, an Indian Baptist preacher, at least in part because of his "preaching up the doctrines of liberty and equality."[155]

The politics of religion and ethnic identity boiled over in Mashpee. As the Indians signaled their independence by forming a Baptist congregation,

Hawley persuaded the General Court to take away the enclave's autonomy, arguing that only his firm hand could stop disruptive intermarriages and religious dissent among the Indians.[156] Leaders of surrounding towns also voiced their fears that without Hawley's control Mashpee "would soon be a Receptacle of Thieves, vagabonds & Robbers and become a nusance to the neighboring Towns & villages — especially if men of no religious principles ["Deists, or infidels" was crossed out] who make it their business to ridicule the Scriptures & the Christian religion should be permitted to have the managing of their interests & concerns."[157] The legislature responded in 1789 by reinstituting the guardianship system abolished twenty-five years earlier, and appointing a five-member board of overseers with Hawley at its head.[158] But the political, ethnic, and religious battles continued long after Hawley's death in 1807, until Mashpee regained its autonomy in 1834.[159]

The similarities in Hassanamisco and Mashpee membership, despite the enclaves' radically different circumstances, demonstrate how the emerging New England Indian identity included a set of values and attributes with three focal points: family, place, and behavior. Those claiming membership in the community were judged by where they lived, by the origins of their parents, and by whether their conduct met with the community's social standards. A strikingly similar pattern exists among the modern Lumbees of North Carolina. Descendants of Cherokees, Cheraws, and other southeastern natives, the Lumbees have persisted as an Indian group apart from their Anglo- and African American neighbors despite their lack of traditionally "Indian" customs. The Lumbees accept intermarriage, particularly if the newcomer fits into the community, yet any suggestion of "mixed-bloodedness, such as 'mulatto' or 'half-breed' or 'mestizo' . . . is viewed by Indians as unacceptable and insulting." While outsiders, particularly whites, are baffled by what makes a Lumbee, the ethnic boundaries are clear to those inside the community. "It is the way of doing and being that is 'Indian,' not what is done or the blood quantum of the doer." Conduct rather than appearance creates the Lumbee "blueprint": pride, "uppityness," cohesiveness, "talking Indian" (dialect), and keeping one's word. Owning land in Robeson County, the center of Lumbee population, is also a critical ethnic marker.[160]

Indians developed an ethnic community in response to their unfortunate dispersion and the overwhelming increase of intermarriage between native women and African American men. Social and cultural markers varied slightly between groups, but generally set high boundaries and granted women a large measure of power in order to defend an enclave's resources and ensure its survival. They barred "foreigners" from claiming community land, but gave full status to the children of "mixed" offspring and to immigrants from other Indian enclaves. A Gay Head leader, Zaccheus Howwoswee, told a state official in the mid-nineteenth century that "wishing our voters to be the native indians of the soil not foreigner[s] you will understand what I mean by native Indian of the soil if [they] come from another indian settlement we do not call them foreigners."[161] While the walls against outsiders were less rigid in the eighteenth century, Indians in southern New England created by the time of the Revolution an expansive community with ethnic instead of geographic, political, or racial boundaries. The ultimate irony, of course, is that by the nineteenth century the offspring of mixed marriages (probably including Howwoswee) were those who reinforced Indian ethnic boundary markers.

)(

Minority groups often feel the need, as their members become significantly acculturated, to build ethnic distinctions between themselves and the dominant society. Indian enclaves in eighteenth-century eastern Massachusetts thus developed their cultural boundaries as they developed closer ties to the regional economy and material culture. While Indian men feared that many of their women (like William Brown's grandmother) married "foreigners" to "change [their] mode of living . . . [and gain] comfortable homes," native men also increasingly built cabins and bought English goods.[162] But because Indians were able to maintain (or create) a traditional core in their culture, young men preferred to work as whalers, emulating the ancestral male duties of hunting, fishing, and fighting. Women also found aboriginal work roles in the market economy, making and peddling traditional and adapted crafts (baskets, mats, and brooms), selling their skills to heal with herbs, and working as domestics. Indians also worked for different goals than whites or free blacks: not to make fortunes or a new life, but to return to their village with enough to build and furnish a comfortable home, perhaps even to buy farm tools and animals.

The socioeconomic changes were particularly notable in Mashpee, the largest Indian enclave in eastern Massachusetts. The Mashpees developed close ties to the regional economy, perhaps because of the influx of newcomers, or perhaps because the pressure of neighboring whites on their resources, including the degradation of rivers by the construction of mills upstream, caused many to seek a living outside the reserve.[163] At the beginning of the century, Mashpee's leaders could boast that they kept their young men at home, but by midcentury a growing number left for whaling ships. Gideon Hawley noted that maritime work "gets them into a distaste for tilling the ground," and indeed Mashpee men may have moved into the whaling trade in part because the only alternative, given a decline in fishing and hunting on the reserve, was English-style farming with its hated gender roles.[164] And at midcentury the Indians began to complain that, due to English encroachments, they had "no land to plant."[165] Whaling soon affected the enclave's material culture. The trade brought not only new income but also new tastes, as men discovered a wide range of cultures among their fellow sailors and in distant places. Mashpee homes began to fill with colonial furniture and goods, and wood-framed houses quickly outnumbered wigwams.[166]

Whaling was one of the few marketable skills possessed by Indian men, and natives were eagerly courted by ship owners and captains.[167] The seamen's rough egalitarianism offered a refuge for natives against the prejudice and scorn that they faced on land, as a man's strength, ability to endure deprivation, and social skills — virtues encouraged in aboriginal societies — were worth far more than his color, wealth, religious beliefs, or formal education. Indian men found a home in the maritime plebeian culture not only because whaling had strong aboriginal roots, but also because the long voyages and dangerous nature, "a great gamble, a dance with doom," held echoes of hunting and fighting.[168] Anglo-American reformers frequently decried the violent habits and immoral behavior of sailors of all races as well as those who socialized with mariners. By the end of the century, Hawley was complaining that "the long whaling voyages of my Indians injures their morals and when they come home there is little else but drinking whoring fighting etc etc. I generally rejoice with almost all my neighbors when they are gone again."[169]

In the wake of the yellow fever epidemic, Nantucket whaling captains looked to Martha's Vineyard for Indian seamen to replace those from their own island and to supplement white crewmen. Crevecoeur noted in the early 1760s that the Chappaquiddick Indians "often go, like the young [white] men of the Vineyard, to Nantucket and hire themselves for whalemen or fishermen."[170] Another visitor, Englishman Edward Kendall, found that among Gay Head men whaling was

> their favourite employ, to which they give themselves, and to which they are anxiously solicited. Ship-owners come to their cottages, making them offers, and persuading them to accept them, and so rarely is Gay Head

visited for any other purpose, that this was supposed, at the light-house to be my errand. This business of inviting the Indians is a sort of crimping, in which liquor, goods and fair words are plied, till the Indian gets into debt, and gives his consent. . . . On the one hand, great advantages are taken of his folly, his credulity, and his ignorance; on the other, he torments the ship or share-owner with his indecision and demands.[171]

The whaling trade caused demographic, social, and economic instability in Indian enclaves as large numbers of men spent long periods far from home. The demographic instability is highlighted by Chappaquiddick numbers: in 1761, sixty-five Indians lived on the islet "besides some not residing there," but only three years later twenty-one more natives were reported in the census.[172] In 1807, Kendall found only fifteen Gay Head men and boys farming, "the rest being at sea, in the fisheries."[173] Alcohol and credit added to the social and economic problems of native families and communities. The Englishman noted that the Gay Head whalemen's "obstinate addiction to spiritous liquors makes their case still worse; hence, an Indian, that goes to sea, is ruined, and his family is ruined with him."[174] Two white guardians reported that the Chappaquiddick Indians

are the most improvident beings. It is not uncommon for them to go to Nantucket to engage on a whaling voiage around Cape Horn sell half their voiage profit for half its probable value to furnish themselves with cloathing, then a Quarter for money to spend in Liquor, & then an eighth to another so on that when they return from the voiage they have not a cent to receive & are often in Debt. Tho' their voiage amounted to the sum of Three or Four, or Five Hundred Dollars. Their Families [as a result] suffering for the necessaries of Life.[175]

A group of Christiantown Indians similarly complained that their men were "sent [on] Long voiages to Sea by those who practice in a more soft manner that of Kidnaping who when they Return with ever so great success they are still In debt & have nothing to Receive and their wives & Children are in a great part Supported by those of the town who are Left behind."[176]

Indian women also found their world changed by closer connections to the regional economy. Their autonomy and power increased with the men's maritime labor. Gideon Hawley remonstrated about the Mashpee women who "in many instances are in fornication, adultery etc. more vicious than the males. They frequently tempt our young whalemen upon their return from their long voyages. And when their husbands are gone they have been found with child by a man in their absence."[177] Hawley also complained that "many of our young females go to Boston for months together . . . to the injury of their morals."[178] Of course, since missionaries often worried that Indians would be corrupted by "white trash," Hawley may have been outraged that Mashpee women were acting as independently as "common" white women. And issues of sexuality aside, women in New England maritime communities often possessed a high degree of socioeconomic independence.[179] On the other hand, if native women *were* more aggressive than white women, did their behavior reflect aboriginal morals? Unfortunately, we lack comprehensive information on native societies before the English came along to change their ways.

Indian women, like their men, did adapt certain aboriginal gender roles to the regional market economy, as they found an increasing demand for the crafts that their mothers and grandmothers had taught them as children. In 1764, Abigail Moheag, a sixty-four-year-old Natick widow, told the General Court that she had been in the business for many years of making "Brooms Baskets and horse Collars," and had been fairly successful at supporting herself.[180] At this time, the few remaining Middleborough Indians "obtained a meagre subsistence by the sale of brooms and baskets which they manufactured."[181] The trade involved weaving brooms, baskets, and mats during the winter, then strapping them to one's back and walking from village to village, selling the goods door to door. It entailed long days and miles of travel regardless of weather, without the money or social standing to obtain decent food or lodging. One native basket maker and seller, Anne Wampy, a Pequot from southern Connecticut, was later described by a white man who knew her when he was a boy.

> When she started from her home she carried upon her shoulders a bundle of baskets so large as almost to hide her from view. In the bundle would be baskets varying in size from a half-pint up to five or six quarts, some made of very fine splints, some of coarse, and many skillfully ornamented in various colors. Her baskets were so good that she would find customers at almost every house. And after traveling a dozen or twenty miles and spending two or three days in doing it her load would be all gone. Then she would start on her homeward journey, and, sad to relate, before she had reached her home a large part of what she had received for her baskets would have been expended on strong drink.[182]

The broom and basket trade, harsh as it was, created another incentive to develop or strengthen ties with distant families and enclaves, to spin new webs of communities that cut across old divisions between villages and tribes. Few basket and broom makers were able to sell their goods in so short a time, so connections between native enclaves and families in the region could literally be lifesaving measures and were carefully cultivated.

Some Indian women also earned reputations for their medical skill among whites as well as natives. Hannah Dexter became well-known around Natick "as a doctress, well-skilled in administering medicinal roots and herbs."[183] Rebecca Davis of Punkapoag "gained some money by the sale of a salve, which she prepared from herbs according to the prescription of some ancient medicine-man."[184] The only detailed state census of Indians, taken in the middle of the nineteenth century, shows two female and one male "Indian Doctor": Amey Robinson or Freeman of Dudley, Charlotte White of Dartmouth, and William Perry of Fall River (Troy).[185] Not all was revealed by that survey, for no occupation was listed for doctor Rebecca Davis. While some Indian doctors were young men, such as William Perry, and Peter Brand of Natick, older women seemed to gain special respect for their healing skills; at the time of the survey, Robinson was fifty-six years old, White was eighty-four, and Davis was seventy-one. During this period, folk medicine was an effective and accepted remedy and, like black women in the south, Indians were perceived as having special skills and knowledge of local herbs. The adaptive nature of culture is highlighted by two ironies: these women were of "mixed" ancestry, and the ecology of the region had changed so dramatically since colonization that many of the "Indian" herbal cures must have been English or African rather than native.

Weaving was another native skill transformed by closer ties to the dominant economy. Aboriginal women had sewn clothing from plants and animal hides, and after colonization their granddaughters learned to weave cloth. That skill became marketable when an infant textile industry emerged in southern New England before the Revolution, in the form of a "putting out" system organized by entrepreneurs who, through store-keepers, distributed raw materials to households and gave credit for the finished product. But women who turned wool and cotton into cloth needed more expensive tools than did Indian basket and broom makers. They and their families also needed reputations as sober, upright citizens who were good credit risks — hardly the reputation of Indians in eighteenth century Massachusetts. Yet at least two Natick women did work as weavers. Mary Paugenet (Poignet) reportedly owned a loom, various weaver's tools, and large amounts of wool when she died in 1757.[186] Esther Sooduck, who died twenty years later, was described as a weaver by those administering her estate; she owned two spinning wheels and two looms in addition to furniture, pewter, flatware, spectacles, and two Bibles. Sooduck's income must have been barely enough to survive on, however, for her house was described as "at best but a mere shelter," and the thirty acres on which it lay was "wholly unfit."[187]

An Indian woman's basic needs might be met by weaving and selling baskets, brooms, or cloth. The slightest extra cost or unforeseen problem, however, such as an extended illness, could force her to seek the assistance of relatives or friends. An increasing number of Indians in Massachusetts, however, particularly the elderly women in Natick, had no children or relatives near their homes. They were therefore forced to sell their land or, if they lacked land, to depend on the charity of their neighbors. Abigail Moheag made a decent living from her wigwam until 1762 when she was "laid low" by a "long fever." Without children, and only a "remote cousen" to claim as a relative, she lacked the necessary safety net of relations upon which laborers and farmers relied in times of need. As a result, she ran up huge debts to the strangers who nursed her.[188]

At least one Indian community seemed to adapt well to the region's capitalist economy. Gay Head was renowned for its outstanding crops of corn, rye, oats, and potatoes, and the community raised large herds of livestock, including cows, sheep, hogs, and, most notably, horses. The Indians (or their guardians) rented out surplus pasture to whites, who came with their cattle from throughout the Vineyard and even from the mainland.[189] But the Gay Headers continued to hold much of their reserve in common, like their cousins in Mashpee and elsewhere on the Vineyard.

> Any native could, at any time, appropriate to his own use such portion of the unimproved common land, as he wished, and, as soon as he enclosed it, with a fence, of however frail structure, it belonged to him and his heirs forever. . . . the most singular and most creditable fact, in connection with this, is, that, while one proprietor has but half an acre, and another has over a hundred acres, there is no heart-burning, no feeling that the latter has more than his share.[190]

The market for Gay Head resources created conflict, however, within the Indian community, as in Christiantown two decades earlier. In 1767, about a third of Gay Head's adults complained to the General Court about the actions of some of their community. A large cedar fence purchased for the community "is taken away from us and kept by some among us and we Denyd any part thereof." Even worse, "some among us (who are Designing men) take in so many Creatures" from English cattlemen, that there was no land left for the others to lease. As a result, "we cannot hire our Rights out and are Deprived altogether of our Interest the Profits of the whole neck almost being taken by a few Dishonest persons." These petitioners asked for a guardian to help their "poor and Ignorant" community. The veracity of their petition, however, is cast into doubt by the General Court's inaction, for normally the legislature would leap at the chance to intervene and bring order to an Indian enclave.[191]

)(

By the end of the colonial period, the descendants of the original inhabitants of eastern Massachusetts had developed a new sense of themselves and their community, as demographic, economic, and social pressures reshaped old ties and kinship loyalties into a modern ethnic identity. Families and individuals were no longer part of the bear or beaver clans, nor members of the Nipmuc, Massachusett, or Wampanoag tribes. The old boundaries were shattered by Anglo-American political and economic dominance and dissolved by intermarriage and market forces. A new pan-Indian identity emerged, distinct from notions of race, political allegiances, or even residence. Ironically, the dominant pattern of intermarriage meant that matrilineal descent replaced bilateral or patrilineal descent as the primary route of Indian ancestry. A regional Indian ethnic network emerged by the Revolution, largely invisible to whites, as scattered families and communities came together through marriages with outsiders, or migrated to obtain work, sell goods, or find better places to live. The surviving native enclaves acknowledged their responsibilities as centers for this new network. While population decline and vanishing enclaves seemed to point to the doom of natives in Massachusetts, Indians were able to build a new community that would ensure their survival.

"Collecting the scattered remains"

In 1780, the French visitor to the United States, J. Hector St. John de Crevecoeur, wrote that the Indian survivors of King Philip's War

> retired to their ancient villages, collecting the scattered remains of nations once populous, and in their grant of lands reserved to themselves and posterity certain portions which lay contiguous to them. There forgetting their ancient manners, they dwelt in peace; in a few years, their territories were surrounded by the improvements of the Europeans,

in consequence of which they grew lazy, inactive, unwilling, and unapt to imitate or to follow any of our trades, and in a few generations either totally perished or else came over to the Vineyard, or to [Nantucket], to reunite themselves with such societies of their countrymen as would receive them.[1]

Crevecoeur's ethnocentric view of the Indians' fate represents certain truths. After the shattering conflict, many of the Indians imprisoned on Deer Island, and some of those who had fled the region during the war, "retired to their ancient villages" where they "collected the scattered remains" of their clans, tribes, and Christian networks. Most of the surviving villages maintained "lands reserved to themselves," but then lost those lands and seemed to disappear after being "surrounded by the improvements of the Europeans." Some from the "perished" enclaves moved to the larger, surviving villages "to reunite themselves with such societies of their countrymen as would receive them," while others maintained social and kinship connections as they lived in colonial towns or cities. In this manner, between King Philip's War and the American Revolution, Indians in eastern Massachusetts united in a new ethnic community. While the first half century of English colonization forced many alterations in native life, even more dramatic modifications came in the subsequent century as English settlers engulfed the Indian enclaves. By 1775, demographic decline, migration between enclaves, and intermarriage with African Americans completely scrambled old boundaries. Indian enclaves adapted to the Bay Colony's geographic, demographic, and economic expansion while maintaining a few critical social and cultural boundaries. Not all were successful, of course: many groups were too small, easily devastated by disease and war, or allowed too much of the dominant culture and too many settlers to penetrate their boundaries. But others survived by gradually incorporating pieces of Anglo-American culture, creating occasionally useful links with provincial officials, assimilating the offspring of intermarriages, and gaining needed income and regional links by sending individuals to labor outside the enclave.

As "outsiders" in the English colony, Indians in Massachusetts did not shape the American Revolution; they did not serve on town committees of correspondence or committees of safety, nor did they represent their villages in the provincial congress. But Indians did participate in the Revolution, and saw their own struggles reflected in the war. Crispus Attucks, of course, was one of the incipient rebellion's first martyrs, and large numbers of

Indian men went to fight for independence. Many Mashpee women became widows during the war, and in fact part of the hostility between Gideon Hawley and his Mashpee congregation came from his loyalist leanings. Those who suffered through the war hoped that the republic's "liberty and social happiness" would bring better times.

The Indians' deep involvement in the Revolution can be glimpsed in the Mashpees' efforts to regain the autonomy lost in 1789. Their protests adopted the language of republican ideology, charging that the state government, by reinstating the guardianship system over their community, had

> imposed Restraints on the Inhabitants, which were ever considered by them as an impingment of that freedom to which as men they were justly entitled. At the Commencement of the late Revolution, when a high sense of civil liberty, and the oppressive policy of an arbitrary Court roused the Citizens of America to noble and patriotic exertions in defence of their freedom, we anticipated the time when a liberal and enlightened spirit of philanthropy should extend its views and its influence to the increase of liberty and social happiness among all ranks and classes of mankind. We supposed a just estimate of the rights of man would teach them the value of those privileges of which were deprived, and that their own sufferings would naturally lead them to respect and relieve ours.[2]

The Mashpees wielded the Declaration of Independence ("all men are created equal") and Article I of the Bill of Rights — but to no avail. Only their resort to armed force in 1834 would gain the desired autonomy.

Indian communities survived the Revolution in three forms: autonomous villages with reserved lands, enclaves within English towns, and scattered households. First, Mashpee and the other large coastal Indian communities, such as Christiantown, Chappaquiddick, Gay Head, and Herring Pond, barred white settlers from their reserves and continued to hold their lands in common. Their lands were protected by the state law that barred its sale to outsiders. Their relative isolation, often-abundant resources, sizable populations, and location along the coast gave these enclaves considerable advantages in the struggle to survive. Their white neighbors continued to trespass and to poach the wood, fish, and wildlife that was scarce outside the Indian reserves, and so, as in the eighteenth century, Indian groups frequently sought and occasionally received the General Court's assistance. Gradually, most of these enclaves formalized previously amorphous land holding in severalty and marketed resources found on the reserves. At the same time, the communities' lands retained a critical, even sacred significance, as their members furiously objected to efforts by white guardians to meet debts by selling reserved land, and refused to approve legal changes that would allow individuals to sell land to whites.[3]

Second, a number of Indian groups within English towns lacked legal protection for their lands, and would seemingly disappear between 1790 and 1825. Yet the Teticut-Assawompsett, Indiantown, and Potawaumacut descendants, identities, and land claims remained painfully alive. These enclaves were particularly vulnerable to the continuing pressure of white settlers. Yarmouth whites openly flouted the terms of the town's 1713 agreement establishing Indiantown. The Indians finally complained to the legislature in 1820 that they were "wholey distitute of land" and "very apprst [oppressed] and deprest" — for town officials prosecuted natives who tried to exercise their traditional right to cut wood in the town.[4] Similarly, in 1799 Ralph Micah told the General Court that he was the only man left in Potawaumacut, was quite elderly, and could no longer care for the many women and fatherless children in the community nor guard the wood on their land from white poachers.[5] Twenty years later the towns of Harwich, Orleans, and Brewster asked to sell Potawaumacut lands that remained within their borders, as the Indians were "nearly Extinct . . . they are dead or removed away to other parts of the Commonwealth and that of late, there has been several returned to said Towns as Town Paupers . . . and we Expect Similar cases will Occur" in the future.[6] These communities seemed on their deathbeds, yet families and individuals frequently and mysteriously reappeared.

Third, by 1780, a few Indian communities existed as loose networks of families living near their former reserves or in neighborhoods of the growing cities. They lacked communal land but retained common accounts from the sale of all or much of their land during the previous century. Members of the Natick, Hassanamisco, and Punkapoag communities could draw funds from the accounts when necessary for medical bills or other needs. Their moneys were often invested, sometimes quite badly, by state-appointed guardians in an effort to sustain the accounts. Over several generations these families and their connections faded into the often undifferentiated sea of "people of color." Some lived on the outskirts of towns, rarely seen or acknowledged, seeking work or selling traditional crafts wherever possible. By the middle of the century, only one Hassanamisco family remained in Grafton, most had lived for generations in other towns, and some were recorded (perhaps by their own preference) as "colored" rather than "Indian."[7] When a family formed by generations of intermarriages left an

Indian enclave, and little remained of the lands that had helped cement the community, the way was open for parents and their children to abandon their Indian ties. They lacked the support of a cohesive, settled community, and were hard put to survive more than one or two generations.

Regardless of the circumstances of their group, Indians in Massachusetts survived by balancing their often-competing needs for community and a livelihood in the changing economy. Most found themselves "forced to go from place to place to git our living." Men living along the coast worked as mariners, primarily whaling; others tried to find work as laborers near their homes, but could be forced to travel long distances. In some enclaves, men usually went to sea until they earned enough to buy the animals and tools necessary to farm at home. Only a few worked as skilled laborers, and, like freed African Americans, Indians were barred from the new factories. Women worked in the fields, sold crafts, or worked as domestics in nearby towns or in Boston or New Bedford, often finding mates among the increasing African-American urban population. Both men and women frequently left the reserves, often for years at a stretch, driven by social or economic needs, making the boundary between "wandering" and "settled" Indians a porous one.

Indian groups remained outside the social and political mainstream of the Commonwealth. Indians were not taxed and could not vote; the legislature appointed guardians to control their finances and to encourage their "reform." While their guardians occasionally proved annoying, Indians generally saw their unique legal status as an important protection for their land and resources. Ironically, the broader reform movements imbedded in or emerging from the Second Great Awakening, particularly temperance and abolitionism, reshaped the Indians' struggle to endure during the second quarter of the nineteenth century. At critical moments Indians were able to find political allies; more generally, romanticism became a potent force that Indian groups could manipulate to their advantage.

In the wake of the Civil War and the Fourteenth Amendment, the rhetoric of equal rights for all, which the Mashpees and some other Indian groups had earlier embraced, became a tool to subvert the surviving native communities. In 1870, the Commonwealth of Massachusetts eliminated the legal distinctions that had served to protect Indians reserves, giving individuals the vote and removing all restrictions on the sale of their lands. Several Indian communities quickly disappeared; only Mashpee and Gay Head survived the century relatively intact. Like many aspects of Indian-white relations in Massachusetts, this foreshadowed national policy.

Seventeen years later, Congress moved to detribalize the "conquered" tribes of the Trans-Mississippi West. Reformers from New England shaped and advocated the policy to assimilate the "savages," and the law was named for its chief sponsor, Senator Henry L. Dawes of Massachusetts.

NOTES

INTRODUCTION

1. Francis Jennings, *The Invasion of America: Indians, Colonialism, and the Cant of Conquest* (Chapel Hill: University of North Carolina Press, 1975), 325.

2. *The Compact Edition of the Oxford English Dictionary*, 2 vols. (New York: Oxford University Press, 1971).

3. James Merrell, *The Indians' New World: Catawbas and Their Neighbors from European Contact through the Era of Removal* (Chapel Hill: University of North Carolina Press, 1989); Helen C. Rountree, *Pocahontas's People: The Powhaten Indians of Virginia Through Four Centuries* (Norman: University of Oklahoma Press, 1990); Daniel Usner, *Indians, Settlers, and Slaves in a Frontier Exchange Economy: The Lower Mississippi Valley Before 1783* (Chapel Hill: University of North Carolina Press, 1992).

"GOTTEN OUR LAND"

1. Elsie Brenner, "Sociopolitical Implications of Mortuary Ritual Remains in Seventeenth-Century Native Southern New England," in *The Recovery of Meaning: Historical Archeology in the Eastern United States*, ed. Mark P. Leone and Parker B. Potter Jr. (Washington DC: Smithsonian Institution, 1988), 147–81.

2. William Cronon, *Changes in the Land: Indians, Colonists, and the Ecology of New England* (New York: Hill and Wang, 1983), 90.

3. Neal Salisbury, *Manitou and Providence: Indians, Europeans, and the Making of New England, 1500–1643* (New York: Oxford University Press, 1982), 225.

4. James Axtell, *The European and the Indian: Essays in the Ethnohistory of Colonial North America* (New York: Oxford University Press, 1981), 251–52, 266–70.

5. Nathaniel Shurtleff, *Records of the Governor and Company of the Massachusetts Bay in New England*, 5 vols. (Boston: 1853–54), 2:176–77, 178.

6. Harold von Lonkhuyzen, "A Reappraisal of the Praying Indians: Acculturation, Conversion, and Identity at Natick, Massachusetts, 1646–1730," *New England Quarterly* 63 (1990): 400–404.

7. Neal Salisbury, "Red Puritans: The 'Praying Indians' of Massachusetts Bay and John Eliot," *William and Mary Quarterly* 3d ser., 31 (January 1974): 32–33.

8. Daniel Gookin, "Historical Collections of the Indians in New England," MHSC, 1st ser., 1 (1792), 166, 184.

9. Gookin, "Historical Collections," 184–85.

10. Gookin, "Historical Collections," 186–87.

11. Gookin, "Historical Collections," 185–93.

12. Gookin, "Historical Collections," 191–92.

13. John Martin, *Profits in the Wilderness: Entrepreneurship and the Founding of New England Towns in the Seventeenth Century* (Chapel Hill: University of North Carolina Press, 1992), 27–28.

14. Elizabeth A. Little, "Indian Politics on Nantucket," in *Papers of the Thirteenth Algonquian Conference*, ed. William Cowan (Ottawa: Carleton University, 1982), 285–96.

15. Edward Byers, *The Nations of Nantucket: Society and Politics in an Early American Commercial Center, 1660–1820* (Boston: Northeastern University Press, 1986), chap. 1 and 2.

16. Gookin, "Historical Collections," 196–200.

17. Virginia DeJohn Anderson, "King Philip's Herds: Indians, Colonists, and the Problem of Livestock in Early New England," *William and Mary Quarterly*, 3d ser., 51 (1994): 601–24.

18. Daniel Gookin, "An Historical Account of the Doings and Sufferings of the Christian Indians in New England, In the Years 1675, 1676, 1677," American Antiquarian Society *Transactions and Collections* 20 (1836): 450–51, 453, 456–67, 475.

19. Gookin, "Doings and Sufferings," 463–65, 471, 473–74, 480–85, 490–92.

20. Gookin, "Doings and Sufferings," 474, 485, 495–97.

21. "Leift Lion Gardener His Relation of the Pequot Warres," MHSC, 3d ser., 3 (1833), 154–55.

"THEIR PROUD & SURLY BEHAVIOR"

1. MA 30:261a.

2. Gookin, "Doings and Sufferings," 517–19, 532.

3. Gookin, "Doings and Sufferings," 519–20.

4. H. Halsey Thomas, ed., *The Diary of Samuel Sewall, 1674–1729*, 2 vols. (New York: Farrar, Straus and Giroux, 1973), 1:47.

5. Gookin, "Doings and Sufferings," 456.

6. Gookin, "Doings and Sufferings," 520–21, 533.

7. Kevin McBride and Mary Soulsby, "The Native Americans," in *Heritage and Horizons: Woodstock Remembers 300 Years* (Woodstock CT: n.p., 1986), 18.

8. William Lincoln and C. C. Baldwin, eds., *The Worcester Magazine and Historical Journal*, 2 vols. (Worcester: Charles Griffin, 1826), 2:148.

9. Gookin, "Doings and Sufferings," 533.

10. Joseph Willard, "Indian Children Put to Service, 1676," NEHGS *Register*, 8 (1854), 270–73.

11. Thomas, *Diary of Samuel Sewall*, 2:659, 683–84, 728, 778.

12. MA 30: 223a, 228, 229, 230a, 231–32, 234, 236b, 239, 239a, 244.

13. MA 1:266.

14. Yasu Kawashima, "Legal Origins of the Indian Reservation in Colonial Massachusetts," *American Journal of Legal History*, 13 (1969): 44.

15. MA 30:243, 261.

16. Thomas, *Diary of Samuel Sewall*, 1:90, 162.

17. Russell Thornton, *American Indian Holocaust and Survival* (Norman: University of Oklahoma Press, 1987), 44, 45, 54, 66.

18. Cotton Mather, *India Christiana* (Boston, 1721), 41, 91–92.

19. Gookin, "Historical Collections," MHSC, 1st ser. 1, 1 (1792), 181, 195.

20. Grindal Rawson and Samuel Danforth, "Account of an Indian Visitation, A.D. 1698," MHSC, 1st ser., 10 (1809), 134; MA 30:279a, 265.

21. Gookin, "Historical Collections," 184; Gookin, "Doings and Sufferings," 532.

22. MA 31:38; Commissioners' Minutes, 11 October 1708, SPG, ms. 7953.

23. MA 31:24; MA 30:275a; Gookin, "Historical Collections," 166, 184.

24. MA 30:247, 260a, 262a; John Eliot, "Dying Speeches & Counsels of such Indians as dyed in the Lord" (Cambridge, 1685), 4; Gookin, "Historical Collections," 190.

25. Gookin, "Historical Collections," 184–93; MCD 9:27–29, 374–75, 1096; MCD 10:557.

26. MA 30:488–89.

27. Kathleen Bragdon, "Social History and Native Texts" (paper presented at the annual meeting of the American Society for Ethnohistory, Oakland CA, Nov. 1987; cited with permission).

28. MA 30:305.

29. Gookin, "Historical Collections," 190.

30. Nathaniel Shurtleff, *Records of the Governor*, 5:531, 532–33.

31. Kathleen Bragdon, " 'Another Tongue Brought In': An Ethnohistorical Study of Native Writings in Massachusett" (Ph.D. diss., Brown University, 1981), 150–51.

32. John Dunton, *Letters Written From New-England, A.D. 1686* (Boston: The Prince Society, 1867), 217.

33. MA 30:280, 285–86, 287.

34. MA 30:261a, 261.

35. MA 30:276.

36. Commissioners' Minutes, 9 Aug. 1795, SPG, ms. 7953.

37. John Eliot to Robert Boyle, 22 April 1684, MHSC, 1st ser., 3 (1794), 185.

38. William Kellaway, *The New England Company, 1649–1776; Missionary Society to the American Indians* (New York: Barnes and Noble, 1962), 120.

39. Samuel Sewall, Boston, to William Ashurst, London, 1 Nov. 1716, SPG, ms 7955, letter 41.

40. Cotton Mather, *Magnalia Christi Americana, or, the Ecclesiastical History of New England,* 2 vols., (Hartford, 1852; reprint ed., New York, 1967), 2:439.

41. Rawson and Danforth, "Indian Visitation," 41.

42. Quoted in Axtell, *Invasion Within,* 240.

43. MA 30:503.

44. MA 30:502, 503, 504.

45. Adam Winthrop, Boston, to Joseph Williams, London, 10 Nov. 1712, SPG, ms. 7955, letter 19a.

46. Kellaway, *New England Company,* 236–37.

47. MA 30:493; MA 31:126–27.

48. Eliot to Boyle, 185.

49. Von Lonkhuyzen, "A Reappraisal of the Praying Indians," 409.

50. Jean O'Brien, "Community Dynamics in the Indian-English Town of Natick, Massachusetts" (Ph.D. diss., University of Chicago, 1990), 175.

51. MA 30:261a.

52. MA 30:261a.

53. Testimony of Joseph Foster of Billerica, Piambow, and Thomas Tray, Job: Indian v. Cyprian Stevens, theft of beaver skins, Middlesex County Court of Common Pleas, folio 96, group 4.

54. Dunton, *Letters Written From New-England,* 217–18.

55. MA 31:345–58.

56. Thomas, *Diary of Samuel Sewall,* 1:253–54.

57. MA 30:315a.

58. "In the Matter of the Dudley Indians, Brief, Before the House Judiciary Committee of Massachusetts," circ. 1890, photocopy, Nipmuc Tribal Acknowledgement Project, Worcester.

59. MA 30:358–59, 368.

60. Ann Plane, "Awasunkes, the 'Squaw Sachem' of Saconet" (paper presented at the annual meeting of the 1994 American Historical Association, San Francisco, 1994; cited with permission).

61. MCD 9:374–76; MCD 10:557.

62. MA 30:315a.

63. MA 30:314, 314a; *AR* 1703–1704, Ch. 121.

64. MA 30:247.

65. MA 30:307a.

66. MA 30:361, 361a.

67. MA 30:276, 277a.

68. MA 30:279b.

69. MA 30:457.

70. MA 30:457.

71. MA 30:240, 288, 291, 299; MA 113:252, 260–62, 304–305; Charles Hudson, *History of the Town of Marlborough* (Boston: T. R. Martin & Son, 1862), 92–95.

72. Job: Indian v. Cyprian Stevens; testimony of Joseph Moor and Thomas Carter of Sudbury, Natick Indians v. claims of Ensign John Grout, Middlesex County Court of Common Pleas, folio 106 group 2.

73. MA 30:257–57a.

74. MA 30:258.

75. MA 30:260a.

76. MA 30:259a.

77. Thomas Doughton, "In the Matter of John Wampas," typescript, Nipmuc Tribal Acknowledgement Project.

78. MA 30:263–64.

79. MA 30:262a, 263–64; Dennis A. Connole, "Land Occupied by the Nipmuck Indians of Central New England, 1600–1700," *Bulletin of the Massachusetts Archaeological Society* 38 (1976): 14–20.

80. MA 30:263–65.

81. MA 30:263–64.

82. MA 30:276a.

83. Shurtleff, ed., *Records of the Governor* 5:442.

84. Doughton, "In the Matter of John Wampas."

85. John F. Martin, *Profits in the Wilderness*, 95; AR 1716, Ch. 33, 16 June 1716; AR 1718, Ch. 160, 14 Feb. 1718, Ch. 48, 1 July 1718.

86. James Thompson, *A Memorial of the One Hundredth Anniversary of the Incorporation of the Town of Barre, June 17, 1874* (Cambridge: John Wilson and Son, 1875), 37.

87. Martin, *Profits in the Wilderness*, 88–99, 267.

88. Samuel Eliot Morison, *Harvard College in the Seventeenth Century*, 2 vols. (Cambridge: Harvard University Press, 1936), 1:340–60; Thomas, *Diary of Samuel Sewall*, 1:394. Thus the building constructed of the bricks from the Indian College was named for the man who, with Joseph Dudley, profited from his negotiations to buy Nipmuc lands.

89. Rawson and Danforth, "Account of an Indian Visitation," 129–34.

"ENCOURAGED TO A MORE NEIGHBOURLY, AND FIXED HABITATION"

1. Commissioners' Minutes, April 1700, SPG, ms. 7953.

2. Gookin, "Historical Collections," MHSC, 1st ser., 1 (1792), 200.

3. Joseph Hinckley, "Letter to William Stoughton and Joseph Dudley [2 April

1685]," MHSC, 4th ser., 5 (1861), 133; Rawson and Danforth, "Indian Visitation," MHSC, 1st ser., 10 (1809), 133–34.

4. Henry W. Litchfield, *Ancient Landmarks of Pembroke* (Pembroke: George Edward Lewis, 1909), 65. The legend combines early seventeenth-century epidemics; the "triumph" of Christianity; large-scale movement out of Mattakeesitt, either between 1685 and 1700 and/or earlier; and the "last" Pembroke sachem, Patience Keurp, who was born about 1700 and died in 1788.

5. Ebenezer W. Pierce, *Indian History, Biography, and Genealogy: Pertaining to the Good Sachem Massasoit of the Wampanoag Tribe and His Descendants* (North Abington, MA: Zerviah Gould Mitchell, 1878), 213–14.

6. Thomas Weston, *History of the Town of Middleboro Massachusetts* (Boston: Houghton, Mifflin and Company, 1906), 12.

7. Samuel Sewall to William Ashhurst, 21 May 1728, SPG, ms. 7955/2, letter 81.

8. MA 30:478; MA 31:15–15a, 45, 73–74.

9. 1861 Senate Report 96, 79–81.

10. Gookin, "Historical Collections," 198–99; Hinckley, "Letter to William Stoughton," 133.

11. Thomas, *Diary of Samuel Sewall* 1:165.

12. Special Collections, Indians, the Pilgrim Society, Plymouth.

13. Rawson and Danforth, "Indian Visitation," 132–33.

14. Jack Campisi, *The Mashpee Indians: Tribe on Trial* (Syracuse: Syracuse University Press, 1991), 78, 80.

15. Gookin, "Historical Collections," 197–98.

16. Hinckley, "Letter to William Stoughton," 133; Cotton Mather, *Magnalia Christi Americana* 2:439.

17. Rawson and Danforth, "Indian Visitation," 132–33.

18. Gideon Hawley, "Biographical and Topographical Anecdotes," MHSC, 1st ser., 3 (1794), 189.

19. Rawson and Danforth, "Indian Visitation," 133; Richard Bourne, Mashpee, to William Ashhurst, London, 15 March 1724, SPG, ms. 7955, letter 74a.

20. Gookin, "Historical Collections," 196–99.

21. Hinckley, "Letter to William Stoughton," 133.

22. Mather, *Magnalia Christi Americana*, 2: 437–38; Rawson and Danforth, "Indian Visitation," 133.

23. MA 30:353.

24. Massachusetts Historical Commission, *Historic and Archaeological Resources of Cape Cod and the Islands* (Boston: State Printers, 1987), 85–86.

25. MA 30:491.

26. AR 1715, Ch. 130, 6 Dec. 1715.

27. Rawson and Danforth, "Indian Visitation," 132.

28. Elizabeth Little, "History of the Town of Miacomet," *Nantucket Algonquian Studies*, 12 (1988).

29. Daniel Vickers, "The First Whalemen of Nantucket," *William and Mary Quarterly*, 3d ser., 40 (1983): 560–83.

30. Matthew Mayhew, *A Brief Narrative of the Success Which the Gospel hath had Among the Indians of Martha's Vineyard* (Boston, 1694), 23–24, 28–29; Rawson and Danforth, "Indian Visitation," 131–32.

31. Rawson and Danforth, "Indian Visitation," 131–32.

32. Experience Mayhew, *Indian Converts, or Some Account of the Lives and Dying Speeches of a Considerable Number of Christianized Indians of Martha's Vineyard* (London: J. Osborn and T. Longman, 1727), 34; Rawson and Danforth, "Indian Visitation," 132.

33. Charles E. Banks, *The History of Martha's Vineyard*, 3 vols. (reprint, Edgartown: Dukes County Historical Society, 1966), 1:22–23.

34. 1856 House Report 47, Feb. 1856, 12–14, 23–26; Rawson and Danforth, "Indian Visitation," 132.

35. Kellaway, *New England Company*, 240–41, 244.

36. Ronda, "Generations of Faith," 378–79.

37. Experience Mayhew, *Indian Converts*, 33–34, 44–48.

38. Rawson and Danforth, "Indian Visitation," 131.

39. Kellaway, *New England Company*, 152–53.

40. MA 31:24, 91–92, 394; Thomas, *Diary of Samuel Sewall*, 2:708.

41. Commissioners' Minutes, 7 Oct. 1706, SPG, ms. 7953.

42. Commissioners' Minutes, 14 Feb. 1709, 6 Nov. 1711, SPG, ms. 7953.

43. Commissioners' Minutes, 3 July 1712, SPG, ms. 7953.

44. Commissioners' Minutes, 3 July 1712, SPG, ms. 7953; Thomas, *Diary of Samuel Sewall*, 2:694.

45. Correspondence from New England, 10 Feb. 1713, SPG, CAC 121.

46. Commissioners' Minutes, 27 April 1708, 11 Oct. 1708, SPG, ms. 7953.

47. MA 32:354; AR 1755–56, Ch. 228, 26 Dec. 1755.

48. Thomas, *Diary of Samuel Sewall*, 1:586, 589, 2:858.

49. Sewall to Ashhurst, 4 March 1717, SPG, ms. 7955, letter 43.

50. Sewall to Ashhurst, 28 Oct. 1719, SPG, ms. 7955, letter 53.

51. Samuel Sewall, "Sewall's Letter-Book," 2 vols., MHSC, 6th ser., 1 (1886), 400–401.

52. Quoted in Bragdon, " 'Another Tongue Brought In'," 27.

53. Ronda, "Generations of Faith," 378–79.

54. Rawson and Danforth, "Indian Visitation," 129–30; Sewall to Ashhurst, 21 May 1728, SPG, ms. 7955, letter 81.

55. Bragdon, " 'Another Tongue Brought In'," 29–30.

56. Thomas, *Diary of Samuel Sewall*, 2:750–751; Kathleen Bragdon, "Language, Folk History, and Indian Identity," (paper presented at the Gay Head Wampanoag History Conference, 1992).

57. Mather, *India Christiana*, 39; Kathleen Bragdon, "Native Christianity in

18th Century Massachusetts: Ritual as Cultural Reaffirmation," (paper presented at the 1983 Laurier Conference, Canada).

58. Zaccheus Macy, 1792, quoted in Alexander Starbuck, *The History of Nantucket: County, Island, and Town* (reprint ed., Rutland VT: Charles E. Tuttle, 1969), 122–23.

59. William Simmons, *Spirit of the New England Tribes: Indian History and Folklore, 1620–1985* (Hanover NH: University Press of New England, 1986), 122–24, 125–27, 174–34.

60. Banks, *History of Martha's Vineyard*, 1:53.

61. Mather, *Magnalia Christi Americana*, 2:439.

62. Commissioners' Minutes, April 1700, SPG, ms. 7953; MA 31:126–27.

63. Litchfield, *Ancient Landmarks of Pembroke*, 77.

64. Thomas, *Diary of Samuel Sewall*, 1:465.

65. Experience Mayhew, "Present Conditions of the Indians on Martha's Vineyard," in Mather, *India Christiana*, 93–94.

66. Mayhew, "Conditions of the Indians," 94.

67. 1861 Senate Report 96, 15–21.

68. Vickers, "First Whalemen of Nantucket," 571–74, 576.

69. Thomas, *Diary of Samuel Sewall*, 2:749–50.

70. Rawson and Danforth, "Indian Visitation," 133.

71. Rawson and Danforth, "Indian Visitation," 132; Elizabeth Little, "The Writings of Nantucket Indians," *Nantucket Algonquian Studies* 3 (1981): 7.

72. MA 30:493.

73. Ronda, "Generations of Faith," 378–79.

74. Elizabeth Little, "Probate Records of Nantucket Indians," *Nantucket Algonquian Studies* 2 (1980): 28.

75. Rawson and Danforth, "Indian Visitation," 130.

76. Mather, *Magalia Christi Americana*, 1:432–33, 437–38.

77. 1856 House Report 47, 12–13.

78. Ives Goddard and Kathleen Bradgon, *Native Writings in Massachusett*, 2 vols. (Philadelphia: American Philosophical Society, 1988), 1:134–35.

79. 1856 House Report 47, 43–45.

80. 1856 House Report 46.

81. Thomas, *Diary of Samuel Sewall*, 2:751–52.

82. 1856 House Report 48, 10–12.

83. Goddard and Bragdon, *Native Writings in Massachusett*, 1:96–97; MA 31:10, 17–19.

84. Daniel Mandell, " 'Standing By His Father': Thomas Waban of Natick, circ. 1630–1722," in *Northeastern Native Lives*, ed. Robert Grumet (Amherst: University of Massachusetts Press, forthcoming).

85. Goddard and Bragdon, *Native Writings in Massachusett*, 1:301, 335; Natick Town Records; Jean O'Brien, "Community Dynamics in the Indian-English

Town of Natick, Massachusetts, 1650–1790" (Ph.D. diss., University of Chicago, 1990), 182.

86. Daniel Mandell, " 'To Live More Like My Christian English Neighbors': Natick Indians in the Eighteenth Century," *William and Mary Quarterly*, 3d ser., 48 (1991): 559–60.

87. Goddard and Bragdon, *Native Writings in Massachusett*, 1:287, 301.

88. MA 31:31.

89. Goddard and Bragdon, *Native Writings in Massachusett*, 1:329.

90. Sewall to Ashhurst, 1 Nov. 1716, SPG, ms. 7955, letter 41; Sewall to Ashhurst, 28 Oct. 1719, SPG, ms. 7955, letter 53.

91. Sewall to Ashhurst, 17 Feb. 1720, SPG, ms. 7955, letter 55.

92. *AR* 1719, Ch. 87, 21 Nov. 1719.

93. MA 30:451–52.

94. MA 30:493b.

95. MA 31:11–12.

96. MA 31:53.

97. *AR* 1703–4, Ch. 121.

98. *AR* 1711, Ch. 56, 21 July 1711.

99. *AR* 1710, Ch. 58, 27 July 1710; *AR* 1711, Ch. 56, 21 July 1711; MA 31:7–8, 13–14, 61–61a.

100. Thomas, *Diary of Samuel Sewall*, 1:532; *AR* 1705–6; Ch. 10.

101. Stephen Badger, "Historical and Characteristic Traits of the American Indians in General," MHSC, 1st ser., 5 (1798), 38.

102. William Apess, "The Experiences of Five Christian Indians," in *On Common Ground*, ed. Barry O'Connell (Amherst: University of Massachusetts Press, 1990), 119.

103. Badger, "Historical and Characteristic Traits," 38, 39.

104. MA 30:456, 458a.

105. Starbuck, *History of Nantucket*, 142–43; Vickers, "First Whalemen of Nantucket," 577–78.

106. Sewall, "Sewall's Letter-Book," 1:326.

107. Ashhurst to Sewall, 1 Nov. 1701, SPG, Copyletter Book 1688–1760, film 171, frames 29–33.

108. MA 30:474–75.

109. MA 30:443; 113:437.

110. MA 31:91–92, 113:437.

111. *AR* 1708, Ch. 73, 27 Oct. 1708.

112. MA 31:49–50; 113:437.

113. MA 113:437–38.

114. MA 113:438.

115. MA 113:438.

116. Goddard and Bragdon, *Native Writings in Massachusett*, 1:14–15.

117. MA 113:439–40.

118. MA 113:437.

119. MA 31:91–92.

120. MA 31:91–93.

121. MA 31:317–18.

122. MA 31:68–71.

123. *AR* 1717, Ch. 151, 10 Feb. 1718.

124. *AR* 1714, Ch. 11, 4 June 1714.

125. MA 30:363.

126. Starbuck, *History of Nantucket*, 143.

127. Sewall to Ashhurst, 9 March 1708, SPG, ms. 7955, letter 6.

128. *AR* 1761–62, Ch. 198; 27 Nov. 1761.

129. *AR* 1724, Ch. 88, 19 June 1724.

130. Sewall to Ashhurst, 9 March 1708, SPG, ms. 7955, letter 6; Loose Court Minutes, 2 May 1711, SPG, ms. 7952; William Taylor, Boston, to Ashhurst, 1712, SPG, ms. 7955, letter 18.

131. Documents relating to Unpassed Senate Legislation, no. 6568, 1820, Massachusetts Archives, Boston.

132. Commissioner's Minutes, 15 Oct. 1711, SPG, ms. 7953.

133. Thomas, *Diary of Samuel Sewall*, 2:751.

134. Sewell to Ashurst, 8 May 1714, SPG, ms. 7955, letter 27.

135. Sewall to Ashurst, 10 Sept. 1715, SPG, ms. 7955, letter 34.

136. Thomas, *Diary of Samuel Sewall*, 2:801–2.

137. MA 31:31–33.

138. MA 31:29–30.

139. MA 31:39–41a.

140. MA 31:38.

141. *AR* 1724, Ch. 244, 4 Dec. 1724.

142. MA 31:38.

143. Commissioners' Minutes, 11 Oct. 1708, SPG, ms. 7953; MA 31:126.

144. MA 31:122–23.

145. MA 31:124–25.

"TO LIVE MORE LIKE MY
CHRISTIAN ENGLISH NEIGHBORS"

1. MA 31:135.

2. *AR* 1736, Ch. 171, 25 Jan. 1736.

3. MA 31:245.

4. MA 31:394.

5. MA 31:320–22.

6. *AR* 1729–30, Ch. 100, 26 Nov. 1729; *AR* 1735–36, Ch. 131, 5 Dec. 1735.

7. *AR* 1735–36, Ch. 131, 5 Dec. 1735.

8. Mandell, "Christian English Neighbors," 564; Bragdon, "Another Tongue Brought In," 145.

9. Thomas W. Baldwin, comp., *Vital Records of Natick, Massachusetts to the Year 1850* (Boston: New England Historical and Geneological Society, 1910); "A Record of Those Who Have Been Received Into Full Communion With the Church of Natick," Bacon Free Library, South Natick, typescript.

10. *AR* 1724, Ch. 27, 6 June 1724.

11. 12 May 1729, "Accounts of Hassanamisco Indian Trustees," JME, 2:2; *AR* 1734–35, Ch. 47, 21 June 1734.

12. *AR* 1735–36, Ch. 261, 23 March 1736.

13. "Accounts of Hassanamisco," 2:26.

14. MA 32:6–7; *AR* 1730, Ch. 28, 3 July 1730.

15. Adam Winthrop, Boston, to Sir Robert Clarke, London, 30 March 1733, SPG, ms. 7955/2, letter 94.

16. *Town Records of Dudley, Massachusetts, 1732–1754* (Pawtucket: The Adam Sutcliffe Co., 1893), 18.

17. MA 31:113.

18. 1861 Senate Report 96, 103; 1857 Senate Report 10, 2–3.

19. Joseph Bourne, Mashpee, to Sir William Ashhurst, 15 March 1724, SPG, ms. 7955, letter 74a.

20. Ezra Stiles, "An Account of the Potenummecut Indians . . . June 4, 1762," MHSC 10 (1809), 113.

21. *AR* 1720–25, Ch. 208, 2 Dec. 1724; *AR* 1720–25, Ch. 39, 9 June 1725.

22. *AR* 1720–25, Ch. 116, 18 June 1725; *AR* 1720–25, Ch. 54, 11 June 1725.

23. Weston, *History of the Town of Middleboro*, 90–91.

24. Mandell, "Christian English Neighbors," 564–65.

25. Quoted in Samuel Hopkins, *Historical Memoirs Relating to the Housatunnuck Indians* (Boston: S. Kneeland, 1753), 92.

26. Hopkins, *Historical Memoirs*, 92–93.

27. Thornton, *American Indian Holocaust*, 53–54.

28. David Hackett Fischer, *Albion's Seed: Four British Folkways in America* (New York: Oxford University Press, 1989), 71, 76.

29. Peter A. Thomas, "Cultural Change on the Southern New England Frontier, 1630–1665," in *Cultures in Contact: The Impact of European Contacts on Native American Cultural Institutions, AD 1000–1800*, ed. William W. Fitzhugh (Washington, DC: Smithsonian Institution Press, 1988), 153–54.

30. Natick Proprietors' Records, microfilm, Morse Library, Natick; Jean O'Brien, "Community Dynamics in the Indian-English Town of Natick, Massachusetts, 1650–1790" (Ph.D. diss., University of Chicago, 1990), 157–66.

31. *AR* 1718, Ch. 77, 4 Nov. 1718; *AR* 1722, Ch. 228, 14 Dec. 1722.

32. *AR* 1722, Ch. 206, 7 Dec. 1722; *AR* 1724, Ch. 27, 5 June 1724.

33. *AR* 1722, Ch. 30, 6 June 1724.

34. MA 31:117–18, 120–21; *AR* 1727, Ch. 88, 28 June 1727; *AR* 1727–28, Ch. 36, 12 Dec. 1727, and Ch. 52, 19 Dec. 1727.

35. *AR* 1728–29, Ch. 3, 31 May 1728; *AR* 1728–29, Ch. 128, 19 June 1728; "Accounts of Hassanamisco," 2:1.

36. "List of Indians of Hassanamisco as found in the Records of the same from June 25, 1725, to 1800," JME, box 1, folder 1; "Accounts of Hassanamisco," 2; Benjamin Heywood, Hassanamisco trustee, to Estes How of Worcester, 16 Jan. 1812, JME, box 1, folder 1.

37. MA 31:117; Frederick Hoxie, *A Final Promise: The Campaign to Assimilate the Indians, 1880–1920* (New York: Cambridge University Press, 1989), 70–78.

38. MA 32:415–16; Jack Campisi, *The Mashpee Indians: Tribe on Trial* (Syracuse: Syracuse University Press, 1991), 82.

39. *AR* 1734–35, Ch. 3, 4 June 1734; *AR* 1731–32, Ch. 58, 30 July 1731.

40. Chappaquiddick to General Court, Unpassed Senate Legislation, no. 2532, Massachusetts Archives.

41. Christiantown to General Court, 25 Dec. 1824, Unpassed House Legislation, no. 9419, Massachusetts Archives.

42. Zaccheus Howwoswee, Mashpee, to James Earle, Worcester, 25 August 1859, 27 Jan. 1860, JME, box 2, folder 3.

43. *AR* 1734–35, Ch. 3, 4 June 1734.

44. *AR* 1722, Ch. 190, Nov. 26.

45. *AR* 1735–36, Ch. 233, 15 Jan. 1736; *AR* 1737–38, Ch. 93, 8 Dec. 1737, Ch. 29, 17 June 1737, Ch. 186, 26 Dec. 1737; MA 31:219, 263.

46. *AR* 1728–29, Ch. 52, 12 June 1728, Ch. 172, 14 Aug. 1728; *AR* 1737–38, Ch. 93, 8 Dec. 1737.

47. *AR* 1729–30, Ch. 116, 5 Dec. 1729.

48. MA 31:175.

49. MA 31:263.

50. MA 31:348.

51. MA 31:403.

52. MA 31:135.

53. *AR* 1728–29, Chs. 51, 176, 224; *AR* 1729–30, Chs. 108, 116, 130, 135.

54. MA 31:254.

55. Mandell, "Christian English Neighbors," 568–71; T. H. Breen, "An Empire of Goods: The Anglicization of Colonial America, 1690–1776," *Journal of British Studies* 25 (1986): 467–99.

56. Mandell, "Christian English Neighbors," 569–70.

57. Christopher L. Miller and George R. Hammell, "A New Perspective on Indian-White Contact: Cultural Symbols and Colonial Trade," *Journal of American History* 73 (1986): 316–17.

58. Mandell, "Christian English Neighbors," 568–71; Philip Greven Jr., *Four Generations: Population, Land, and Family in Colonial Andover, Massachusetts* (Ithaca: Cornell University Press, 1970), 225. Greven was not able to adjust the estate values from Andover for currency fluctuations, so for comparisons I left those from Natick also uncorrected. Deflating the values to a constant value, pounds sterling, shows that the Indian estates were worth even less. The figures that I used to calculate constant values for Natick's records are in John J. McCusker, *Money and Exchange in Europe and America, 1600–1775: A Handbook* (Chapel Hill: University of North Carolina Press, 1978), 140–41.

59. *AR* 1738–39, Ch. 39, 21 June 1738.

60. Badger, "Historical and Characteristic Traits," 38–39.

61. MA 33:409–10, 513–14.

62. Mandell, "Christian English Neighbors," 568–69; Gloria Main, "Inequality in Early America: The Evidence from Probate Records of Massachusetts and Maryland," *Journal of Interdisciplinary History* 7 (1977): 561, 567.

63. Terry Anderson, "Economic Growth in Colonial New England: 'Statistical Renaissance'," *Journal of Economic History* 39 (1979): 257.

64. *AR* 1730, Ch. 28, 3 July 1730.

65. *AR* 1735–36, Ch. 261, 23 March 1736.

66. *AR* 1738–39, Ch. 121, 27 Dec. 1738.

67. WCP, 41125.

68. WCP, 36457.

69. "Accounts of Hassanamisco," 2:14–28, 53.

70. Land sale petitions in *AR* and MA 31.

71. *AR* 1737–38, Ch. 92, 8 Dec. 1737.

72. *AR* 1724, Ch. 193, 27 Nov. 1724.

73. *AR* 1725, Ch. 362, 10 Dec. 1725; MA 31:128; *AR* 1726–27, Ch. 294, 30 Dec. 1726.

74. *AR* 1729–30, Ch. 115, 5 Dec. 1729.

75. *AR* 1735–36, Ch. 117, 25 Nov. 1735.

76. MA 31:245–46; *AR* 1739–40, Ch. 150, 2 Jan. 1740.

77. MA 31:175.

78. *AR* 1733–34, Ch. 49, 24 Aug. 1733.

79. *AR* 1731–32, Ch. 107, 5 Feb. 1732.

80. *AR* 1733–34, Ch. 145, 5 Feb. 1734.

81. *AR* 1731–32, Ch. 58, 30 July. 1731, Ch. 128, 11 Jan. 1732.

82. MA 31:296–98; *AR* 1740–41, Ch. 175, 3 April 1741.

83. *AR* 1725, Ch. 295, n.d.

84. MA 31:154–55.

85. MA 31:346–47.

86. Badger, "Historical and Characteristic Traits," 38.

87. MA 31:221–24.

88. MA 31:356–57.

89. MA 31:478–79.

90. AR 1735–36, Ch. 99, 2 July 1735, Ch. 280, 24 March 1736.

91. MA 31:299.

92. AR 1735–36, Ch. 280, 24 March 1736.

93. Elizabeth Little, "Probate Records of Nantucket Indians," *Nantucket Algonquian Studies* 2 (1980): 27–28.

94. Reprinted in Starbuck, *History of Nantucket*, 145.

95. Starbuck, *History of Nantucket*, 145.

96. Conversation with Vineyard Indian geneologist Andrew Pierce, 19 Feb. 1993, NEHGS.

97. Ives Goddard and Kathleen Bragdon, *Native Writings in Massachusett*, 2 vols. (Philadelphia: American Philosophical Society, 1988), 1:225.

98. Goddard and Bragdon, *Native Writings*, 153, 157.

99. Goddard and Bragdon, *Native Writings*, 161.

100. AR 1747–48, Ch. 70, 30 June 1747.

101. AR 1747–48, Ch. 69, 30 June 1747.

102. AR 1735–36, Ch. 134, 9 Dec. 1735.

103. AR 1737–38, Ch. 175, 20 Dec. 1737.

104. Sewall to Ashhurst, 3 July 1721, SPG, ms. 7955, letter 62.

105. Clifford K. Shipton, ed., *Sibley's Biographical Sketches of Those Who Attended Harvard College*, 17 vols. (Boston and Cambridge, 1879–), 6:529.

106. Kellaway, *The New England Company*, 237–38; O'Brien, "Indian-English Town of Natick," 203.

107. Shipton, *Sibley's Biographical Sketches*, 6:531.

108. O'Brien, "Indian-English Town of Natick," 221.

109. Shipton, *Sibley's Biographical Sketches*, 6:530.

110. MA 31:136–37.

111. "Report of ye Comittee of ye Honble Comissioners for ye Indian Affairs and of ye Corporation of Harvard College . . . Oct. 23, 1729," *Publications of the Colonial Society of Massachusetts* 16 (1925), 575–77.

112. *Colonial Society*, 577.

113. Samuel Sewall, *Sewall's Letter Book*, 2 vols., MHSC, 6th ser. (1886), 1:401.

114. Shipton, *Sibley's Biographical Sketches*, 6:532.

115. Mandell, "Christian English Neighbors," 562.

116. O'Brien, "Indian-English Town of Natick," 222.

117. MA 31:234–35; AR 1739–40, Ch. 45, 26 June 1739.

118. Shipton, *Sibley's Biographical Sketches*, 4:259.

119. Samuel Dexter, diary, manuscript copy, MHS, 287–89.

120. Shipton, *Sibley's Biographical Sketches*, 4:258.

121. Shipton, *Sibley's Biographical Sketches*, 4:258.

122. Sewall to Ashhurst, 6 Oct. 1724, SPG, ms. 7955, letter 73, and 28 Oct. 1723, SPG, ms. 7955, letter 67.

123. Joseph Bourne, Mashpee, to Ashhurst, 15 March 1724, SPG, ms. 7955, letter 74a.

124. Francis Hutchins, *Mashpee: The Story of Cape Cod's Indian Town* (New Hampshire: Amarta Press, 1979), 66–67.

125. Hawley, "Anecdotes Respecting Sandwich and Marshpee," MHSC, 1st ser., 3 (1794), 191.

126. William Kendall, *Travels Through the Northern Parts of the United States in the Years 1807 and 1808*, 3 vols. (New York: I. Riley, 1809), 2:48–50, 183.

127. MA 31:124.

128. MA 31:143.

129. *AR* 1733–34, Ch. 46, 23 Aug. 1733.

130. MA 31:317–18; *AR* 1741–42, Ch. 39, 30 July 1741.

131. MA 31:320–22.

132. MA 31:323–26; *AR* 1742–43, Ch. 223, 8 April 1743.

133. Starbuck, *History of Nantucket*, 142.

134. Starbuck, *History of Nantucket*, 142–45; MA 31:147.

135. Reprinted in Starbuck, *History of Nantucket*, 146–47.

136. *AR* 1737–38, Ch. 139, 7 Dec. 1737.

137. Banks, *History of Martha's Vineyard*, 3:96.

138. *AR* 1741–42, Ch. 108, 9 Dec. 1741.

139. Goddard and Bragdon, *Native Writings*, 1:329.

140. MA 31:143.

141. MA 31:315–16.

142. MA 31:315–16.

143. *AR* 1733–34, Ch. 46, 23 Aug. 1733.

144. *AR* 1741–42, Ch. 45, 4 Aug. 1741, Ch. 108, 9 Dec. 1741.

145. Sewell to Ashhurst, 21 March 1721, SPG, ms. 7955, letter 61.

146. MA 31:143.

147. Shipton, *Silbey's Biographical Sketches*, 5:445–46.

148. Sewall to Ashhurst, circ. 1712, SPG, ms. 7955, letter 20.

149. Kellaway, *New England Company*, 223.

150. Adam Winthrop, Boston, to Joseph Williams, London, 10 June 1730, SPG, ms. 7955, letter 88.

151. Winthrop to Williams.

152. Winthrop to Williams.

153. Winthrop to Williams, 31 July 1727, SPG, ms. 7955/2, letter 79.

154. Sewell to Ashhurst, 21 March 1721, SPG, ms. 7955, letter 61. The overseer may have been Francis Fullham, who acted as the proprietors' secretary, "assist[ing] them at their Town Meetings, regulating their Affairs, and Entring their Records fairly in a Book"; Sewall to Ashhurst, 17 Feb. 1720, SPG, ms. 7955, letter 55.

155. *AR* 1722, Ch. 153, 14 Aug. 1722; Banks, *History of Martha's Vineyard*, 3:193–94.

156. *AR* 1722, Ch. 201, 4 Dec. 1722.

157. MA 31:129–31.

"GREAT INJURIES & OPPRESSIONS"

1. Badger, "Historical and Characteristic Traits," 38.

2. *AR* 1749–50, Ch. 135, 12 Dec. 1749.

3. Mandell, "Christian English Neighbors," 564.

4. "A List of Names of the Indians . . . Which Live in or Belong to Natick; Taken June 16, 1749," MHSC, 1st ser., 10 (1809), 134–36.

5. MA 33:106–7.

6. Land sale data is from petitions in MA 31–33 and *AR*.

7. MA 31:440.

8. MA 31:385.

9. "Accounts of Hassanamisco," 2:26.

10. MA 31:304–5.

11. MA 32:592.

12. MA 31:600.

13. MA 32:80.

14. WCP, 41125.

15. WCP, 51.

16. MA 31:341–42.

17. MA 31:358.

18. MA 31:343.

19. MA 31:221–24, 553–56b.

20. MA 31:559.

21. MA 31:310; *AR* 1750–51, Ch. 284, 18 April 1751; *AR* 1754–55, Ch. 110, 7 Nov. 1754, Ch. 182, 21 Dec. 1754; MA 33:50–52.

22. MA 32:738–39.

23. MA 33:40–41.

24. MA 32:527–28.

25. MA 31:445–47.

26. *AR* 1748–49, Ch. 13, 3 June 1748; *AR* 1750–51, Ch. 144, 23 Jan. 1751.

27. Teticut land sale petitions, MA 31–33 and *AR*.

28. MA 31:448.

29. MA 31:420–21; *AR* 1742–43, Ch. 236, 15 April 1743.

30. MA 33:222.

31. Anderson, "Economic Growth," 250–52, 257.

32. MA 32:228.

33. Elisha Tupper to Andrew Oliver, Boston, Secretary for the New England Company, 18 Nov. 1761, misc. bound mss., MHS; Franklin B. Dexter, ed., *Extracts*

from the Itineraries and other Miscellanies of Ezra Stiles (New Haven: Yale University Press, 1916), 59, 165.

34. Tupper to Oliver, 18 Nov. 1761, misc. bound mss., MHS.

35. Dexter, *Itineraries of Ezra Stiles*, 165; MA 33:186; Herring Pond Indians to the General Court, 31 Dec. 1844, in Unpassed House Legislation, no. 1698, Massachusetts Archives.

36. A. Williams, Sandwich, to Eliot, Boston, 20 Jan. 1778, New England Company mss, NEHGS.

37. Goddard and Bragdon, *Native Writings*, 1:179.

38. MA 32:424–26.

39. Dexter, *Itineraries of Ezra Stiles*, 167; "Report of a Committee on the State of the Indians in Mashpee and Parts Adjacent [in 1767]," MHSC, 2d ser., 3 (1815), 14.

40. Goddard and Bragdon, *Native Writings*, 1:179.

41. Dexter, *Itineraries of Ezra Stiles*, 167.

42. MA 32:415–16.

43. Mather, *India Christiana*, 88; Banks, *History of Martha's Vineyard*, 1:254.

44. John W. Barber, *Historical Collections* (Worcester: Dorr, Howland, & Co., 1839), 148–50.

45. Goddard and Bragdon, *Native Writings*, 1:173.

46. Goddard and Bragdon, *Native Writings*, 1:140.

47. Goddard and Bragdon, *Native Writings*, 1:173, 175.

48. Goddard and Bragdon, *Native Writings*, 1:140.

49. Shipton, *Sibley's Biographical Sketches*, 6:532; Mandell, "Christian English Neighbors," 562.

50. "A Record of Those Who Have Been Received Into Full Communion With the Church of Natick," typescript, Bacon Free Library, South Natick.

51. William Simmons and Cheryl Simmons, *Old Light on Separate Ways: The Narragansett Diary of Joseph Fish, 1765–1776* (Hanover, NH: University Press of New England, 1982), xxxi.

52. Badger, "Historical and Characteristic Traits," 40.

53. Richard Johnson, "The Search for a Usable Indian: An Aspect of the Defense of Colonial New England," *Journal of American History*, 64 (1977): 644.

54. Gary Nash, *The Urban Crucible: Social Change, Political Consciousness, and the Origins of the American Revolution* (Cambridge: Harvard University Press, 1979), 172.

55. Charles Swift, *History of Old Yarmouth* (Swift: Yarmouth Port, MA, 1844), 143–144.

56. O'Brien, "Indian-English Town of Natick," 351.

57. O'Brien, "Indian-English Town of Natick," 312; MA 32:4, 85; "Names of Indians of Hassanamisco," JME, box 1, folder 1; "Accounts of Hassanamisco," 2:55–60.

58. Baldwin, *Vital Records of Natick*; O'Brien, "Indian-English Town of Natick," 373.

59. "List of Names of the Indians," 134–36.

60. MA 32:424–26.

61. MA 32:710–11.

62. MA 31:656.

63. MA 31:662.

64. MA 31:659–659a.

65. MA 32:318a.

66. MA 32:499–500.

67. AR 1744–45, Ch. 42, 20 July 1744, Ch. 138, 29 Dec. 1744.

68. AR 1746–47, Ch. 11, 5 June 1746.

69. AR 1746–47, Ch. 331, 7 April 1747; AR 1747–48, Ch. 3, 2 June 1747.

70. AR 1748–49, Ch. 135, 21 Nov. 1748; AR 1749–50, Ch. 45, 27 June 1749, Ch. 351, 20 April 1750.

71. Nash, *Urban Crucible*, 244–45.

72. Fred Anderson, *A People's Army: Massachusetts Soldiers and Society in the Seven Years War* (Chapel Hill: University of North Carolina Press, 1984), 101.

73. Badger, "Historical and Characteristic Traits," 41.

74. MA 32:708–9.

75. MA 33:104–5.

76. Ibid., 703–4.

77. AR 1761–62, Ch. 128, 19 Nov. 1761.

78. MA 33:22.

79. Stiles, "Account of the Potenummecut Indians," 112–13.

80. Badger, "Historical and Characteristic Traits," 38, 39.

81. Badger to General Court, 17 Aug. 1791 and 17 Feb. 1798, in Unpassed Senate Legislation, no. 2398, June 1798, Massachusetts Archives.

82. O'Brien, "Indian-English Town of Natick," 223–28; Michael J. Crawford, "Indians, Yankees, and the Meetinghouse Dispute of Natick, Massachusetts, 1743–1800," *New England Historical and Geneological Register* 132 (1978): 282–83. There are thirteen English houses in Hog End shown on a 1749 Natick map; MA 13:380.

83. Crawford, "Meetinghouse Dispute of Natick," 282–89.

84. MA 32:632.

85. MA 32:489–90.

86. MA 32:527–28.

87. MA 31:336–38.

88. MA 33:118, 120.

89. MA 33:400, 419, 424; MA 32:16–16a; AR 1742–43, Ch. 225, 9 April 1742, Ch. 87, 4 June 1742, Ch. 80, 8 Sept. 1742; AR 1750–51, Ch. 53, 29 June 1750.

90. MA 31:463–64; AR 1743–44, Ch. 113, 15 Sept. 1743, Ch. 255, 2 March 1744.

91. MA 31:564.

92. Alice Sachemus Indenture, 1723–26, Special Collections, Indians, Folder 2, the Pilgrim Society, Plymouth.

93. MA 33:151.

94. MA 32:632.

95. MA 31:624–25.

96. MA 31:659–59a.

97. MA 32:409–10, 529–30, 489–90.

98. MA 32:532–34, 527–28.

99. MA 32:419–21.

100. MA 32:494, 510.

101. MA 31:234.

102. Frank G. Speck, "A Note on the Hassanamisco Band of Nipmuc," *Bulletin of the Massachusetts Archeological Society*, 4 (1943), 53.

103. MA 31:485.

104. MA 31:576.

105. MA 33:186.

106. MA 32:245.

107. Goddard and Bragdon, *Native Writings*, 1:373.

108. MA 32:415–16.

109. Mashpee to General Court, 4 Aug. 1757, Gideon Hawley Letters, MHS.

110. MA 33:30–31b.

111. MA 33:10–11a.

112. MA 33:30–31b.

113. MA 33:33c.

114. Reprinted in Starbuck, *History of Nantucket*, 148, 153–55.

115. Reprinted in Starbuck, *History of Nantucket*, 148, 153–55.

116. Reprinted in Starbuck, *History of Nantucket*, 153–55.

117. MA 31:531–49.

118. Reprinted in Starbuck, *History of Nantucket*, 150–52, 155; MA 31:658. The colonists also denied killing any of the Indians' animals "except a few unruly dogs they had which we killed for the more safety of Our sheep."

119. MA 32:166–67, 391–92.

120. MA 32:268–71; Starbuck, *History of Nantucket*, 160–67.

121. MA 32:551–53.

122. Starbuck, *History of Nantucket*, 168–69.

123. Goddard and Bragdon, *Native Writings*, 1:373.

124. MA 31:357–58.

125. MA 31:455.

126. *AR* 1746, 6 Jan. 1746; Yasu Kawashima, "Legal Origins of the Indian Reservation in Colonial Massachusetts," *American Journal of Legal History*, 8 (1969): 46–47.

127. *AR* 1749–50, Ch. 231, 26 Jan. 1750.

128. For similar actions in eighteenth-century Virginia see Rountree, *Pocahontas's People*, 165, 168–69.

129. MA 31:422.

130. MA 31:564.

131. MA 31:567.

132. MA 31:342.

133. MA 31:356.

134. MA 32:738–39.

135. MA 31:553–56b; McCusker, *Money and Exchange in Europe and America*, 140–41.

136. MA 31:476–77.

137. Senate 1861, 90–91.

138. *AR* 1753–54, Ch. 241, 10 Jan. 1754.

139. MA 32:415–16.

140. MA 32:424–26.

141. Mashpee to General Court, 4 Aug. 1757, Hawley Letters, MHS.

142. MA 31:523–24.

143. MA 31:550.

144. Banks, *History of Martha's Vineyard*, 2:13.

145. Goddard and Bragdon, *Native Writings*, 1:173.

146. MA 32:356.

147. MA 33:61–62.

148. Mashpee to Mass. General Court, 28 May 1792, documents relating to Unpassed Senate Legislation, no. 1643/2, 1792, Massachusetts Archives.

149. MA 31:476–77.

150. MA 32:424–26.

151. Goddard and Bragdon, *Native Writings*, 1:173.

152. MA 32:356.

153. *AR* 1753–54, Ch. 360, 18 April 1754.

154. *AR* 1755–56, Ch. 64, 16 June 1755.

155. MA 33:61–62.

156. Goddard and Bragdon, *Native Writings*, 1:173.

157. MA 33:61–63.

158. *AR* 1762–63, Ch. 184, 29 Jan. 1763.

159. *AR* 1760–61, Ch. 319, 28 March 1761.

160. *AR* 1761–62, Ch. 198, 27 Nov. 1761.

161. *AR* 1763–64, Ch. 53, 9 June 1763, Ch. 246, 28 Jan. 1764; *AR* 1764–65, Ch. 27, 7 June 1764, Ch. 76, 14 June 1764.

162. MA 33:237–38a.

163. MA 33:368–70.

164. MA 33:470–71.

165. MA 33:612–14.

166. MA 33:583–85.

167. MA 33:586–88.

168. MA 33:612–14.

169. 1849 House Report 46, 10–11.

170. MA 32:405–6.

171. MA 32:455–58.

172. MA 32:495–97.

173. MA 32:568–70.

174. MA 32:738–39; AR 1756–57, Ch. 215, 20 Oct. 1756.

175. MA 32:774, 33:40.

176. MA 31:341–42, 356–58.

177. AR 1741–42, Ch. 211, 2 April 1742.

178. MA 32:405–6.

179. MA 32:448.

180. MA 31:341–42.

181. MA 31:560–61.

182. MA 32:624–25.

183. MA 32:609–10.

184. MA 32:710–11.

185. MA 32:712.

186. MA 32:715.

187. AR 1756–57, Ch. 125, 26 Aug. 1756, Ch. 523, 16 April 1757.

188. Reprinted in Starbuck, *History of Nantucket*, 148–49.

189. MA 32:415–16.

190. Mashpee to General Court, 4 Aug. 1757, Hawley Letters, MHS.

191. MA 32:424–26.

192. MA 32:452–54.

193. Mashpee to General Court, 4 Aug. 1757, Hawley Letters, MHS.

194. MA 33:144–47.

195. AR 1763–64, Ch. 16, 17, 31 May 1763.

196. AR 1763–64, Ch. 3, 17 June 1763, quoted in Russell Peters, *The Wampanoags of Mashpee* (Somerville, MA: Nimrod Press, 1987), 29.

197. MA 33:398.

198. 1861 Senate Report 96, 93–94.

199. MA 32:614–15.

200. MA 32:620–21.

201. MA 33:36

202. MA 33:113

203. AR 1753–54, Ch. 333, 10 April 1754; AR 1754–55, Ch. 127, 15 Nov. 1754; MA 32:694–95; MA 33:338–39.

204. MA 33:143.

205. MA 32:6–7.

206. *AR* 1746–47, Ch. 179, 12 Nov. 1746; O'Brien, "Indian-English Town of Natick," 217.

207. MA 32:618–19.

208. MA 32:429–30.

209. MA 33:513–14.

210. O'Brien, "Indian-English Town of Natick," 326.

211. MA 32:429–30; *AR* 1755–56, Ch. 25, 7 June 1755; MA 33:5–6, 53–54.

212. *AR* 1749–50, Ch. 195, 13 Jan. 1750; MA 33:59–60.

213. *AR* 1799–60, Ch. 12, 7 June 1759; O'Brien, "Indian-English Town of Natick," 327.

214. Mandell, "Christian English Neighbors," 564; "Note," MHSC, 1st ser., 10 (1809), 136.

215. "Note," MHSC, 136.

216. Badger, "Historical and Characteristic Traits," 39–40.

217. MA 31:310–11.

218. MA 32:122.

219. MA 32:459.

220. Benton, *Early Census-Making.*

221. Badger, "Historical and Characteristic Traits," 40.

222. Douglas L. Jones, "The Strolling Poor: Transiency in Eighteenth Century Massachusetts," *Journal of Social History* (1975): 28–39

223. MA 31:383.

224. MA 33:77–79.

225. MA 31:473.

226. MA 31:562–63.

227. MA 32:230–31.

228. MA 32:375–76.

"INDIANS AND THEIR MIXT POSTERITY"

1. Gideon Hawley, Mashpee, to James Freeman, 2 Nov. 1802, Gideon Hawley Papers, Congregational Library, Boston.

2. Dexter, *Itineraries,* 59.

3. Benton, *Early Census-Making.*

4. "Account of the Number of Indians at Natick, 1778," New England Company records, NEHGS, box 3, folder 63.

5. MA 33:188–90.

6. MA 33:555–56; *AR* 1771–72, Ch. 132, 22 April 1772.

7. *AR* 1773–74, Ch. 49, 25 June 1773.

8. MA 33:204–5.

9. MA 33:509–9a, 513–14.

10. MA 33:159–60.

11. *AR* 1763–64, Ch. 33, 3 June 1763.

12. MA 33:553–57.

13. Natick Indians to General Court, March/May 1806, documents relating to Resolves of 1808, Ch. 262, Passed Legislation, Massachusetts Archives.

14. Various receipts, JME, box 1, folder 1; "Accounts of Hassanamisco," 2:1–32.

15. MA 33:157–58.

16. *AR* 1769–70, Ch. 89, 6 April 1770.

17. MA 33:525–26.

18. "Accounts of Hassanamisco," 2:105.

19. "Resolves of the legislature regarding the sale of Hassanamisco Indian land," JME, box 1, folder 5; Worcester, Leicester, and Framingham town clerks to John Milton Earle, 1859, JME, box 1, folder 1.

20. Speck, "Hassanamisco Band of Nipmuc," 50–56.

21. *AR* 1762–63, Ch. 184, 29 Jan. 1763.

22. Dexter, *Itineraries of Ezra Stiles*, 228.

23. MA 33:463.

24. Dexter, *Itineraries of Ezra Stiles*, 228.

25. *AR* 1762–63, Ch. 184, 29 Jan. 1763.

26. John Chamberlain, Dudley, to the Massachusetts legislature, in documents relating to Unpassed Senate Legislation, no. 2151, 12 Feb. 1796, Massachusetts Archives.

27. 1849 House Report 46, 43.

28. 1861 Senate Report 96, 103.

29. O'Brien, "Indian-English Town of Natick," 293–94.

30. O'Brien, "Indian-English Town of Natick," 293; MA 33:518–20.

31. MA 33:597–99.

32. O'Brien, "Indian-English Town of Natick," 295.

33. Badger, "Historical and Characteristic Traits," MHSC, 1st ser., 5 (1798), 39.

34. *AR* 1784, Ch. 11, 7 June 1784.

35. MA 33:518–20.

36. Benton, *Early Census-Making*.

37. MA 33:468–69.

38. MA 33:224–25.

39. MA 33:355.

40. MA 33:456; *AR* 1769–70, Ch. 13, 6 July 1769; *AR* 1773–74, Ch. 67, 29 June 1773; *AR* 1775–76, Ch. 982, 4 May 1776.

41. MA 33:456.

42. MA 33:468.

43. 1861 Senate Report 96, 76–77.

44. Benton, *Early Census-Making*.

45. Dexter, *Itineraries of Ezra Stiles*, 166.

46. Dexter, *Itineraries of Ezra Stiles*, 165.

47. Lamont D. Thomas, *Rise to Be a People: A Biography of Paul Cuffe* (Urbana: University of Illinois Press, 1986).

48. O'Connell, *On Our Own Ground*, xxiv–xxix.

49. MA 33:118, 120.

50. Peter Oliver, Middleborough, to Andrew Oliver, Boston, Jan. 1762, misc. bound mss., MHS.

51. MA 33:223.

52. AR 1763–64, Ch. 139, 29 Dec. 1763; MA 33:450–51, 477–78, 541–42; AR 1769–70, Ch. 87, 6 April 1770.

53. Weston, *Town of Middleboro*, 13.

54. 1827 House Report 68, 5.

55. East Bridgewater to General Court, 1826, in documents relating to Resolves of 1826, Ch. 54, Passed Legislation, Massachusetts Archives.

56. AR 1762–63, Ch. 195, 3 Feb. 1763.

57. MA 33:269–75.

58. Dexter, *Itineraries of Ezra Stiles*, 166.

59. 1861 House Report 216, 6–8.

60. 1861 Senate Report 96, 6.

61. Dexter, *Itineraries of Ezra Stiles*, 59; Benton, *Early Census-Making*; Anonymous, "Report of a Committee on the State of the Indians in Mashpee and Parts Adjacent [in 1767]," MHSC, 2d ser., 3 (1815), 14.

62. Anonymous, "Mashpee and Parts Adjacent," 14; 1849 House Report 46, 46.

63. Stiles, "Potenummecut Indians," 112–13; Benton, *Early Census-Making*.

64. MA 33:622–27.

65. Anonymous, "Mashpee and Parts Adjacent," 14–16; Benton, *Early Census-Making*.

66. AR 1726, Ch. 194, 2 Dec. 1726; AR 1743–44, Ch. 235, 21 Feb. 1744; AR 1744–45, Ch. 250, 5 April 1745.

67. MA 33:23–24.

68. MA 33:324–25.

69. MA 33:319–20.

70. MA 33:409–10.

71. MA 33:509–9a, 513–14.

72. O'Brien, "Indian-English Town of Natick," 413, 419–20.

73. MA 33:503–4, 524.

74. 513–14.

75. O'Brien, "Indian-English Town of Natick," 404.

76. 1861 Senate Report 96, 68–69.

77. Elisha Tupper, Sandwich, to Andrew Oliver, Boston, 18 Nov. 1761, misc. bound mss., MHS; Benton, *Early Census-Making*; MA 33:561.

78. A. Williams, Sandwich, to Eliot, Boston, 20 Jan. 1778, New England Company records, NEHGS, box 3, folder 62.

79. Dexter, *Itineraries of Ezra Stiles*, 167.

80. Benton, *Early Census-Making*.

81. Anonymous, "Mashpee and Parts Adjacent," 14.

82. "Numbers of the Indians, mulatoes, and Negroes belong to Mashpee June 24 1776," Hawley Letters, MHS.

83. Hawley to William Phillips, Boston, 24 June 1776, New England Company records, NEHGS, box 3, folder 53.

84. Anonymous, "Mashpee and Parts Adjacent," 13.

85. Mashpee vital records, Gideon Hawley Papers, Congregational Library, Boston; Hawley to James Freeman, 2 Nov. 1802, Hawley Papers, Congregational Library.

86. Anonymous, "A Description of Mashpee, in the County of Barnstable, September 18th, 1802," MHSC, 2d ser., 3 (1815), 6.

87. Anonymous, "Mashpee and Parts Adjacent," 13.

88. Dexter, *Itineraries*, 167; Anonymous, "Mashpee and Parts Adjacent," 14; "Numbers of the Indians . . . 1776," Hawley Letters, MHS.

89. William Sturtevant, "Two 1761 Wigwams at Niantic, Connecticut," *American Antiquity* 40 (1975): 437.

90. Mashpee petition in documents relating to Unpassed Senate Legislation, no. 1419a, 1791, Massachusetts Archives.

91. Hawley to William Phillips, 26 Dec. 1776, New England Company records, NEHGS, box 3, folder 59.

92. Hawley to Phillips, 15 July 1776, New England Company records, NEHGS, box 3, folder 54.

93. Hawley to Shearjashub Bourne, 15 Dec. 1788, Samuel Phillips Savage Papers, MHS 2:208.

94. J. Hector St. John de Crevecoeur, *Letters From an American Farmer* (1782; reprint, New York: Penguin Books, 1981), 123; Barber, *Historical Collections*, 148–50.

95. Goddard and Bragdon, *Native Writings in Massachusett*, 1:7–8; Benton, *Early Census-Making*; documents relating to Unpassed House Legislature, no. 8029, 1816.

96. MA 33:348–50, 390–92.

97. Elizabeth Little, "The Nantucket Indian Sickness," *Papers of the Twenty-First Algonquian Conference*, ed. William Cowen (Carleston University, Ottowa, 1990): 181–96.

98. Mashpee vital records, Hawley Papers, Congregational Library.

99. Crevecoeur, *Letters From an American Farmer*, 118, 122.

100. Little, "Nantucket Indian Sickness," 189.

101. Zaccheus Macy, "A Short Journal of the first settling of the Island of Nantucket," MHSC, 1st ser., 3 (1794), 159; Kendall, *Travels Throughout the Northern Parts*, 2:211.

102. Starbuck, *History of Nantucket*, 120.

103. William D. Piersen, *Black Yankees: The Development of an Afro-American Subculture in Eighteenth-Century New England* (Amherst: University of Massachusetts Press, 1988), 1–19, 59–61; "Number of Negro Slaves in the Province of the Massachusetts-Bay, Sixteen Years Old and Upward, Taken by Order of Government, in the Last Month of the Year 1754, and the Beginning of the Year 1755," MHSC, 2d ser., 3 (1815), 95–97.

104. Gideon Hawley to James Freeman, 2 Nov. 1802, Hawley Letters, MHS.

105. Kendall, *Travels Through the Northern Parts*, 2:179.

106. Benton, *Early Census-Making*. The Massachusetts census of 1764 aggregated all ages among blacks and Indians. Censuses from Rhode Island and Connecticut in 1774 provide separate figures for Indian adults and adolescents/children. Both show more boys than girls but about 1.6 adult women for every man—and when aggregated show more balanced female-male ratios than Massachusetts. Anonymous, "Number of Indians in Connecticut . . . January 1, 1774," MHSC, 1st ser., 10 (1809), 117–18; Anonymous, "Number of Indians in Rhode Island . . . Taken Between the 4th of May and the 14th of June, 1774," MHSC, 1st ser., 10 (1809), 119.

107. William J. Brown, *The Life of William J. Brown* (Providence, 1883), 10–11.

108. Benjamin Allen, Christiantown guardian, to Massachusetts Legislature, in Unpassed Senate Legislation, no. 12207, 1846, and no. 13034, 1850, Massachusetts Archives.

109. 1861 Senate Report 96, 32.

110. Mass. Provincial Laws, 1705–6, Ch. 10.

111. Thomas, *Diary of Samuel Sewall*, 2:532.

112. *The Laws of the Commonwealth of Massachusetts, From November 28, 1780 . . . to February 28, 1807*, 3 vols. (Boston: Thomas & Andrews and Manning & Lorring, 1807), 1:324, act of 22 June 1776.

113. Badger, "Historical and Characteristic Traits," 43.

114. Hawley to Thomas Cushing, 24 June 1776, Savage Papers, MHS.

115. Hawley to Bourne, 15 Dec. 1788, Savage Papers, MHS.

116. Hawley to Gov. John Hancock, Boston, 8 July 1791, Hawley Letters, MHS.

117. Hawley to John Davis, 17 Oct. 1794, Savage Papers, 2:214, MHS.

118. 1861 Senate Report 96, 109.

119. MA 32:429; William Biglow, *History of the Town of Natick, Mass.* (Boston: Marsh, Capen, & Lyon, 1830), 44.

120. Ann Marie Plane and Gregory Button, "The Massachusetts Indian Enfranchisement Act: Ethnic Contest in Historical Context, 1849–1869," *Ethnohistory* 40 (1993): 597.

121. Fredrick Barth, "Introduction," from *Ethnic Groups and Boundaries: The Social Organization of Cultural Difference*, ed. Barth (Boston: Little, Brown and Company, 1969), 16.

122. Barth, "Introduction," 9–10.

123. "Depositions regarding whether a negro man by name of Aaron was ever married to Sarah Muckamugg," JME, box 1, folder 4.

124. O'Brien, "Indian-English Town of Natick," 291, 326.

125. MA 33:143.

126. "Depositions regarding," JME, box 1, folder 4.

127. O'Brien, "Indian-English Town of Natick," 291; Elizabeth Senah, Dudley, to Massachusetts General Court, 4 Dec. 1783, in documents relating to Resolves of 1784, Ch. 11, 7 June 1784, Passed Legislation, Massachusetts Archives.

128. O'Brien, "Indian-English Town of Natick," 326–27; AR 1773–74, Ch. 129, 25 Feb. 1774.

129. Badger, "Historical and Characteristic Traits," 44.

130. MA 33:143.

131. Dexter, *Itineraries of Ezra Stiles*, 203, 262.

132. 1861 Senate Report 96, 101.

133. Speck, "Hassanamisco Band of Nipmuc," 51–52.

134. Grafton Birth Records, Grafton Town Library; MA 32:592–93, MA 33:102.

135. Note on sale of Sarah Burnee's lands, 5 May 1752, JME, "Accounts for Hassanamisco," 2:66, Grafton Marriage Records, Grafton Town Library.

136. Benjamin Heywood, statement of facts concerning estate of Abigail Burnee, JME, box 1, folder 1.

137. Heywood, statement of facts, JME, box 1, folder 1; documents relating to Resolves of 1811, Ch. 159, Passed Legislation, Massachusetts Archives. Indian property could not be transferred to non-Indian ownership without the General Court's permission, and after Fortune died in 1795 the Hassanamisco guardians refused to fulfill the will. But in 1811, after a lawsuit by the white man's heirs and a request by the town of Grafton for part of Burnee's estate to assist Indian paupers, the legislature ordered the funds to be divided between two claimants.

138. Barth, "Introduction," 10.

139. Grafton Marriage Records.

140. MA 33:538; Hassanamisco accounts, Unpassed Senate Legislation, no. 1671/52, 1793, Massachusetts Archives.

141. WCP, 36457; request to inventory estate of Cesear and Patience Gimbee, 9 May 1800, and plan of Gimbee farm, JME, box 1, folder 1.

142. WCP, 23875.

143. *Rise to Be a People*, 3–13, 110, 121.

144. Petition to General Court by thirty-one Mashpee men (no women), July 1788, in documents relating to Acts of 1788, Ch. 38, 30 Jan. 1789, Passed Legislation, Massachusetts Archives.

145. Hawley to Freeman, 26 May 1796, Hawley Letters, MHS.

146. Howwoswee to John Milton Earle, 27 Jan. 1860, JME, box 2, folder 3.

147. Hawley to Bourne, 15 Dec. 1788, Savage Papers, MHS; Hawley to Freeman, 26 May 1796, Hawley Letters, MHS.

148. Hawley to Hancock, 8 July 1791, Hawley Letters, MHS.

149. Kendall, *Travels Through the Northern Parts*, 2:181.

150. Hawley to Cushing, 24 June 1776, Savage Papers, MHS; Kendall, *Travels Through the Northern Parts*, 2:179–80.

151. Josiah Fiske, report, Committees and Commissions, Accounts of Indian Guardians, box 2, file 1, Massachusetts Archives.

152. Simmons, *Spirit of the New England Tribes*, 116.

153. Simmons, "Spirit of New England Tribes," 19; Mashpee vital records, Hawley Papers, Congregational Library.

154. Hawley to Sewall, 15 Sept. 1779, Hawley Letters, MHS.

155. Hawley to Cushing, 24 June 1776, Savage Papers, MHS; n.a., 1807, Savage Papers, 2:228, MHS; Hawley, report to legislature, 2 Sept. 1795, Savage Papers, 2:218, MHS.

156. Hawley to General Court, 7 Jan. 1789, in documents relating to Acts of 1788, Ch. 38, Passed Legislation.

157. Justices of peace, selectmen, and other inhabitants of Barnstable, Sandwich, and Falmouth, to the General Court, 22 Dec. 1788, in documents relating to Acts of 1788, Ch. 38, 30 Jan. 1789, Passed Legislation, Massachusetts Archives.

158. Acts of 1788, Ch. 38, 30 Jan. 1789.

159. William Apess, "Indian Nullification of the Unconstitutional Laws of Massachusetts Relative to the Marshpee Tribe" (1835), in O'Connell, *On Our Own Ground*, 163–274.

160. Karen Blu, *The Lumbee Problem: The Making of an Indian People* (New York: Cambridge University Press, 1980), xii, 27, 30–33, 46–47, 62–63, 142–43.

161. Howwoswee to Earle, 27 Jan. 1860, JME, box 2, folder 3.

162. Brown, *Life of William J. Brown*, 11.

163. Mashpee to legislature, 29 Dec. 1788, documents relating to Acts of 1788, Ch. 38, 30 Jan. 1789, Passed Legislation, Massachusetts Archives; Isaiah Icanus, Mashpee, to Massachusetts Senate, 13 June 1791, in Unpassed Senate Legislation, no. 1419a, Massachusetts Archives.

164. Hawley to Freeman, 15 Nov. 1802, Hawley Letters, MHS.

165. MA 32:415–16.

166. Kendall, *Travels Through the Northern Parts*, 2:180.

167. Kendall, *Travels Through the Northern Parts*, 163–66, 194–95.

168. Marcus Rediker, *Between the Devil and the Deep Blue Sea: Merchant Seamen, Pirates, and the Anglo-American Maritime World, 1700–1750* (New York: Cambridge University Press, 1987), 293.

169. Hawley, report to legislature, 2 Sept. 1795, Savage Papers, 2:218, MHS.

170. Crevecoeur, *Letters From an American Farmer*, 133.

171. Kendall, *Travels Through the Northern Parts*, 2:194–95.

172. *AR* 1761–62, Ch. 198, 27 Nov. 1761; Benton, *Early Census–Making.*

173. Kendall, *Travels Through the Northern Parts,* 2:194.

174. Kendall, *Travels Through the Northern Parts,* 2:195.

175. Joseph Thaxter and Frederick Baylies to the legislature, 22 Sept. 1818, Committees and Commissions, Accounts of Indian Guardians, box 3, folder 15, Massachusetts Archives.

176. Christiantown to the legislature, 29 Jan. 1805, Acts of 1804, Ch. 84, Passed Legislation, Massachusetts Archives.

177. Hawley, report to legislature, 2 Sept. 1795, Savage Papers, 2:218, MHS.

178. Crevecoeur, *Letters From an American Farmer,* 157–60.

179. Hawley to Freeman, 2 Nov. 1802, Savage Papers, MHS.

180. MA 33:300–301.

181. Weston, *History of the Town of Middleboro,* 13.

182. John Avery, *History of the Town of Ledyard, 1650–1900* (Norwich, CT: Noyes and Davis, 1901), 259–60, quoted in O'Connell, *On Our Ground,* 153.

183. Biglow, *History of the Town of Natick,* 83.

184. Daniel Huntoon, *History of the Town of Canton* (Cambridge: John Wilson and Son, 1893), 39.

185. 1861 Senate Report 96, li, lix, lxx.

186. MCP, 17061.

187. MCP, 20860.

188. MA 33:300–301.

189. Barber, *Historical Collections* 148–50; 1827 House Report 68, 7.

190. 1849 House Report 46, 20–21.

191. MA 33:416–17.

EPILOGUE

1. Crevecoeur, *Letters From an American Farmer,* 123.

2. Documents relating to Acts of 1795, Ch. 48, Passed Legislation, Massachusetts Archives.

3. 1861 Senate Report 96.

4. Documents relating to Unpassed Senate Legislation, no. 6568, Massachusetts Archives.

5. Micah to the General Court, documents relating to Unpassed House Legislation, no. 4847, Massachusetts Archives.

6. Harwick, Orleans, and Brewster committees to Massachusetts Legislature, 18 May 1818, documents relating to Readers of 1818, Ch. 212, 27 Jan. 1819, Passed Legislation, Massachusetts Archives.

7. 1861 Senate Report 96.

BIBLIOGRAPHICAL ESSAY

Little has been published on Indians in eighteenth-century eastern Massachusetts. The following brief review of sources and literature for that people, period, and place will be useful to those who wish to read further in the field. My discussion is limited to works that were particularly significant for this study.

PRIMARY SOURCES

The four volumes of Indian documents in the colonial records in the Massachusetts Archives, nos. 30–33, are a treasure trove of information and form the backbone of this book. Most of the authentic native voices in this work are from the many letters written by or for Indians to the General Court and stored in the archives. Particularly revealing are the petitions from Natick Indians asking the legislature's permission to sell land to whites; many provide painful details of conditions in their families and community. The many published volumes of *The Acts and Resolves, Public and Private, of the Province of Massachusetts Bay* not only contain the laws passed affecting Indians, but also transcripts of some of the petitions from the archives and others apparently lost, along with reports from investigative committees.

Most of the Indians in Massachusetts in the eighteenth century were not literate, and many of those who could read and write did so in a written form of Massachusett developed by John Eliot. All of the extant documents in that language have been translated into English by Ives Goddard and Kathleen Bragdon in *Native Writings in Massachusett*, 2 vols., *Memoirs of the American Philosophical Society*, vol. 185 (Philadelphia: American Philosophical Society, 1988). Since an oral culture remained prominent among Indian groups in the region, few kept town records. Natick was the most prominent exception: Thomas Waban's notes on town meetings and the "Natick Indian Proprietors' Book of Records, 1723–1787" have been microfilmed and deposited in the Morse Library, Natick. Natick also boasts the only record of Indian church members in the eighteenth century; a typescript of "A Record of Those Who Have Been Received Into Full Communion With the Church of Natick" can be found in the files of the History Room of the Bacon Free Library, South Natick.

Hassanamisco was the only other enclave to leave a substantial body of records: notes by white trustees on payments to and for Hassanamiscos, Indian land allotments, and other useful data can be found in the John Milton Earle Papers, American Antiquarian Society, Worcester. Similarly, few Indians left probate records, which provide useful information on an individual's economic condition and material culture. The vast majority come from Natick Indians; they can be found, along with those left by colonists, in the Middlesex County Probate Records, Massachusetts Archives. A few Hassanamiscos also left wills, which are in the Worcester County Probate Records.

Census data from the American colonies is extremely rare, and almost nothing remains from Indian groups. Like so much other documentation, the most complete figures are from Natick, where white ministers kept birth, marriage, and death records, beginning in 1721, that have been compiled by Thomas Baldwin in *Vital Records of Natick, Massachusetts to the Year 1850* (Boston: New England Geneological Society, 1910). The Natick Indians also made one of the rare native censuses: "A List of Names of Indians . . . Which Live in, or Belong to Natick; Taken June 16, 1749," MHSC, 1st ser., 10 (1809), 134–36. The governor of New Plymouth reported on the population and communities of Indians within his colony in 1685: "Thomas Hinckley to William Stoughton and Joseph Dudley," MHSC, 4th ser., 5 (1861), 132–33. Anglo-American ministers Grindal Rawson and Samuel Danforth visited almost every Indian congregation in Massachusetts in 1698; their record of the number attending each meetinghouse provides a fairly reliable census: Rawson and Danforth, "Account of an Indian Visitation," MHSC, 1st ser., 10 (1809), 129–34. Ezra Stiles noted the numbers and conditions of many Indian enclaves in southern New England during his travels in the middle of the eighteenth century; Franklin Dexter, ed. *Extracts From the Itineraries and other Miscellanies of Ezra Stiles, 1755–1794* (New Haven: Yale University, 1916). The first (nearly) complete provincial census came in 1765: Josiah H. Benton, *Early Census-Making in Massachusetts, 1643–1765* (Boston: Goodspeed, 1905). While the 1765 census provides figures on white, black, and Indian populations in almost every town in the province, it does not provide separate data for most of the Indian communities.

Students of Indians in colonial Massachusetts inevitably begin with the 1674 account by Daniel Gookin, the colony's Indian superintendent and John Eliot's colleague, "Historical Collections of the Indians in Massachusetts," MHSC, 1st ser., 1 (1792), 141–226. Gookin continued his peerless description of the colony's Indians during and in the wake of King Philip's War with "An Historical Account of the Doings and Sufferings of the Christian Indians in New England, In the Years 1675, 1678, 1677," American Antiquarian Society *Transactions and Collections* 2 (1836), 432–517.

In the eighteenth century, Massachusetts political and religious leaders showed a surprisingly high level of interest in the surviving Indian enclaves. In addition to the legislature's frequent interventions and investigations, a number of the colony's secular and ecclesiastical elites, such as Peter Oliver, John Quincy, Cotton Mather, and Samuel Sewall, worked with Indians as guardians or as commissioners of the London-based Society for the Propagation of the Gospel in New England (better known as the New England Company). The guardians' extant letters and accounts are in the Indian volumes of the Massachusetts Archives and the *Acts and Resolves*, described above. The minutes of meetings and correspondence of the Boston officials of the New England Company provide a unique (though obviously biased) description of the condition of Indian groups, the province's policy toward the surviving natives, and the often-acrimonious relations between Indians and their white neighbors. Collections of these records can be found in the Guildhall Library, London, and in the New England Historical and Geneological Society, Boston. In 1729, a group of New England Company commissioners and other provincial officials traveled to Natick; their visit and conditions in the town are in the "Report of ye Comittee of ye Honble Comissioners for ye Indian Affairs and of ye Corporation of Harvard College . . . Oct. 23, 1729," *Publications of the Colonial Society of Massachusetts* 16 (1925), 575–77.

In addition to their official correspondence and reports, a number of white ministers made frequent notes on native groups. Samuel Sewall recorded his dealings with Indians in Boston and Cambridge, and kept detailed observations during his visits to Gay Head and Natick, in *Sewall's Letter Book*, 2 vols., MHSC, 6th ser., 1886, and *The Diary of Samuel Sewall, 1674–1729*, ed. H. Halsey Thomas, 2 vols. (New York: Farrar, Straus and Giroux, 1973). Conditions among the Indians on Martha's Vineyard at the turn of the century are described by Matthew Mayhew, *A Brief Narrative of the Success Which the Gospel hath had Among the Indians of Martha's Vineyard* (Boston, 1694), and Experience Mayhew, *Indian Converts, or Some Account of the Lives and Dying Speeches of a Considerable Number of Christianized Indians of Martha's Vineyard* (London: J. Osborn and T. Longman, 1727). Cotton Mather's *Magnalia Christi Americana*, 2 vols. (Hartford, 1852) and *India Christiana* (Boston, 1721) includes reports by the Mayhews on the Vineyard, Samuel Treat on upper and middle Cape Cod, Roland Cotton on the lower Cape, and John Cotton in Plymouth. Ezra Stiles's *Itineraries* is described above.

Two white ministers in eastern Massachusetts whose congregations were largely or entirely Indian wrote on their experiences. Stephen Badger's 1798 review of his half-century among the Natick Indians is an astonishing indictment of white racism and violence against natives; Badger, "Historical and Characteristic Traits of the American Indians in General, and those of Natick in Particular," MHSC, 1st ser., 5 (1798), 33–45. Gideon Hawley began his service in Mashpee in 1765 as an assistant to the native minister Solomon Briant; when Briant died ten years later, Hawley took the pulpit, and while he quickly alienated his congregation by trying to turn them into good Englishmen, he also left many letters and records that provide biased but useful information on Mashpee. Collections of his papers are in the Hawley Papers, Congregational Library, Boston; the Hawley Letters, Massachusetts Historical Society; and the Samuel P. Savage Papers, also in the

Massachusetts Historical Society. Some have been published: "Biographical and Topographical Anecdotes Respecting Sandwich and Marshpee, Jan. 1794," MHSC, 1st ser., 3 (1794), 188–93; and "A Letter From Rev. Gideon Hawley of Marshpee . . . July 31, 1794," MHSC, 1st ser., 4 (1795), 50–56.

SECONDARY SOURCES

Puritan colonization of New England has been controversial ever since Roger Williams clashed with Massachusetts Bay authorities in the 1630s. The subjective nature of historical interpretation has perhaps never been as clear as in the differences between Alden Vaughan, *New England Frontier: Puritans and Indians, 1620–1675* (New York: Norton, 1965, rev. ed. 1979), who celebrated the colonists' fair motives and efforts, and Francis Jennings, *The Invasion of America: Indians, Colonists, and the Cant of Conquest* (Chapel Hill: University of North Carolina Press, 1975), who (using the same documents) condemned the colonists' dishonest, greedy, and savage behavior. Their contradictory views of John Eliot (a potential saint according to Vaughan, an ineffective Machiavellian demon according to Jennings) are particularly striking.

More balanced interpretations of Eliot and his Indian converts can be found in Neal Salisbury, "Red Puritans: The 'Praying Indians' of Massachusetts Bay and John Eliot," *William and Mary Quarterly*, 3d ser., 31 (1974): 30–42, and Harold W. Von Lonkhuyzen, "A Reappraisal of the Praying Indians: Acculturation, Conversion, and Identity at Natick, Massachusetts, 1646–1730," *New England Quarterly* 63 (1990): 396–428. Charles Cohen, a scholar of Puritan conversion narratives, has written an intriguing essay on the persistent gap between native and English worldviews; "Conversion Among Puritans and Amerindians: A Theological and Cultural Perspective," in *Puritanism: Transatlantic Perspectives On a Seventeenth-Century Anglo-American Faith*, ed. Frank Bremer (Boston: Massachusetts Historical Society, 1993), 233–56. On Puritan missions on Martha's Vineyard see James Ronda, "Generations of Faith: The Christian Indians of Martha's Vineyard," *William and Mary Quarterly*, 3d ser., 38 (1981): 369–94.

Recent works on relations between natives and colonists in seventeenth-century New England have reshaped our understanding of the region and the dynamics of intercultural encounters. Neal Salisbury examined how the development of English and aboriginal peoples forged their encounter in *Manitou and Providence: Indians, Europeans, and the Making of New England, 1500–1643* (New York: Oxford University Press, 1982). William Cronon's seminal study, *Changes in the Land: Indians, Colonists, and the Ecology of New England* (New York: Hill and Wang, 1983), shows that the two groups shaped their environment in very different ways, and that the colonists' most fundamental conquest was not political or military but economic and ecological. The natives' efforts to adapt to those changes are explored by Peter Thomas, "Cultural Change on the Southern New England Frontier, 1630–1665," *Cultures in Contact: The Impact of European Contacts on Native American Cultural Institutions, AD 1000–1800*, ed. William Fitzhugh (Washington DC: Smithsonian Institution Press, 1985), 131–61, and Virginia DeJohn Anderson, "King Philip's Herds: Indians, Colonists, and the Problem of Livestock in Early New England," *William and Mary Quarterly*, 3d ser., 51 (1994): 601–24. James Axtell's books offer some of the most balanced and intriguing views of the relationships between Europeans and Indians in the Northeast. See particularly his collection of essays, *The European and the Indian: Essays in the Ethnohistory of Colonial North America* (New York: Oxford University Press, 1981), and his comparison of English and French missionary activity and Indian reactions, *The Invasion Within: The Contest of Cultures in Colonial North America* (New York: Oxford University Press, 1985).

Far less has been written on the natives who remained in Massachusetts after King Philip's War. While Axtell occasionally dips into the eighteenth century, the best overview of the region is still Laura E. Conkey, Ethel Boissevain, and Ives Goddard, "Indians of Southern New England and Rhode Island: Late Period," *Handbook of North American Indians*, vol. 15, *Northeast*, ed. Bruce G. Trigger (Washington, DC: Smithsonian Institution, 1978), 177–89, and includes an excellent map that provided much of the data for the map in this book. While few of the tales recorded by William Simmons in *Spirit of the New England Tribes: Indian History and Folklore, 1620–1984* (Hanover: University Press of New England, 1986) date from the eighteenth century, some of the folklore points to change and continuity in native culture during that period. In addition, his introduction is an excellent overview of Indian history in the region.

A few publications on relations between Indians and provincial authorities cover the eighteenth as well as seventeenth century: William Kellaway, *The New England Company, 1649–1776: Missionary Society to the American Indians* (New York: Barnes and Noble, 1962); Richard Johnson, "The Search for a Usable Indian: An Aspect of the Defense of Colonial New England," *Journal of American History* 64 (1977): 623–51; and Yasu Kawashima, "Legal Origins of the Indian Reservation in Colonial Massachusetts," *American Journal of Legal History* 13 (1969): 42–56.

The Massachusetts Historical Commission's reports on *Historical and Archaeological Resources* provide excellent data on changing settlement and landuse patterns from prehistoric to modern times. Particularly useful were the volumes on *Cape Cod and the Islands* (1987) and *Southeastern Massachusetts* (1982), which show shifts in English and Indian villages after 1600. I used data from maps in these publications, along with the map in Conkey, Boissevain, and Goddard's article in the *Handbook of North American Indians*, to create the map for this book.

Anthropologist Kathleen Bragdon has written a number of studies on Indians in seventeenth- and eighteenth-century Massachusetts, including " 'Another Tongue Brought In': An Ethnohistorical Study of Native Writings in Massachusetts" (Ph.D.

diss., Brown University, 1981); "Probate Records as a Source of Algonquian Ethnohistory," in *Papers of the Tenth Algonquian Conference*, ed. William Cowan (Ottowa: Carleton University, 1979), 136–41; "The Material Culture of the Christian Indians of New England, 1650–1775," in *Documentary Archaeology in the New World*, ed. Mary C. Beaudry (New York: Cambridge University Press, 1989), 126–31; "Crime and Punishment Among the Indians of Massachusetts, 1675–1750," *Ethnohistory* 28 (1991): 23–31. She also coedited *Native Writings in Massachusett*, described above.

Most studies that focus on Indians in Massachusetts in the eighteenth century deal with specific communities. My Ph.D. dissertation, "Behind the Frontier: Indian Communities in Eighteenth-Century Massachusetts" (University of Virginia, 1992), details developments in four Indian enclaves in the province: Natick, Hassanamisco, Punkapoag, and Stockbridge. Natick, John Eliot's flagship "Praying Town" and the best-documented Indian enclave in the province, has drawn particular attention. The most thorough Natick study is Jean O'Brien, "Community Dynamics in the Indian-English Town of Natick, Massachusetts" (Ph.D. diss., University of Chicago, 1990); this work is noteworthy for its geneological work and examination of the relationships between and fates of Natick Indian families. My article, " 'To Live More Like My Christian English Neighbors': Natick Indians in the Eighteenth Century," *William and Mary Quarterly*, 3d ser., 48, (1991): 552–79, places Natick's troubles and decline in the context of problems within the province. The conflict between natives and white newcomers, which focused on the location of the town's meetinghouse, is the subject of Michael J. Crawford, "Indians, Yankees, and the Meetinghouse Dispute of Natick, Massachusetts, 1743–1800" (*New England Historical and Geneological Register* 132, 1978): 278–92.

Mashpee, Nantucket, and Martha's Vineyard have also attracted students of Indian communities. Two books have been published on Mashpee: Jack Campisi, *The Mashpee Indians: Tribes on Trial* (Syracuse: Syracuse University Press, 1991), and Francis G. Hutchins, *Mashpee: The Story of Cape Cod's Indian Town* (West Franklin, NH: Amarta Press, 1979). Elizabeth Little has published a number of studies on Nantucket Indians, including "Probate Records of Nantucket Indians, *Nantucket Algonquian Studies* 2 (1980); "The Nantucket Indian Sickness," *Papers of the 21st Algonquian Conference*, ed. William Cowen, (Ottowa: Carleton University, 1990), 181–96; "The Writings of Nantucket Indians," *Nantucket Algonquian Studies* 3 (1981); and "History of the Town of Miacomet," *Nantucket Algonquian Studies* 12 (1988): 1–34. Daniel Vickers, "The First Whalemen of Nantucket," *William and Mary Quarterly*, 3d ser., 40 (1983): 560–83, is a perceptive study of how colonists on that island were able to entrap Indians in the market economy. A more traditional narrative history, which includes transcripts of many useful but difficult-to-find documents, is Alexander Starbuck's *History of Nantucket* (Rutland, VT: Charles E. Tuttle, 1969). A similar description of Martha's Vineyard is Charles E. Banks, *History of Martha's Vineyard*, 3 vols. (Edgartown, MA: Dukes Historical Society, 1966).

INDEX

Gimbee, Cesear, 191–92

Gookin, Daniel, 15, 17, 21, 28, 30, 32, 36, 47, 143

Gookin, Daniel, Jr., 35

governors, Massachusetts. *See* Massachusetts governors

Grafton, 88–89, 107, 121, 136–37, 192, 206

Great Awakening, 127

guardians, 25, 89, 114, 130, 151, 157, 188, 207; abuse by, 115–16, 118, 150, 152–53; appointment of, 4, 113–14, 130, 143–45, 153; complaints about, 146, 148–49, 152–54, 158, 205; efforts to reform Indians, 143–44, 148; embezzlement by, 115–16, 153, 158; fraud by, 118, 145, 148–49, 150, 152–53; incompetence of, 146, 152, 155–56, 206; and lease of Indian lands, 147–48, 155–56; powers of, 113–14, 143, 144–46, 152–54; secular nature of, 113, 144; subversion of native leaders, 115–16, 155–56. *See also individual groups*

Hannit, Japheth, 56, 59

Harvard Indian College, 47

Harwich, 140

Hassanamisco Indians (also Hassanamissets), 17, 28, 36, 39, 47, 57, 116; adaptation by, 16, 87, 88–89, 97, 120–21; Chabanakongkomun, connections with, 84; church of, 16, 17, 88; and colonists, conflicts with, 107, 136–37; debts, 97, 167, 190; demographics of, 120, 167, 168; economy of, 88–89, 97, 168, 190; emigration by, 188, 191, 206; ethnic boundaries of, 191–92; funds of, 89, 97, 113, 120, 146, 148, 158, 167, 190–92; gender roles among, 89, 120–21; guardians of, 89, 97,

113, 121, 137, 143, 144, 148, 149, 168, 177, 235 n.137; and homeless, 167, 177; and intermarriage, 188–92; and King Philip's War, 21; landholding by, 69, 87, 88–89, 97, 121; land sales by, 88, 97, 120, 167–68, 191, 235 n.137; material culture of, 88–89, 97, 120–21, 167–68; Natick, connections with, 26, 57, 83, 97, 121, 159, 167; networks among, 168, 191–92; and Nipmuc lands, 16, 43–45, 83; population of, 16, 107, 190, 206; and poverty, 120–21, 167–68; resettlement of, 25, 36, 39; and soldiers, 128; and trespass by colonists, 136; wartime restrictions on, 67; widows, 167–68

Hawley, Gideon, 127, 157, 179, 180, 181, 183, 185–86, 193–95, 196, 198–99, 205

Herring Pond Indians, 51, 109, 172; church of, 123, 124; culture of, 124; economy of, 124, 138, 178; and immigrants, 124, 178; landholding by, 124; networks among, 178; and New England Company, 124, 178; population of, 51, 52, 123–24, 178

Hiacoomes, 18

Hill, Nathaniel, 159, 160, 189, 191

homeless: colonists, 161–62; Indians, 95–96, 118, 161–64, 176–78

Hossueit, Zachary, 126, 127

indenture, Indian, 69, 70

Indians: aboriginal culture of, 3, 9–11, 14, 25, 40, 59–60, 85, 91, 95, 96, 101–2, 106, 109–10, 194, 199; acculturation of, 2, 4, 9, 11, 14–15, 18, 20, 23, 25, 48, 49, 68–69, 81, 88–89, 101–2, 178, 184, 200, 204, 205; African Americans and, 4, 165, 183–96; autonomy of, 3, 24, 31, 46–49, 66, 81, 115; and colonists, relations with, 20–23, 25,

48, 50, 66–75, 77–78, 110–16, 118,
132–43, 145; communities, forms
of, among, 5, 10, 14, 50; conflicts
among, 100, 101–4, 112; debts of,
69, 81, 98–99, 101, 118, 132, 134, 135,
161; demographics of, 2, 12, 81, 86,
116, 117, 128, 134, 163; doctors, 200;
economy of, 10, 24, 49, 51, 58, 60–62,
74, 87, 96, 100, 104, 107, 116; folklore
of, 60, 109–10; hunting by, 10, 67,
87; illness among, 86–87, 98–99,
162–63; imprisonment of, 21–22,
99; injury to, 99–100; landholding
by, 10, 25, 49, 60–62, 81, 91–92,
104, 118, 137, 146, 205–6; land sales
by, 4, 45–46, 81, 118, 134; language
of, 35, 52, 58–59, 71, 73, 104, 105,
109, 124; leadership among, 8–9, 10,
11, 12, 25, 47, 62–66, 101–3; legal
status of, 207–8; literacy of, 57, 58;
material culture of, 61, 81, 184, 196;
ministers, 17, 19, 35, 49, 52, 55, 56, 59,
84; population of, 65, 81, 124, 164,
165–66; and poverty, 2, 117–18, 129,
132, 143, 162–64, 171, 177; religion of,
10, 14, 25, 59–60, 109–10; servants,
25–26, 28–29, 135; settlement
patterns among, 3, 9–11, 49–50, 69,
78–79, 82, 84–85; traditionalism of,
3, 5, 9, 11, 15, 81, 85, 100, 116, 124,
137, 161, 178, 196. *See also* alcohol
and Indians; boundary disputes;
churches, Indian; ethnic identity,
Indian; gender roles; intermarriage;
law; migrants; networks, Indian;
poaching by colonists; soldiers,
Indian; trespass by colonists;
whaling, Indians in; women, Indian;
and individual groups
Indiantown (Yarmouth), 128, 205;
network in, 175; population of, 175;

reserve created in, 54, 75; soldiers of,
128
intermarriage: and census flaws, 173,
185–86, 190; "foreigners" and,
195–96; Indian attitudes toward, 185,
191; and Indian ethnicity, 5, 182–96,
206–7; and Indian land, 189–91;
Indian and African American, 4, 159,
165, 170, 173, 182–96, 204; Indian
and white, 186–88, 193–94; laws
concerning, 185. *See also individual
groups*

Josiah, Charles, 31–32

Kendall, Edward, 197–98
Keurp, Patience, 50, 101–2
King George's War (1744–1748), 124,
128–30, 136, 156
King Philip's War (1675–1676), 2,
20–25, 51, 52, 203–4
King's Council, Mashpee's appeal to,
157
King William's War (1689–1697), 39, 51
Kitteaumut, 51–52, 123, 172

landholding. *See under* Indians:
landholding by; *individual groups*
land sales. *See under* Indians: land sales
by; *individual groups*
law, 134–35, 145; colonists' manipulation
of, 13, 41, 70, 132, 134–35, 140, 171;
and Indian land, 71–73, 81, 87,
91–92; Indians' use of, 140
Leaverett, John, 77
Little Compton. *See* Pocasset
livestock, 13, 34; Indian ownership of,
16, 20, 23, 61, 74–75, 92, 94–95, 97,
111–12, 119, 120, 140, 142, 147
Lumbee Indians, 195

Magunkaquag, 17, 21, 26; sale of, by
Natick, 76–77, 87

Maine, 70, 85, 129, 130

manitou, 10, 60, 109

Mannamett, 52, 123

Marlborough, 21. *See also*
Okommakamesit Indians

Martha's Vineyard, 63, 112; annexation
by Massachusetts Bay Colony, 46,
48, 181; and colonists, 18, 112; and
guardians, 144; Indian culture on,
61–62, 63; Indian landholding on,
90; Indian ministers on, 55, 56;
Indian population of, 49, 55, 58,
125, 181; Indians on, 18, 28, 30, 35,
57, 61–62, 100, 106, 197; Indian
settlement patterns on, 55, 56.
See also Chappaquiddick Indians;
Christiantown Indians; Gay Head
Indians

Mashpee Indians, 19, 22, 46, 51–53,
69–70, 109, 114; aboriginal culture
of, 194; adaptation by, 179–81, 194,
196; African Americans among,
158, 179, 185–86, 192–93; Anglo-
American culture, influence of, 125;
and boundary disputes, 74, 139;
church of, 35, 52, 53, 61, 108–9, 157,
179–90, 194–95; demographics of,
178–79; ecology of, 52, 53, 179–80,
197; economy of, 126, 135–36, 147,
179–81, 196; epidemics among,
124; ethnic identity of, 192–95; and
Falmouth, 176, 179; folklore of, 194;
and Gay Head, 126; government of,
53, 158, 179, 195, 205; guardians of,
144, 147, 156–58, 195; immigrants to,
53, 118, 125, 157–58, 179–80, 193–96;
and intermarriage, 183, 185–86,
193–95; landholding by, 89, 91, 125,
135–36, 138–39, 193; land leases, sales
by, 136, 147, 148, 193–94; language
of, 35, 53, 105, 108, 109, 125, 138,

179, 194; material culture of, 125,
180, 194, 197; messenger to London,
157, 176; ministers of, 105, 108–9,
125, 126, 157, 194–95; mulattoes in,
179, 186; networks among, 69–70,
85, 108, 125, 126, 176, 179–81, 182;
and New England Company, 108–9,
124, 125; and poaching, by colonists,
138–39, 143, 156; population of,
52–53, 85, 124–25, 178, 180; and
proprietorship, 89–90, 125, 157–58,
193; reserve created for, 52; resources
of, 53, 69–70, 126, 138, 147, 156;
settlement patterns of, 52–53, 69–70,
125; soldiers of, 68, 85, 124, 125, 129,
156, 179, 181, 193; traditionalism
of, 105, 125, 179–80; trespass of, by
colonists, 74, 138–39, 197; widows,
124, 129, 204–5; women, 193; and
whaling, 147, 181, 196–97; yellow
fever among, 181, 182

Massachusetts Bay Colony: charter,
repeal of, 43, 46; depression in, 96,
123, 161–62; expansion of, 13, 42–43,
46, 48, 50, 53, 54, 71, 80, 81–82, 85,
87; and Glorious Revolution, 46;
inflation in, 4, 123; Nipmuc lands,
purchase of, by, 43–46; population
of, 12, 49, 79, 81

Massachusetts General Court, 27–
28, 37, 43, 45, 49, 53–54, 64–75,
71–74, 79, 81, 99–106, 129, 130,
134–36, 143, 146, 199, 204, 205;
and antimiscegenation laws, 68,
185; and Assawompsett, 72; and
Chabanakongkomun, 148, 149–50;
and Chappaquiddick, 74–75, 150–52;
Indian reserves, creation of, by, 14–
16, 51, 75, 136; and Freetown, 51, 174;
and Gay Head, 64–65, 72–73, 74,
147, 148–49, 201–2; and guardians,

New Plymouth, 12, 19–20, 22, 43, 46, 48, 50, 52, 53, 57, 71, 138
Nipmuc Indians, 16, 17, 21, 23, 25, 27–28, 30, 33, 57, 58, 84; lands, 43–46. *See also* Chabanakongkomun Indians; Hassanamisco Indians
Nonantum, 14, 26, 30, 43
Nukkehkummee Indians, 51, 59, 63, 84

Okohammeh. *See* Christiantown Indians
Okommakamesit, 17, 26, 27, 32, 33, 34
Okommakamesit Indians: 17, 26; and King Philip's War, 21; Marlborough, conflict with, 27; and Natick, 21, 27, 32, 33; sale of, controversy over, 34
orphans, 28. *See also individual groups*
overseers. *See* guardians

Pawtucket Indians. *See* Pennacook Indians
Peabody, Oliver, 66, 104–6, 110, 127, 128
Pegan, Samuel, 84, 97
Pegan, Thomas, 84, 98
Pembroke, 50, 99, 109, 155
Pennacook Indians, 12, 16–17, 21, 27, 67
Pequot Indians, 13, 68
Philip, King. *See* Metacom
Piambow, 32, 33, 38, 44
Pigwacket Indians, 130
Pilgrims. *See* New Plymouth
Plymouth, 51, 135, 178
Plymouth County Indians. *See* Assawompsett Indians; Herring Pond Indians; Mattakeesit Indians; Teticut Indians
poaching, by colonists, 2, 66, 69, 79, 80, 81, 110–14, 115, 118, 127, 132, 137–40, 149, 150–54, 205–6. *See also individual groups*

Pocasset, 51, 59, 83, 85, 176, 178
Pokanoket Indians. *See* Wampanoag Indians
Popmonit, Simon, 53, 62, 69
Potawaumacut Indians, 53–54, 99; and Billingsgate beach, 140, 175–76; and colonists, relations with, 74, 206; land sales by, 131; population of, 85, 206; resources of, 74, 176; and soldiers, 175; and whaling, 132, 139–40, 175; widows, 131–32, 175, 206
praying Indians. *See* Christianity, Indian conversions to
Printer, Abigail, 190
Printer, James, 32, 36, 57, 84
Printer, Moses, 83
proprietorships, 91. *See also* Natick Indians; Mashpee Indians; Teticut Indians
Punkapoag Indians, 15–16, 17, 47, 159; aging of, 121–22, 171; conflicts among, 101, 154; debts of, 121, 153, 171; demographics of, 30, 121–22; economy of, 16, 36, 38, 61, 112–13, 121–22, 171; emigration by, 31, 161, 171; epidemics among, 78, 107; funds of, 100, 101, 121–22, 146, 152–54, 171; guardians of, 100, 114, 121–22, 143, 144, 152–54, 171; homeless, 121, 161; and hunting, 36, 38, 77, 121; illness among, 100, 121–22; land leases, sales by, 31, 77–78, 121–22, 153, 171; leadership among, 31–32, 62–63, 100; networks of, 57, 171–72; and Nipmuc land claims, 43; orphans, 171; poaching, by colonists, 110–11, 113, 114, 152–54, 171; population of, 16, 30–31, 78, 121, 152, 171; and poverty, 121–22, 171–72; settlement patterns of, 24–26, 28, 30–31, 61, 171; and soldiers, 68, 129; and Teticut,